THREE
WISE MEN

A NAVY SEAL, A GREEN BERET,
AND HOW THEIR MARINE BROTHER BECAME A WAR'S SOLE SURVIVOR

BEAU WISE AND TOM SILEO

ST. MARTIN'S
GRIFFIN
NEW YORK

Published in the United States by St. Martin's Griffin, an imprint of St. Martin's Publishing Group

www.stmartins.com

Designed by Omar Chapa

The Library of Congress has cataloged the hardcover edition as follows:

Names: Wise, Beau, 1984– author. | Sileo, Tom, author.
Title: Three wise men : a Navy Seal, a Green Beret, and how their Marine brother became a war's sole survivor / Beau Wise, and Tom Sileo.
Description: First edition. | New York : St. Martin's Press, [2021]
Identifiers: LCCN 2020035341 | ISBN 9781250253446 (hardcover) | ISBN 9781250253453 (ebook)
Subjects: LCSH: Wise, Beau, 1984– | Wise, Benjamin B., 1977–2012. | Wise, Jeremy J., 1974–2009. | Afghan War, 2001—Biography. | United States. Navy. SEALs—Biography. | United States. Army. Special Forces—Biography. | United States. Marine Corps. Marine Division, 3rd. Battalion, 1st—Biography. | Iraq War, 2003–2011—Biography. | Families of military personnel—Arkansas—History—21st century. | Wise family.
Classification: LCC DS371.42 .W57 2021 | DDC 958.104/74092273—dc23
LC record available at https://lccn.loc.gov/2020035341

ISBN 978-1-250-25346-0 (trade paperback)

Our books may be purchased in bulk for promotional, educational, or business use. Please contact your local bookseller or the Macmillan Corporate and Premium Sales Department at 1-800-221-7945, extension 5442, or by email at MacmillanSpecialMarkets@macmillan.com.

First St. Martin's Griffin Edition: 2022

10 9 8 7 6 5 4 3 2 1

Praise for *Three Wise Men*

"It's a great book. Highly recommended." —Jake Tapper, CNN

"It's an important story that everybody needs to hear."

—Anderson Cooper, CNN

"This is what Memorial Day is about."

—Martha Raddatz, ABC News

"After losing my friends in Afghanistan, I resolved to spend the rest of my life honoring the fallen, their families, and my fellow veterans. By writing *Three Wise Men* with Tom Sileo, Beau Wise has not only paid tribute to Jeremy and Ben but all who've served and sacrificed during the post-9/11 wars our military has fought. We are all brothers and sisters in arms."

—Flo Groberg, Medal of Honor recipient and author of

8 Seconds of Courage

"A poignant look at love and loss, sacrifice and honor. I'm reminded of Lincoln's famous letter to the mother who lost her sons 'upon the altar of freedom.'" —Mike Beebe, former governor of Arkansas

"Three lives on separate paths but intertwined by war, this story becomes a modern-day *Saving Private Ryan* when the surviving sibling is barred from the battlefield. With ties to the Osama bin Laden manhunt and the ground fighting in Afghanistan and Iraq, *Three Wise Men* runs the gamut of our current entanglements and legacies. Our nation is forever indebted to the Wise family."

—Michael Golembesky, *New York Times* bestselling author of

Level Zero Heroes and *Dagger 22*

"Many American families have sacrificed much for our freedom, but few if any in modern times have given as much as the Wise family from my home state of Arkansas. Theirs is the story of true heroes—those who gave their lives as well as those who remain to carry on and honor the memory of Jeremy and Ben. It's a story that needs to be told and, more important, needs to be read and shared. It will remind you that America is a great country because of great, God-fearing people who pay a price for all of us."

—Mike Huckabee, former governor of Arkansas

"*Three Wise Men* is a moving and powerful book that relates the humanity and commitment of a family that paid a painfully high price in defense of freedom. The story of service and sacrifice is emotional in and of itself, but the fact that the Wises were my childhood neighbors made it even more emotional for me."

—Matthew J. Shepherd, Arkansas speaker of the house

CONTENTS

PREFACE

THE OLDEST BROTHER

"I can't believe I'm the oldest brother now," U.S. Army Sergeant First Class Ben Wise said in anguish on a sunny but sad 2010 spring day.

Ben and I were sitting next to each other in a limousine bound for the funeral of our big brother, Navy SEAL turned CIA contractor Jeremy Wise.

Ben is my older brother, but he didn't become the oldest until December 30, 2009, when Jeremy was killed by an explosion in Khost, Afghanistan. The two surviving Wise brothers were on leave from our own Afghanistan deployments to attend Jeremy's funeral.

Like Jeremy, Ben was an elite special operations warrior. On that day, however, he was just a grieving sibling. He had chosen to wear a suit instead of his U.S. Army Green Beret uniform. I was in my U.S. Marine Corps dress blues, but like Ben, I didn't feel like I was in the military that day. I was numb not only from a thirty-plus-hour flight home from Afghanistan but from the waves of emotion that accompanied trying to accept that my oldest brother was gone.

As we rode toward the Albert G. Horton Jr. Memorial Veterans Cemetery in Suffolk, Virginia, Ben and I discussed whether we would serve as pallbearers for our brother's funeral. Since we were both stationed on remote forward operating bases in Afghanistan, where internet access was nonexistent and satellite phone signals were poor, we hadn't been able to communicate since the immediate aftermath of Jeremy being killed in action. Because of the top-secret nature of our brother's work, we still didn't know the exact circumstances of his death.

I drifted in and out of the pallbearer conversation as we got closer to the place where Jeremy would be buried. As I looked out one of the limousine's darkened windows, I marveled at the beauty of the water as we went over a small bridge. It reminded me of fishing with my two brothers as we grew up together in rural Arkansas.

For a fleeting moment, I looked forward to fishing together again during our next trip home. That's when I remembered that I would never be on the receiving end of another one of my oldest brother's mischievous smirks. Jeremy was gone.

When the limo pulled into the cemetery, which is about an hour from where Jeremy was once stationed as a member of SEAL Team 4, I noticed some large words carved into a gray stone wall just outside the reception center.

"Honor to the soldier and sailor everywhere, who bravely bears his country's cause," the message read. It was written by President Abraham Lincoln during the height of the Civil War.

Jeremy was a sailor. Ben was a soldier. I was a marine, but even more importantly, I was their little brother.

Less than two years later, I found myself riding inside another limousine, which was driving down the exact same road.

I was looking out toward that same body of water before once again reading Lincoln's quote on the way into the cemetery grounds. It was a much colder, drearier day than my first visit, which was perhaps fitting given the unimaginable circumstances.

This time, Ben wasn't sitting next to me. He was resting inside an American flag–draped casket.

As I buried my head in my hands, I prayed to be awoken from what seemed like a terrible dream. My blank eyes then moved back out the window and toward the place where my two brothers would soon rest side by side for all eternity.

In that surreal moment, I came to the same somber realization that Ben had reached twenty-two months earlier. I was now the oldest living Wise brother.

THREE
WISE MEN

1

WISING UP

"You can hang out with us tonight," Jeremy said.

As the youngest, nothing made me happier than hearing those seven words. It was a crisp, fall 1989 night in southern Arkansas, where we grew up not far from "a town called Hope," as then governor Bill Clinton would make famous a few short years later.

I hurriedly moved my mattress from my room to theirs and slid between their tall pine beds. Jeremy was fifteen years old, while the middle brother, Ben, was twelve. I was only five, which made both my brothers truly larger than life.

With a huge smile on my face as I pulled up my blanket and settled in between my two heroes, our mother, Mary, entered Jeremy and Ben's room.

"Are you camping out with the boys tonight, Beau?" she said with a chuckle.

Jeremy and Ben had already fired up the Nintendo by then, so we each gave my mom a distracted nod before she told us to press Pause on *Duck Hunt*, which all three of us loved to play since the video game involved firing a plastic pistol.

It was time for our nightly military story. While Jeremy and Ben were obviously too old for bedtime stories, I was just reaching the age where I could comprehend the concept of service before self.

After Ben tossed aside the Nintendo gun and Jeremy cleared the finished homework scattered all over his bed, I listened to my brothers ask our mom questions about the Civil War. They especially loved hearing stories about Union and Confederate military leaders like Ulysses S. Grant, Robert E. Lee, William Tecumseh Sherman, and Stonewall Jackson.

My mom was a walking encyclopedia on American conflicts, which greatly excited Ben, who always wanted to find out more about the Wise family's involvement in our nation's wars.

Ben first asked about our grandfather John Morgan, who served in the U.S. Army Air Forces in World War II. Jeremy then asked about Great-Uncle Darwin, who fought in the bloody WWII battle of Guadalcanal.

Uncle Darwin was a U.S. Marine Corps Raider and Purple Heart recipient. While subsequently fighting the Japanese at Saipan, he was shot in the back of the head but initially—and incredibly—survived when the bullet ricocheted and glanced off the inside of his helmet.

Instead of going home, Uncle Darwin chose to stay with his unit and finish his combat tour. What he couldn't have realized is that the head wound would later become infected. The decision to stay and fight in the Pacific would ultimately cost him his life several years later.

"He never, ever quit," said my mom to a wide-eyed Jeremy, who I could tell was enthralled by the notion of fighting until the end.

My personal favorite story was that of Great-Great-Uncle Lyon, a Marine Corps doughboy who fought in the harrowing Argonne Forest during World War I.

Uncle Lyon was one of the original Teufel Hunden, or Devil

Dogs, the German nickname for the select few doughboys who—outnumbered and outgunned—assaulted heavily fortified positions in the legendary Battle of Belleau Wood.

These little stories loomed large for all of us, but especially Ben. His passion and pride in our family roots was something I would definitely share, but not until much later in life.

After Jeremy briefly shifted the conversation back to World War II and military leaders like Generals Dwight D. Eisenhower and Douglas MacArthur, my mother told us it was time for bed. All of us knew that meant it was time to lower our heads in prayer.

"Lord, please protect my three sons," said our mother, who also offered a prayer for our ten-year-old sister, Heather.

Even though my brothers and I would eventually feel driven to serve in combat, we weren't big on GI Joes or running through the town of El Dorado's many dirt roads playing war. We did watch a lot of action films, but our overall interest in the military didn't go much further than our family history. Jeremy did teach me to fire a .22-caliber rifle, and as country boys, we certainly enjoyed hunting and fishing. Our biggest passion, however, was music.

Jeremy and Ben both played guitar, with Ben mostly "slapping the bass." I was the drummer. While our parents were thrilled that all three boys eventually joined the church band, they were less enthusiastic about our increasingly loud jams of hit songs by the popular hard rock band Van Halen.

As we became better musicians, especially Ben, even our parents couldn't stop our instruments from blasting out tunes like "Ain't Talkin' 'Bout Love" or our deeply Christian mother's least favorite Van Halen song, "Runnin' with the Devil."

For similar religious reasons, Halloween was not an officially sanctioned holiday in the Wise household. Neither was the mischief that usually came with it. A few years after I was born,

Harvest Festival—not Halloween—was the holiday's name at our church functions.

"Beau!"

My mother's call echoed through our colonial-style redbrick two-story home but went unanswered as she looked for her children. All four of us were hiding around the house on Halloween night.

"Shhhhh," Jeremy whispered with his index finger over his mouth, trying to conceal his laughter before turning toward me. "It's okay," he assured me. "She'll never find you."

I was only five, but I knew for sure that "never" was a long time. Eventually, our mom was going to find me.

Jeremy was the oldest brother, but he also had a nose for trouble. Don't get me wrong; he was bright, ambitious, outgoing, and known all around our Arkansas small town for his infectious smile. He was also opinionated to the point of being stubborn and was a highly skilled debater. Those qualities, coupled with our always special relationship, basically meant that Jeremy could convince me to do anything he wanted when we were kids.

Even if he would talk his gullible, naive little brother into doing stupid things for his and Ben's entertainment, the fun and games would always stop if trouble arose. That's when Jeremy would instinctively step forward, raise his hand, and take the blame.

My mom was still shouting our names throughout the house, and even at a young age, I could sense that her occasional Irish temper was about to reveal itself on that so-called Harvest Festival night. In addition to her irritation, I also knew at least one of us was in big trouble.

Since I had only done what Jeremy had told me to do, I wasn't exactly sure which crime we'd committed had put us on the lam.

All that I remember is following Jeremy into my sister's room, where he proceeded to rifle through her dresser to find a brown paper bag. Sure enough, it was Heather's Halloween candy, which she had immediately hidden from her three brothers.

Minutes later, I was stuffing my face with my sister's treats on the floor of Jeremy and Ben's room. As soon as Heather alerted our mom to the theft and the search began, I emerged as the prime suspect even though I was far from the heist's mastermind.

I started to figure out where this was headed as Jeremy swiftly ushered me toward a trapdoor roughly three feet off the ground. It was the laundry chute.

Shortly after we had moved into the house, Jeremy and Ben had discovered that I was small enough to crawl up and down the vertical square chute. This enabled me to move to and from my parents' upstairs bathroom to the laundry room directly below.

To Jeremy especially, this was quite amusing. In fact, on more than one occasion, he would encourage me to sneak up the chute into the master bath and uncover certain "secret" or confiscated items, such as his Red Ryder BB gun or hidden Christmas presents in the closet. Jeremy was undoubtedly the most playfully mischievous young man I had ever known.

"She'll never find you, Beau," he repeated, no longer trying to conceal his laughter.

Jeremy picked me up and set me on the edge of the trapdoor. I put my legs inside, but just before I could brace myself against the wall, Jeremy slammed the door closed and immediately began trying to conceal my presence.

Nearly simultaneously, my mom marched in. "Where is he?" she demanded.

"Where's who?" Jeremy asked with his patented smile.

"I know he's up here somewhere," said my mother, who I could hear walking around the bathroom and closet space as she moved around clothes and boxes.

"Oh . . . you mean Beau?" Jeremy said to my mother, who wasn't convinced. Again, he attempted to nudge the chute door closed with his elbow in passing while trying to stay in between our mom and my secure, undisclosed location.

What Jeremy didn't know is that I'd never gotten the opportunity to brace myself inside the chute. With every subtle nudge of the door, I lost more and more of my seat.

Instead of an easy fall down the chute, I was looking at a plunge through the darkness toward what I could only pray was a pile of soft dirty laundry.

"Jeremy, I'm not going to ask you again!" my mom said even more firmly. "Give Heather back her Harvest Festival candy and tell me where Beau is!"

Heather was usually very tolerant of our shenanigans, but this was not such an occasion. My mother had come to her rescue.

I managed to get one butt cheek back onto the ledge before Jeremy once again told my mom he had no idea what she was talking about.

This time—less subtly than before—he elbowed the door completely closed.

My fate was now in the hands of Sir Isaac Newton and the unlikely possibility that my mother was behind on laundry that week. As I plummeted downward, my cry of terror faded into the distance before I thankfully crashed into a high pile of bedsheets and comforters.

As I popped out of the trapdoor in the laundry room, I was surprised to find Ben waiting.

Ben was the second child in our little quartet. Three and a half years younger than Jeremy, he was more of an introverted intellectual. Being closer to Jeremy in size and age as a child, Ben seemed to view me as more of a nuisance than any sort of equal.

Although our relationship would eventually grow as strong as any other in the family, it was initially more distant in comparison to my relationship to Jeremy or Heather. Ben and I were perhaps the most alike in terms of personality and facial features, which was perhaps the biggest reason for our childhood clash.

Sometimes—and this particular Halloween was one of those occasions—Ben would join Jeremy in his mischief. Clearly playing along, Ben picked up the candy bag I had dropped during my fall and pointed outside. As if he were an Arkansas Razorbacks quarterback running a play with his fullback, Ben then handed the stolen goods back to me.

"Go, Beau, go!" Ben said, beginning to laugh to the point of tears.

I quickly ran out the back door and banged a hard left, heading for a row of honeysuckle bushes. Concealed in this little hidden path, I could avoid punishment indefinitely . . . or at least until I got hungry for something other than Jolly Ranchers, Snickers bars, and those honeysuckles.

Our closest neighbors had a son, John, and daughter, Rose, who were both a year apart from me in age. My first thought after arriving in the honeysuckle row was to make a break for John and Rose's house before realizing I would have to pass in full view of my home's back door and windows to get there, revealing my whereabouts.

Alone with my thoughts, I started to realize the extent of betrayal both my brothers had most likely perpetrated against me. I had been set up.

As the night got even darker and my father's "dually" pickup truck coasted into the driveway after a long day at work, I heard my stomach growl. That's when I decided that it was time to face the music.

Mustering all my courage, I went back inside the house. Both of my seemingly invincible brothers were leaning over the counter—still laughing—while our five-foot-one mother began administering our punishment in the form of her belt on their backsides.

As usual, Jeremy had taken the lead and confessed to planning the Halloween heist. Ben had admitted his role as well.

After their corporal punishment was complete, my mother turned toward me.

"Give me the candy, Beau," she said.

I handed over the crinkled, half-full bag, which she immediately returned to Heather before dismissing Jeremy and Ben.

"Next time, maybe don't eat all your candy on the night of Harvest Festival," my mom said.

"Yes, ma'am!" they said in unison.

Looking disappointed with the ineffective result of the punishment, Heather gave Jeremy a swift jab in the arm as my two brothers exited the kitchen, still laughing despite being on the receiving end of my mom's belt. My sister sighed and went back to her room—candy in hand—shortly thereafter.

My parents, who seemed to have temporarily forgotten I was there, locked eyes and laughed quietly to themselves. Just then, my dad, Jean, leaned over his seat at the head of the kitchen table and opened his arms.

"Come here, buddy," he said warmly to his terrified five-year-old son. "Did you get framed?"

My mom had already returned to a pot on the stove, no longer concealing her amusement at the night's events as her laughter grew.

"Stay out of that laundry chute, okay?" my dad said. "I don't want you falling and getting hurt."

"Yes, sir," I gratefully replied.

My father was, for the most part, mild mannered in nature and at times a bit stoic. At the time, he was one of a handful of reconstructive plastic surgeons in South Arkansas, which meant that my dad expected nothing but good behavior and academic excellence.

Even though he was a man of discipline, Dr. Jean Wise had a soft spot for his children, especially the youngest.

"Stop doing everything your two brothers tell you to do," my dad said. "Now run along and play."

"Yes, sir," I once again replied as my father patted me on the back.

Wasting no time, I sprinted back upstairs, ready to confront my much bigger brothers. My ill-advised urge to fight them vanished immediately after opening the door, however. They greeted me like an inmate just out of prison, much like the scene in *Goodfellas* when a young Henry Hill is congratulated by much older gangsters for getting arrested and being released.

"Duuuude!" Ben said. "Good job, Beau."

"Gave me a scare, little brother!" Jeremy exclaimed. "Thank God Ben put those bedsheets at the bottom of the laundry chute!"

While I was still upset at my brothers as I plopped down on a beanbag, Jeremy handed me a Kit Kat bar and the *Duck Hunt* gun to make peace.

"I'll always have your back, Beau," Jeremy said.

Ben and I fought more in the next couple of years than the rest of our lives put together. There was a growing rivalry between him and Jeremy as well.

Ben was built like our dad: short and stocky with dark blond hair and steel-blue eyes. People jokingly called him Jean Jr. Jeremy, on the other hand, was already five foot ten with green eyes. He also walked with his chest puffed out like a rooster, which would later become his nickname in the navy. Whatever Jeremy's hair looked like when he woke up on a given morning, that would be his style for the day.

I was growing into a frame more like Jeremy's than Ben's, who wouldn't have his big growth spurt until much later in adolescence. This was in part responsible for our early rivalry, which led to us fighting over just about everything. I would often challenge Ben, and he would usually patronize me.

One day, things got more physical than normal.

I don't remember exactly what started the fight, but when it started to escalate, Ben pushed me away in a rather nonchalant fashion. I retaliated, and he answered with minimal effort and a condescending laugh aimed at letting me know that he wasn't even trying.

In the background, Jeremy was laughing at his little brothers and even antagonizing us a bit. "Watch out, Ben. I think Beau's gonna get you this time," Jeremy said.

That was when I threw the first punch. This time, Ben didn't hold back while retaliating. He hit me so hard that I flew into the wooden door of an armoire with an oval mirror in the center.

I heard the frame crack, but fortunately, the glass didn't break. All the air in my lungs seemed to leave me, and all that I could think of was how badly I wanted to hurt Ben, even though I was barely able to breathe.

Jeremy was usually reluctant to break up our fights, probably because watching two smaller kids beat up on each other was entertaining. This time, however, Jeremy seemed to realize that things had gotten out of hand when he sprang from his resting position on the bed and restrained me. "Wait here," Jeremy said in a forceful tone as he sat me down on the bed and led Ben out of the room.

To this day, I have no idea what Jeremy told Ben in private. But when the two of them returned, Ben walked into the room first, wearing a completely different expression from before. He slowly reached out his arms and embraced me. "I'm sorry, brother," he said. "Can you forgive me?"

Before I could answer, Jeremy stepped beside both of us and placed his hands on the shoulders of his younger brothers. Ben then stared at the floor and placed his hand on my opposite shoulder as we waited for the oldest to break the silence.

"Guys, listen to me," Jeremy began. "Someday, we'll be old. We also might be fat, bald, and broke. Maybe our wives will leave us and we'll have absolutely nothing left in the world. But even then, we'll be lucky—and do you know why?" he continued. "We'll always have each other. No matter what happens, you'll always have two brothers to lean on."

Jeremy's speech was brief but of enormous consequence. My relationship with Ben was instantaneously transformed, as he became more tolerant of me and I began to once again see him as a role model, much like I had always viewed Jeremy. It was the first of many times Jeremy would teach me to remember what's truly important in life: family and specifically the privilege of having two big brothers.

Our parents originally met in Southern California. They got married when my father was in medical school at the University of California at Irvine, but both my mother's and father's families were rooted in the southeastern part of the country.

The two eventually took the advice of my grandfather, shortly after Jeremy was born, and moved to South Arkansas to begin a private medical practice in otolaryngology. My dad was a specialist in reconstructive plastics and the most brilliant man I have ever known.

There was only one thing that my father was more diligent about than his profession: his family. As an only child, he was in awe of his father, Floy, a University of Arkansas alum, football player, and professor. Still, my dad often spoke about how much he wanted a brother and sister. I think the *Leave It to Beaver* childhood my siblings and I were provided was the very life our father wished he had as a child.

My dad never served in the military, but he always had a great respect for the family's history of stepping forward in wartime. His attitude about service, along with my mom's nightly stories, planted the seeds for Jeremy's interest in historical generals and admirals.

As Jeremy's high school graduation year approached, his interest in military academies became more apparent. Before Jeremy finished any other college applications, he had completed the required paperwork for the U.S. Naval Academy in Annapolis and U.S. Military Academy at West Point.

One day as we were driving home from school, Ben, Heather, and I piled in the back seat of my mother's car; Jeremy sat in the front seat. That's when she handed him a large envelope. Without speaking, Jeremy sat in the passenger seat and stared at the return address, which read, "United States Military Academy."

After pausing, Jeremy opened the envelope.

"It's an acceptance letter!" he said.

My mom brimmed with excitement before shouting, "Jeremy, you did it!"

Jeremy's tense expression faded as he relaxed in his seat, as if he had just finished a marathon. The long journey he had anticipated since around the time I was born was now ahead of him, and the current Wise generation's chapter in the U.S. military was about to begin.

Jeremy's high school graduation from our little Christian school in El Dorado was a bit of a letdown for him since he missed being valedictorian by a small margin. My oldest brother's standard of excellence was higher than that of anyone I've ever known. My parents, of course, did not share in Jeremy's disappointment. They were extremely proud of their straight-A, firstborn son.

After the main portion of graduation, Jeremy was recognized by the principal of the school and asked to step forward. The principal then reached below the podium and pulled out an appointment letter to the United States Military Academy at West Point, which was signed by Governor Clinton.

Our patriotic little community rewarded Jeremy with a standing ovation. To Ben, Heather, and especially their little brother, this moment solidified Jeremy's giantlike image.

Later that fall, it was finally time to send Jeremy off to West Point. Early one morning, the whole family crammed into my dad's little Piper six-seat aircraft and flew to a tiny airport in Newburgh, New York, to take Jeremy to his appointed place of duty. We rented a van from there and headed for the historic military post, which George Washington once called America's single most important stronghold.

As we were navigating through the academy grounds, the little van crested the last hill as the entire family gasped at the sight of the beautiful Hudson Valley campus. Jeremy's knees were shaking up and down as he glared ambitiously out the side window.

When we finally found the family parking area, everyone got out and started hugging Jeremy and saying goodbye. He was nervous, something I rarely ever saw from my oldest brother, even at that age. I was the last to say goodbye.

As Jeremy dropped to a knee and wrapped his arms around me, I started to feel a bit emotional. The thought of not having him around to get me in and out of trouble was suddenly becoming very real.

"Goodbye, Skello!" said Jeremy, using a nickname he and Ben had affectionately bestowed to gently mock my adolescent physique— or lack thereof. For perhaps the first time I could remember, I didn't really mind the nickname.

Jeremy then stood up, grabbed his bags, said he loved us, and waved one last goodbye before heading toward a large building. My mom's military stories suddenly had a whole new meaning as we watched Jeremy and his formation turn toward the archway and disappear from view.

Ben and I observed with curiosity, intrigue, and perhaps even a bit of envy. It was our first real exposure to military life.

The following semester, Jeremy was doing poorly at West Point. While his grades were up to par, the rigid structure of military academy life—especially the strict emphasis on timeliness and a flawless appearance—was new and difficult for my oldest brother. Jeremy, who had always been opinionated and boisterous at times about his views, also clashed with a few professors. He eventually decided to drop out of West Point, which would haunt him for many years to come.

"I'm a quitter," he later told me. "No matter what I do or where I go, in my mind, I'll never let this go."

Eventually, Jeremy and Ben both settled into a private Central Arkansas school called Hendrix College. There, they both began the pursuit of natural science degrees and excelled in both academics and athletics.

Both my brothers were nevertheless unfulfilled—especially Jeremy, even after being accepted to medical school. Quitting West

Point continued to gnaw at him, while Ben firmly believed he had a lot more to prove.

As I started high school in a town called Hope, I missed my big brothers each and every day. Even as they struggled to find their path, I had a feeling that mine would eventually follow in their footsteps.

2

THE FIGHT

By late 1999, Ben had dropped out of college and moved into a town house with Jeremy and Heather in Little Rock. I was the only child still at home, and I started getting into a bit more trouble than my parents were used to seeing from any of their children.

Between seventh and ninth grades, I had gone from As and Bs to Cs and Ds. I was running with the wrong crowd, partying too much, and even smoking the occasional joint. My siblings were all frustrated with my behavior, with Jeremy going so far as threatening to drive home from Little Rock to kick my ass if I didn't clean up my act. As usual, my big brother was right.

One holiday weekend, Jeremy, Ben, and Heather came home for a visit. Within minutes of their arrival, Jeremy (instead of kicking my ass, thankfully) pulled his bass guitar and amplifier out of the back of his Jeep Cherokee and hauled it inside, where my drum set and Ben's gear were already waiting.

Moments after Jeremy plugged in his bass, we were jamming out to Van Halen, Queen, Led Zeppelin, and finally Jeremy's personal favorite, Black Label Society. It sounded absolutely terrible, but we didn't care. The Wise brothers were back together.

Ben and I practiced together nearly every night. I was the first child in the family to be afforded any type of formal musical education due to the fact that our school didn't offer the program back when Jeremy and Ben were students. I had chosen percussion and drums around the same time that Ben put down his six-string for a bass.

The roles in our house had also shifted. Ben had always taught me about music, but now I was bringing the music home to him. I was helping him understand theory on as primitive a level as I was capable of understanding at the time.

My brothers were once again home for a weekend when I stumbled upon Ben playing the bass introduction to the 1995 hit song "Hey Man Nice Shot" by the alternative rock band Filter. Ben would often hum the song's lyrics before squeezing his rifle's trigger during hunting trips, but loved playing the song's distinctive bass chords even more.

I could tell Ben was focused on playing his favorite song and didn't want to intrude, but in addition to sheets of music scattered around the room, I noticed what looked like military-themed brochures and a mountain of paperwork. While I thought about interrupting to inquire, I decided to go to bed and simply ask Ben about it the next day.

Before I got a chance to talk to Ben the next morning, I walked in on my two brothers while they were in the middle of a heated argument. Jeremy was red in the face and screaming at the top of his lungs at Ben, who looked like smoke was coming out of his ears.

"So what's your brilliant plan?" Jeremy yelled.

"Ranger, I guess," Ben said.

"You *guess?*" Jeremy screamed. "Tell me something, Ben: Do you have the slightest fucking clue what you're getting yourself into? What's the minimum run time or distance? Tell me, do you even know what it is? You don't exactly look like you've been running five miles a day."

Amid all the screaming, I realized they were arguing about Ben joining the military. Maybe that was what the brochures were all about.

Then I remembered seeing all that paperwork. *Had Ben really gone ahead and signed his life away without consulting anyone?* Surely he would have told Jeremy, me, or our father first, or so I'd thought.

While Ben loved military history, I had rarely heard him discuss actually joining the armed forces. Jeremy, on the other hand, had long been fascinated by the Navy SEALs and specifically Basic Underwater Demolition / SEAL (BUD/S) training. Even as he was graduating college and being accepted to medical school, my oldest brother seemed far more consumed with getting information about becoming a SEAL than a doctor like our dad.

Now Jeremy was suddenly confronted with one of his younger brothers not only enlisting before he did but without doing what Jeremy believed was the bare minimum amount of research.

"What dirty used car salesman sold you this crock of shit, Ben?" Jeremy said, flipping through pages of what I soon realized was an official U.S. Army Ranger contract.

As Jeremy understood well from many years of special operations research, a "Ranger contract" did *not* mean a given soldier was guaranteed a spot in Ranger School. You might be forwarded the opportunity someday, but that was it. Once the contract was signed, the army could ultimately do as they pleased with your job and future.

Jeremy was getting angrier and angrier as he pressed Ben for an explanation that made sense. Why would Ben have signed such a contract without first ensuring that he had given himself every possible advantage toward Ranger School if that was where he wanted to end up? By this point, Jeremy looked like he wanted to lay into Ben, who seemed like he wanted Jeremy to take the first shot.

"My bad, bro," Ben sarcastically said to Jeremy. "I didn't know I needed your approval to wipe my ass."

"No," said an emphatic Jeremy, who jumped up off the couch. "Apparently, you just need someone to teach you how to do it!"

That was it for Ben, who had been trying to hold his tongue and temper up to that point. Without hesitation, he threw a sharp right jab at Jeremy, who dodged late but successfully, as the punch glanced off the side of his face.

Using all his considerable might, Jeremy then pulled Ben's shirt and coat toward him before slamming his second-youngest brother into the wall. Ben tried to fight back, but Jeremy was simply too strong after many years of lifting, running, swimming, collegiate rugby, wrestling, and preparation for BUD/S. Ben got the only reminder he needed about how tough Jeremy was as he was pressed up against the wall.

The point had been made as Jeremy lowered Ben from the wall. My oldest brother won the fight without throwing a single punch.

"I'll be fine," said Ben, who was referencing his career rather than the aftereffects of being slammed into a wall.

"What happens when you fail?" Jeremy said. "Are you an open contract?"

Ben was silent and refused to look his still-enraged big brother in the eye. He also didn't want to admit that he didn't even know what the term *open contract* meant, which further underscored the heavy amount of military research Jeremy had done compared to Ben.

Open contract is a term for someone who enlists without requiring any particular military occupational specialty (MOS) in their initial contract. If you fail in whatever school your contract specifies, assuming you get an unguaranteed spot in the given school to begin with, it's understood that the branch of service in which you enlist gets to decide where you go and what you do from that point forward.

"So what happens when the army picks your job for you, Ben?" Jeremy said. "Good luck doing a job that fucking no one signs up for. Did you ever stop and think about how the army fills those jobs? Do you think you're the only guy who wants to be a Ranger or a Green Beret?"

Jeremy relentlessly harped on that point even after Ben revealed that he had received a substantial bonus to enlist. The relatively brief conflict in Kosovo had just ended, and the army was trying hard to keep its ranks filled in peacetime.

"They offered you a big fat bonus because you might get to go to an elite school that you're not prepared for," Jeremy hammered home. "They know you're going to fail, which is why the contract is conditional on graduation. You and I both know you'll never fucking see graduation day at Ranger School, which is why you should call the recruiter right now and ask him to delay your MEPS [Military Entrance Processing Station] date," Jeremy continued. "Dude, you are not . . . fucking . . . ready."

"You think you know everything, don't you?" said Ben, who was still fuming as he finally locked eyes with Jeremy.

"Do what you want, Ben," Jeremy said. "I hope you prove me wrong."

"What you don't understand is that I'm leaving . . . *period*," Ben said in his firmest tone of the argument. "And at least I'll be doing what I want to do with my life."

Ben was clearly taking a shot at Jeremy, who was going to medical school instead of training to become a Navy SEAL. It was immediately clear that those words deeply hurt my oldest brother, too.

There was a brief period of silence as Jeremy processed the slight and Ben realized he had just taken things too far. Without saying anything else, Ben stomped right by me and slammed the door.

Jeremy, for his part, did remember there was a ghost in the corner before leaving the room. "Hey, Beau," he said. "I'm sorry you had to see that."

He then asked if I wanted to go grab something to eat. As we drove to a local fast-food restaurant in his small, two-door Cherokee, I began to realize that Jeremy didn't really think all military recruiters were crooked used car salesmen, as he had emphatically conveyed to Ben. Jeremy was simply using scare tactics to try to convince Ben to try to cancel or delay his contract.

My oldest brother wasn't his normal, social self during our drive down Main Street. His left elbow was propped on the window ledge of the driver-side door with his hand on his forehead, nervously rubbing his brow while his right hand was on top of the wheel. He seemed to stare miles down the road before finally breaking the silence.

"I was too hard on him," Jeremy said. "I'm always too hard on him—I really don't know why."

"You're a great brother, Jeremy," I said.

"Thanks, Beau, but I've never been the brother to Ben that I've been to you," he said. "It's not like I love him less or anything. He's just so fucking impulsive that he drives me nuts. I just want him to think shit through for once."

After he sighed and placed both hands on the wheel, I began to see that Jeremy was just as mad at himself as he was with Ben. I was also pretty sure that he was still pondering Ben's final comment about going to medical school when we all knew his heart was elsewhere.

Jeremy had recently suffered a knee injury and for the last few months had been stubbornly running with an awkward stride that produced shin splints that evolved into stress fractures. It may have been the only reason that he hadn't already gone to BUD/S.

I could tell Jeremy was still reflecting on Ben's comments as he stared off into the distance.

"So what do you think is going to happen to Ben?" I finally asked Jeremy.

"The path ahead of Ben is a tough one that starts at Fort Benning in Georgia," Jeremy said. He went on to explain that Ben signed what's known as a RIP contract, which stands for Ranger Indoctrination Program. While noting that Ben had lettered in soccer and swimming at Hendrix, Jeremy also pointed out that Ben hadn't stayed in peak physical condition since leaving school.

"Let's be honest, he's gotten a little pudgy," Jeremy said of Ben. "A RIP is no joke, either. We're talking about Rangers here, Beau. Ben's in for a shit ton of calisthenics, running, and hiking. He hasn't done any of the prep."

As Jeremy continued describing the rigorous qualifications of Ben's contract, I realized he had known the answer to every single question that he had stumped Ben with back at the house. That's how much time and effort Jeremy had already put into his military career before enlisting.

"The basic training he'll do first isn't designed to prepare you for Ranger School. It's designed to break you down," Jeremy explained. "I mean, sure, he'll shed some fat and maybe condition his legs, but that's about it."

"It's the army, though, right?" I said with confusion. "I thought basic training was supposed to be tough."

"Oh, I'm sure it is, but you have to remember that not everyone that enlists goes to basic training or boot camp in shape," Jeremy said. "You still have to account for that kid playing video games and eating Hot Pockets in his mother's basement. That kid who just saw a 'Be All That You Can Be' commercial on TV—that's who basic is designed for. It's not designed to build an ideal Ranger candidate. It's set up to give you the tools to become a soldier if you've got the guts. Otherwise, everyone would be a Ranger, right?"

Jeremy then outlined what would happen if Ben survived basic training. He would go straight into Jump (Airborne) School, and if he didn't fail or get injured, he would roll straight into the Ranger indoctrination test (INDOC) that a soldier is required to pass to gain entrance to Ranger School.

"I think he'll have some downtime in Jump School, and he'd better use it to work out and prepare for that INDOC test," Jeremy said.

"Did you tell him that?" I asked.

"Heck no. I've already done enough damage," Jeremy said. "Any idea that I could offer, he'd probably refuse just to spite me."

Either way, Ben had already signed all the paperwork at the Little Rock MEPS. No matter what Jeremy, Heather, my parents, or I thought about his decision, Benjamin Brian Wise was now a U.S. Army recruit.

"Ben's already taken the oath," Jeremy said, shaking his head. "He's going to have to learn the hard way."

During Jeremy's ongoing planning phase, enlisting in the navy was simply a path to BUD/S. If he was going to commit to this plan, his mentality was BUD/S or death.

Even though he was almost certainly right about Ben's "piss-poor planning," Jeremy had failed to see the most important thing: Ben wanted to serve.

Above all else, our brother wanted front lines, camaraderie, and a uniform. Out of all three of us, Ben enlisted for the most purely patriotic reasons. No one was going to talk him out of it, not even Jeremy.

I hesitated before telling Jeremy, who had just picked up some cheeseburgers from Sonic, what I really thought.

"Here's the thing—I'm proud of him, Jeremy," I stammered.

After washing down the first bite of his cheeseburger, Jeremy nodded in agreement. "Me, too, Beau," he said. "At least the army might help him grow up. If that doesn't do it, infantry school will for sure."

"School of Infantry is eight weeks after boot camp, right?" I said.

"No. In the army; it's four weeks after basic training, and it's called ITB [Infantry Training Brigade]," Jeremy said, shooting me a concerned look. "Where did you hear it was eight weeks?"

"Marine Corps," I said.

"Hold on!" Jeremy yelled as he swerved his Cherokee off Main Street and onto a dirt road. His maneuver resulted in soda spilling all over me.

"What the heck, Jeremy?" I said before demanding an explanation.

Jeremy put the vehicle in park and stared right into my eyes. "Have you been talking to a recruiter, too?"

"Uh, well, sort of," I stammered.

"It's a simple question," he said. "Did you, or did you not?"

"Yes, I talked to one," I said, knowing Jeremy would probably fly off the handle just like he had with Ben. "They came to my school!"

This was only partially true. I had first met the recruiter at school, but all the information I had gotten about the School of Infantry, as it's called in the Marine Corps, had been over the phone.

Jeremy stared at me intently before putting his head in his

hands. Instead of screaming at me some more, his tone turned somber.

"Look, I'm sorry, Beau," Jeremy said, probably reflecting on the recent conversation with Ben. "But you should go to a real school—college—before thinking about the infantry kind. Dad's right about a lot of things, and this is one of them. Maybe we'll become doctors like him, or maybe we won't. But without that bachelor's degree, you don't have many options."

"That's all I'm doing, Jeremy," I said. "I'm just exploring some options."

"But you didn't go to a recruiter's office or anything like that?" he said.

"No," I said, becoming agitated.

"Okay, one last thing and I'll leave it alone," Jeremy said. "Why Marine Corps? I'm curious."

"Listening to Mom's stories about Uncle Darwin and Uncle Lyon," I said.

"That's not a good reason, Beau," Jeremy said. "Doing something just because a couple of family members did it is a bad idea."

"Well, that's not all," I interjected. "Did Dad ever tell you that he was contemplating the Marine Corps?"

Our father was a private pilot and an aviation enthusiast. During the Vietnam War, he had contemplated serving in the military through a marine officer flight program. When the recruiter told him that the shortest contract was six years, however, he decided to hold off.

In our dad's mind, the Marine Corps made the most sense for a pilot. He once told me that if there was a high probability of being shot down, as was the case in Vietnam, he'd rather be a stranded marine than anything else.

"I think the whole 'every marine is a rifleman' thing is pretty cool," I said to Jeremy. "I get why I shouldn't just do it for family reasons, but, dude . . . we've got Marine Raider blood in us. That's pretty badass."

"It is pretty cool, I'll give you that," Jeremy said, no longer seeming as irritated. "If you're thinking Marine Corps, we will talk to Nathan and Jonathon, but only *after* you get a bachelor's degree."

Nathan and Jonathon were the only cousins we had nearby while growing up in Arkansas. Nathan had already enlisted in the Marine Corps, and was in the reserves at the time while finishing school. Jonathon had been accepted to the U.S. Naval Academy.

Still, Jeremy's most recent comment irritated me, as it insinuated that he was trying to take control of my future.

"What do you mean 'we' will talk to Nate and Jon?" I said.

"Sorry, I meant 'you.' Just you," Jeremy said. "After college, talk to Nate, if you've got your heart set on the Corps. If you have any other questions, all I ask is that you *please* come to me before talking to another recruiter. If I don't have the answers, I'll find the guy who does, okay, dude?"

Honestly, Jeremy didn't really have anything against recruiters. He was just terrified that, like the events that just unfolded with Ben, someone would talk me into making a hasty decision.

Jeremy then suggested that in college I study music instead of medicine since I was clearly more passionate about the former. I nodded silently, starting to feel as if I were being held hostage in a vehicle that hadn't moved since we'd started what seemed like an endless debate.

That's when Jeremy, who didn't want to make the same mistake twice in one night, took the hint. He turned his Jeep back onto the main road and started driving through the Arkansas heat.

"I love you, Skello," Jeremy said.

"I love you, too, Jerms," I replied.

In 2000, my family flew to Columbus, Georgia, to attend Ben's basic training and ITB graduation.

We were all so proud of him. Ben had been appointed a squad leader and maintained that coveted status for the duration of basic and ITB.

I would never forget my first look at Ben's face after ITB. He weighed less than 150 pounds and was almost unrecognizable due to suddenly protruding cheekbones. I hadn't seen him that thin for at least a decade, if not longer.

Always the quiet professional, Ben was stoic the whole trip home. With both his brothers thinking about military careers, however, Ben had no choice but to humor us. I was also struck by how well Jeremy and Ben were getting along after their big fight just a few months earlier.

"So where will you go now, Ben?" our mom asked.

"Well, if all goes well, I'll come back to Fort Benning and start Jump School," he explained. "With some hard work and a little bit of luck, I'll pass INDOC and then be assigned to one of the three Ranger battalions."

As it turned out, the little bit of luck that Ben needed didn't materialize. Even though he was able to avoid getting injured, he wound up getting sick during Jump School and failed his physical fitness test for Ranger INDOC. As a result, he was ordered to report to the U.S. Army's Second Infantry Division at Fort Lewis in Washington State.

By the next time the Wise brothers were together, it had become clear that almost all of Jeremy's predictions about Ben's career had come true. As a result, I was worried about Jeremy unleashing a torrent of *I told you so*s on Ben.

To my surprise, it didn't happen. Jeremy knew Ben had just finished even more training and would be assigned to a mechanized infantry unit, where he would drive Stryker tactical fighting vehicles and operate turret weapons. The skills Ben was honing impressed Jeremy, who knew that if there was ever another war, Ben would be on the front lines.

In Washington State, Ben would later fall in love with the Puget Sound and a beautiful young woman named Traci, who eventually became his wife. He also made numerous friends for life while starting a long, distinguished army career. Even though he was disappointed with himself for not getting into Ranger School, Ben would nevertheless find a fruitful, noble path in life.

Meanwhile, both Jeremy and I were becoming more envious of Ben by the day. As he had promised during the big fight, Ben was doing what he wanted to do with his life. Jeremy—who was still in medical school—most certainly was not. Despite my father's and oldest brother's advice, I wasn't sure college was where I wanted to be, either.

3

THE DECISION

"Jeremy, shouldn't you be studying?" my brother's classmate Paul Sebastian asked him in the fall of 2001.

"In a minute, dude," said Jeremy, his head buried in a Navy SEAL workout manual. "I gotta finish lifting."

Jeremy had just started his second academic year of medical school in Little Rock, which was about two hours from where we grew up. It was his third overall year at University of Arkansas for Medical Sciences (UAMS) after failing several classes as a first-year med student. From the start, Jeremy's heart wasn't set on following in our dad's footsteps and becoming a doctor.

Even though succeeding at UAMS wasn't terribly important to Jeremy, he soldiered on rather than turn in his white coat. Potentially being viewed as a quitter was abhorrent to every bone in my oldest brother's body, especially after West Point, which still haunted him.

Staying in medical school also seemed like Jeremy's only realistic option after developing those knee and shin splint problems. Although he was running farther and faster than he had in years thanks to a buddy who helped correct his stride, Jeremy wasn't yet able to run at the level he had reached before the injuries.

Still, joining the military and specifically becoming a SEAL were never far from Jeremy's mind, especially at twenty-eight years old. The cutoff for entering BUD/S training was his current age, which meant that every morning Jeremy woke up that year at UAMS, the first thing he heard was a ticking clock.

Jeremy made up for every extra mile he couldn't run by following an almost superhuman SEAL swimming and weight lifting routine that would have genuinely impressed the likes of Michael Phelps and Arnold Schwarzenegger. While I was in awe of Jeremy's physical prowess, the exorbitant amount of time he spent in his apartment's makeshift gym and nearby indoor pool was beginning to frustrate Paul, who was himself a U.S. Navy recruit.

"Jeremy, we have a test tomorrow," Paul said as the clock neared midnight. "At some point, you're going to need to study."

"Later," Jeremy said between deep breaths as he attacked an expensive weight machine that he couldn't really afford while bogged down with student loans from college and now medical school.

Paul had also been forced to repeat his first year at UAMS with Jeremy and didn't want it to happen again. Having already completed boot camp, Paul had his sights set on becoming a navy doctor. He had spent almost every day of medical school going to class and hanging out with Jeremy, who was already one of his best friends.

Anyone who was around my oldest brother was almost instantly drawn to his magnetic personality, and Paul was no exception. Only a few days before their unsuccessful study session, Jeremy had accidentally broken Paul's nose during an impromptu Greco-Roman wrestling match at the YMCA in Little Rock. With his nose smashed in and blood all over the passenger's seat as the culprit drove him to the hospital, all Paul could do was laugh as Jeremy lightened the mood by quoting movie lines.

With his black-and-blue eyes getting heavier as he tried to convince Jeremy to study, Paul finally got fed up with his buddy's workout antics as the clock struck 1:00 a.m. Their med school exam was just seven hours away.

"Jeremy, sit down and open your anatomy book!" Paul yelled. "You've spent almost eight hours working out today. Enough is enough."

Huffing and puffing, Jeremy heeded his friend's advice and joined the late-night study session. For the next few minutes, he distractedly flipped through the pages of his textbook while half listening to Paul's predictions about what the professor would include on the test.

It only took about a half hour for Jeremy's thoughts to wander to the previous October's bombing of the U.S. Navy guided missile destroyer USS *Cole* in Yemen, which the former Clinton and current Bush administrations agreed was the work of an organization called al Qaeda. The terrorist group was led by an elusive leader named Osama bin Laden, who had been thrust into the spotlight after the almost simultaneous 1998 bombings of U.S. embassies in the African nations of Kenya and Tanzania.

Seemingly out of nowhere, Jeremy interrupted Paul, who was quizzing him on the medical subject they were about to be tested on.

"Hey, dude, have you heard about what these terrorists are doing in North Africa and the Middle East?" he said. "I've been reading a book about it."

Paul rolled his eyes, threw his hands in the air, and stood up. "This is the book you should be reading!" he said, pointing to their textbook. "What is going on with you, Jeremy? Do you want to flunk out completely this time? I don't."

Barely reacting to Paul's uncharacteristic outburst beyond sporting a wry smile, Jeremy replied calmly as he cooled down from another intense workout. "This is what motivates me," he said, holding up his daily training manual. "I want to be a Navy SEAL."

"It's World War III, bro!"

Those were the first five words I heard upon walking into my second-period class at Hope High School on September 11, 2001.

Since the pronouncement was made by a guy who was widely regarded as a stoner—and who was probably high at the moment—I didn't give his dramatic phrasing much thought until I saw our teacher wheeling a television into our classroom. That's when I—along with millions of other American men, women, and children—first saw the smoke.

I was confused when I saw the fiery clouds billowing above New York City, along with the Pentagon and what appeared to be a wide-open field in Pennsylvania.

What the heck is going on? Are we really at war? My teenage mind was suddenly swimming with worst-case scenarios before arriving at the most important question of all.

Where is Ben?

I knew I couldn't simply go to the school pay phone and call my brother, since he was at Fort Lewis, one of the U.S. Army's largest infantry hubs. If he wasn't already on a plane headed for whatever country had just attacked us, he was probably somewhere out in the field for a training mission, which was often the case on weekdays.

As I refocused on the harrowing images filling the TV screen, I became even more baffled when I saw the second World Trade Center tower collapse into a massive cloud of smoke, fire, and debris at 9:28 a.m. central time.

To a kid from rural Arkansas, the Twin Towers were the backdrop of movies like *Superman* and—like the Man of Steel himself—seemingly invincible. Like most Americans that day, I simply couldn't believe my eyes. All I felt was despair as I watched one of the worst days in American history unfold from a classroom in a town called Hope.

After school, I hurried over to my father's medical office, which you could spit and hit from my high school's computer lab. I was anxious to ask him about Ben and whether he had been able to reach him.

Dr. Wise was with a patient, which meant I spent the next half hour watching more 9/11 coverage with my dad's audiologist and longtime business partner, Jim Davidson.

"What the heck is happening, Jim?" I asked. "Who did this to us?"

"I'm not really sure, but I think they're looking at Afghanistan," he said.

Jim was a mild-mannered, rational guy whom my father had met years earlier while they were working together at a VA hospital. Normally stoic, Jim's eyebrows tensed up before he finished his thought. "I don't know much about this stuff, but I do think we need to go over there and get whoever did this," he said.

The idea of our country going to war, like my grandfather and great-uncle had done sixty years earlier, was suddenly becoming very real.

If that was indeed the case, Ben would almost certainly be on the front lines if he wasn't already boarding a flight out of Washington State.

Fort Lewis—now Joint Base Lewis-McChord—is the spearhead of the West Coast army as far as infantry is concerned. There's a Ranger battalion there, Special Forces, and a massive infantry division along with scouts and mechanized units. While the East Coast infantry is scattered around bases like Forts Campbell,

Benning, Bragg, and Drum, Lewis-McChord was and is where you will find most of the army's western war fighters.

Ben would be at the heart of America's response to 9/11, and as I would later find out, watching Special Forces soldiers head straight into the killing fields would help launch Ben's quest to become a Green Beret.

My dad and I were never able to speak to Ben on 9/11, nor did we remember to ask whether he was in the field or in the barracks when he found out two hijacked jets had been flown into the World Trade Center. But one thing was certain: the attention of my parents and my entire family shifted mostly to Ben and when—not if—he would leave for his first combat deployment.

Like me, Jeremy was sitting in a classroom when news of the terrorist attacks began to circulate. Upon stepping out of class to try to get more information, he almost immediately ran into Paul, who knew his life was about to change, since he was already in training to become a navy doctor.

Both medical school students were smart enough to know America was going to war. Even though Little Rock was a long way from lower Manhattan, Paul and Jeremy also felt a deep sense of responsibility to avenge the horrors of that terrible day.

In an otherwise quiet hallway at UAMS in Little Rock, Arkansas, two grown men hugged each other and cried. Their country had been attacked, and they would not stand idly by as their generation was called to serve.

Ten days later, on September 21, 2001, the world was definitively told who was responsible for the terrorist attacks on our country. President George W. Bush also outlined what was coming next for the U.S. military while speaking to a joint session of Congress.

"Our war on terror begins with al Qaeda, but it does not end there," President Bush said. "It will not end until every terrorist group of global reach has been found, stopped, and defeated."

Every terrorist group? That meant Ben would probably wind up deploying to not just Afghanistan but other unnamed countries where terrorists were planning attacks that could kill even more Americans than the nearly three thousand murdered on 9/11.

To me, President Bush's speech was the moment 9/11 first felt like my generation's Pearl Harbor. It also came with the sobering realization that at least one of my brothers—and many more men and women like them—would probably spend a significant portion of their adult lives at war.

The commander in chief's words were undeniably poignant but also changed the lives of countless military families, including my own.

Great harm has been done to us. We have suffered great loss. And in our grief and anger we have found our mission and our moment.

Freedom and fear are at war. The advance of human freedom, the great achievement of our time, and the great hope of every time, now depends on us.

Our nation, this generation, will lift the dark threat of violence from our people and our future. We will rally the world to this cause by our efforts, by our courage. We will not tire, we will not falter, and we will not fail.

Ben was watching the president's speech at Fort Lewis. I was watching the speech at home with our mom and dad, who I could tell were both thinking about not just one son that was already in

the army but their firstborn who was watching the address in Little
Rock with one foot already out the door of medical school.

It is my hope that in the months and years ahead, life
will return almost to normal. We'll go back to our lives
and routines and that is good.

Even grief recedes with time and grace.

But our resolve must not pass. Each of us will remember what happened that day and to whom it happened.
We will remember the moment the news came, where we
were and what we were doing.

Some will remember an image of a fire or story or
rescue. Some will carry memories of a face and a voice
gone forever.

And I will carry this. It is the police shield of a man
named George Howard who died at the World Trade
Center trying to save others.

It was given to me by his mom, Arlene, as a proud
memorial to her son. It is my reminder of lives that ended
and a task that does not end.

I will not forget the wound to our country and those
who inflicted it. I will not yield, I will not rest, I will not
relent in waging this struggle for freedom and security for
the American people.

The course of this conflict is not known, yet its outcome is certain. Freedom and fear, justice and cruelty,
have always been at war, and we know that God is not
neutral between them.

It's hard to adequately express the profound impact President
Bush's words had on me that night. Not in a political sense, as for

most of us who lived through 9/11, the immediate aftermath was not about being a Republican, Democrat, or Independent. It was about being a good American and grieving for the victims and their families.

Even though I wanted to quit high school, pick up a weapon, and go to war, the effect 9/11 had on a kid like me paled in comparison to my oldest brother, who was already straddling the imaginary fence between medical school and the military before America was attacked.

From the moment I stepped into my dad's office immediately following the attacks, I could sense not only concern for Ben but, for the first time, a sense of resignation about what would come next for Jeremy.

My father still desperately wanted at least one son to become a doctor, and with Jeremy in his third year at UAMS, my dad's dream was closer than ever to becoming reality. Just by looking in my father's eyes as we watched President Bush's speech, however, it was obvious how quickly 9/11 had changed everything for Jeremy, Ben, and our entire family.

Ben barely said anything when we first got a chance to talk on the phone after the president's address. True to form, Ben was the quiet professional ready to go wherever the army sent him. He also made clear—in as few words as possible—that becoming a Green Beret was the next order of business if and when he returned from battle. Wherever and whenever he deployed, Ben would also have his sights set on reaching what he viewed as the highest level of military excellence.

Jeremy, on the other hand, had a lot to say when I visited him for the first time since 9/11 at UAMS. As soon as I walked into my brother's room, I saw the white coat he had earned during his second academic year of medical school lying on the floor.

To me, the white coat symbolized where Jeremy was in the weeks and months after 9/11. When my oldest brother wanted to accomplish something in life, he was all in. That just never felt like the case in terms of becoming a doctor, and even before talking to him that night, it seemed like he wanted out.

Despite the events of 9/11, my dad had firmly dug his heels into the position that if Jeremy had made it this far in medical school, he might as well finish his studies. Then he would have more options not only as a civilian but inside the military if he decided to enlist.

I had heard many of their telephone arguments back home (only my father's side, of course), and what my dad said actually seemed to make a lot of sense. Finishing med school and joining the military did not have to be mutually exclusive; Jeremy still had the option of doing both.

My mother had joined me on this particular trip to Little Rock, where Jeremy lived with our sister, Heather, whose room was downstairs from Jeremy's living area and provisional workout center. As soon as my mom and sister sat on the couch and launched into girl talk, Jeremy invited me upstairs to play the popular video game *StarCraft*.

Instead of starting up his computer, Jeremy shut the door behind us. I could immediately tell he had something serious to say. At the same time, I couldn't help but notice how much bigger my brother had gotten since the last time I had seen him. Clearly, he had been hitting the gym extremely hard over the last few months.

After opening up a thirty-pack of Pabst Blue Ribbon, which he could easily crush by himself before getting up and running five miles the next morning, Jeremy hit me with his big news.

"Dude, I'm gonna do it," he said in a hushed tone so our mom wouldn't hear him. "I'm gonna go to BUD/S."

Completing BUD/S was required for anyone who wanted to become a Navy SEAL.

Even though I'd known this was coming, I gathered my thoughts and began trying to talk some sense into my much older and stronger big brother.

"Okay, Jeremy, I get it," I began. "But you're in your third year of medical school—"

"Second," he interjected.

"Okay, fine, you're technically in your second year, but you've been here for three, and you've gotten through the hardest part and earned your white coat," I continued. "Dad's right—just fucking graduate!"

Jeremy gave me the same sardonic smile as that Halloween night when he'd put me on the edge of the laundry chute. I could already sense that, as usual, he knew something his youngest brother didn't.

Still, as he sipped his PBR, I pressed forward. "What about your student loans?" I said. "I don't know a lot about money, but do you really want to spend the next ten years paying for a degree you'll never get to use?"

"I owe fifty grand right now," he said. "If I become a SEAL, I get a $50,000 bonus."

Clearly, the financial argument wouldn't have much of an effect on Jeremy.

"Either way, it doesn't matter," continued my still-smiling brother. "As you'll find out one day, some things are bigger than money."

I could tell he had already made his decision and that it was final. "If you go to BUD/S and it doesn't work out, will you ever go back to med school?" I said.

"The only way I won't make it through is if I heatstroke or if I fuck up my knee again," Jeremy said.

"Okay, so if that happens, will you come back and finish?" I said.

"No," Jeremy said. "Dad's right: to graduate from medical school and become a doctor, I've got to be in or out. As of tomorrow, I'm out," he concluded.

Nothing was going to stop Jeremy by that point, but out of respect for our father, I tried one last time. "It's two more years," I said. "Then you'll pretty much be a doctor and can do whatever you want."

The smile was even bigger. Jeremy appreciated what I was trying to do on behalf of our dad, but he wouldn't have any of it. "In two years, I'll be thirty, Beau," he said. "You know what that means, right?"

Jeremy went on to explain that anyone older than twenty-eight had to receive a special waiver to attend BUD/S, which Jeremy believed would put him at an immediate disadvantage with both instructors and his peers if he was even able to obtain the waiver in the first place.

"Why does it have to be the SEALs?" I said. "Why can't you use all the stuff you've learned here and become a navy doctor like Paul?"

His smile fading, Jeremy put his beer down and looked me right in the eye. "Because I want to kick down doors, blow shit up, and shoot people in the face," he said in a manner that was—to put it mildly—extremely blunt. "Those people trapped in the World Trade Center couldn't fight back. I can."

"You can be a doctor, though, Jeremy," I said. "That's important and saves lives, too."

The smile had fully vanished as Jeremy cut me off one last time. By this point, it was abundantly clear that 9/11 was the last straw in Jeremy's long struggle to find his life's calling.

"Twenty years from now, I'm going to look back and say one

of two things: 'I could have been a doctor' or 'I could have been a Navy SEAL,'" Jeremy said. "I can't live with the latter."

That was it. Before my parents, Ben, Heather, or I could try one last time to change his mind, Jeremy had traded in his white medical school coat for a U.S. Navy dress uniform of the same color.

A few months later, Jeremy stood cold, tired, soaking wet, and almost completely naked on the now famous Navy SEAL beach at Naval Amphibious Base Coronado in Southern California.

He was in the middle of the water training regimen known as *surf torture*, which was designed to push even the toughest warriors on the planet to mental and physical limits they never knew existed. For Jeremy and many of his classmates, it was the hardest part of not only Hell Week but BUD/S itself.

Exhausted and shivering as an instructor screamed orders directly in his ear, the thought of quitting never entered Jeremy's mind. While some SEALs might scoff at that notion, it was 100 percent true in my oldest brother's case.

Rather than look at the large bell any SEAL recruit could ring if he wanted to give up and leave BUD/S, Jeremy's bloodshot eyes focused on the brightest objects visible on the beach at 3:30 a.m.: the lights of San Diego across the bay and a U.S. Navy ship at sea.

As his mind and body threatened to give out, Jeremy zeroed in on those shining lights and began using them as a unique form of motivation. If he ultimately ended up working in an office building or aboard a ship, that would mean his mission to finish BUD/S had ended in failure.

Even though both scenarios would have been easier and a lot warmer, my oldest brother was exactly where he wanted to be by the spring of 2002. At long last, Jeremy Jason Wise was training to become a Navy SEAL.

4

GHOST SOLDIERS

"Dear Jerms," Ben, who was deployed to Iraq with the U.S. Army's Fifth Battalion, Twentieth Infantry Regiment, First Brigade Combat Team (Stryker), wrote to Jeremy in January 2004. "I smell like a bag of dead cats, but apart from that, things are good."

Ben, a sergeant, was serving in a scout platoon during the Iraq war's first-ever Stryker deployment. He was riding around in an armored vehicle somewhere in northern Iraq—almost certainly in the vicinity of Mosul—when he wrote this particular letter.

Jeremy, for his part, had already started the brutal Navy SEAL training regimen in Coronado. He was probably the only member of his class to be getting real-time dispatches from a brother serving in an active war zone, which helped motivate him to excel even further at BUD/S.

"Good luck with your training," Ben wrote. "Benny out."

From November 2003 to Thanksgiving 2004, the letters and phone calls Jeremy and I received from Ben left no doubt that his infantry deployment to Iraq was kinetic, high risk, and often flat-out crazy. Not only was it the first combat tour by a Wise brother, but it wound up being the longest and perhaps the most action-packed.

From participating in the hunt for deposed Iraqi leader Saddam Hussein's generals to battling murderous Sunni jihadist Abu Musab al-Zarqawi's al Qaeda in Mesopotamia and the vicious insurgent militia of radical Shiite cleric Muqtada al-Sadr, Ben was squarely in the middle of perhaps the defining yearlong stretch of the entire Iraq war.

Six months after President Bush's decision to publicly declare the end of major combat operations, Ben arrived at the end of Saddam's rule and the dawn of the insurgency. While every American had heard of Baghdad in 2003, Ben also fought in places like Mosul, Samarra, and Fallujah before the names of those violent cities began dominating nightly news coverage. Ben's platoon, which navigated thousands of miles of terrain riddled with booby traps, improvised explosive devices (IEDs), suicide bombers, and snipers, would bear witness to the carnage for more than a year.

The Iraq war's now infamous pair of triangles—the Sunni Triangle northwest of Baghdad and the Triangle of Death to the south—was first filled with the tire tracks, footprints, and blood left by soldiers like Ben and his brothers-in-arms. Serving for more than a year at the height of the Iraq war would change Ben's life forever, both as a human being and as an American soldier.

The Strykers arrived in the Sunni Triangle in early December 2003. As a member of a scout platoon, Ben was trained—and eager—to dismount and perform reconnaissance missions. Most of the time, however, he was performing the roles of vehicle commander or turret gunner inside a medium-weight "armored" Stryker vehicle with four fellow soldiers.

I put the word *armored* in quotes because early in the deployment, the Stryker vehicles were woefully underprepared to defend Ben and his army brothers from IEDs, rocket-propelled grenades (RPGs), and other insurgent weapons of choice. It took several months for

Ben's vehicle to be equipped with armored plates and birdcage-like wiring that would wind up saving his life several times over.

As Ben's platoon often joked, they were guinea pigs sent into the fire without the army truly knowing how these Stryker vehicles would perform in a modern war zone. Ben and his teammates were extremely lucky to make it through the opening months of his deployment in one piece.

In fact, Ben was almost seriously wounded before his unit even crossed into Iraq. It was in Kuwait where a fellow soldier, Sergeant Jesse Williams, accidentally discharged his M4 carbine assault rifle while he and Ben were cleaning their weapons. The round landed squarely between Ben's legs, just inches from his manhood.

After patting himself down to make sure no bullet fragments slipped through, my quiet, mild-mannered middle brother, who was even more timid than usual while learning the ropes on his first combat deployment, understandably showed an uncharacteristic level of emotion.

"Jesse, if I get my balls shot off before we even get in-country, I'm gonna kick your ass!" Ben snapped.

After Jesse profusely apologized, it didn't take long for him, Ben, and the rest of the unit to start howling with laughter. The incident became a running joke for the entire deployment, especially since Jesse—as Ben would later share—was one of the bravest, toughest soldiers he ever fought alongside. "The baddest guy in the platoon," he would often say. Ben and Jesse ultimately became close friends.

Less than three years later, Jesse would return to Iraq, where he was killed by an enemy sniper, leaving behind his wife, Sonya, and their daughter, Amaya. Jesse's multiple deployments, constant courage, and ultimate sacrifice embodied the selflessness of our post-9/11 military generation.

Jesse, Ben, and the Strykers crossed into Iraq from Kuwait less than a week before the capture of Saddam Hussein. They were preparing to actively search for the deposed dictator's retired officers and Ba'ath Party members until three words uttered by Coalition Provisional Authority leader and top diplomat L. Paul Bremer—"We got him"—stunned Iraq, the United States, and the world.

The Stryker-led mission targeting Saddam's henchmen, nicknamed Operation Ivy Blizzard, was postponed for a few days so U.S. military leaders and politicians could evaluate the effect of Saddam's capture on the country he'd once ruled with an iron fist. Unfortunately, the unofficial cease-fire wouldn't last long.

Just two days after Saddam's December 13, 2003, capture, U.S. Army general Ray Odierno gave the green light for a small army unit to go into Samarra, a city about eighty miles north of Baghdad that would eventually be regarded by many as the heart of the Sunni Triangle. The platoon chosen for this unpredictable, risky mission was none other than Ben's.

Fortunately for my brother, the mission was subsequently delegated to a different platoon that would strike a hidden IED while also encountering a motorcycle gang that was wielding assault rifles. The soldiers also took RPG and mortar fire before killing eleven insurgents in the subsequent fighting, according to Mark J. Reardon's *From Transportation to Combat: The First Stryker Brigade at War.*

While the Americans suffered no casualties that day, it was abundantly clear to Ben and his fellow soldiers that, much like the controversial MISSION ACCOMPLISHED banner that flew aboard the USS *Abraham Lincoln* as President Bush spoke, the capture of Saddam Hussein would not mark the end of the U.S.-led war in Iraq.

"The next year is gonna be fun," said one of Ben's teammates in a sarcastic tone.

"Hey, Wise, it's your brother calling from Iraq!" a BUD/S instructor shouted from the distance as Jeremy was going through another torturous exercise on the SEAL beach. "Take five and go talk to him."

To put it mildly, BUD/S training is not usually interrupted by calls from back home. With a family member deployed, exceptions were sometimes made, at least in Jeremy's case. While the instructors were notorious for being the military's ultimate hard-asses, they also had the foresight to recognize the value in a future SEAL learning firsthand about daily life in a war zone where he would almost certainly wind up deploying.

Jeremy had supreme confidence in his own abilities, but when Ben called from the battlefields of Samarra, Mosul, or Fallujah, he knew it was time to shut up and listen.

"How are you, dude?" Jeremy said.

"My nuts are still intact, bro," Ben joked while referencing the close call in Kuwait, which he had told Jeremy about in a previous letter. "How's BUD/S?"

"Just glad to be here," Jeremy said.

During pre-BUD/S workouts a few months earlier, Jeremy had become severely overheated while running on a beach berm. Jeremy had told my parents he was up late the night before reading training manuals and drinking coffee, but knowing my brother, I suspected he had gone out with the guys for a few drinks at McP's Irish Pub or one of the other well-known watering holes on picturesque Coronado Island.

Either way, Jeremy had suffered heatstroke, which put both his life and his dream career in great peril. No matter the circumstances, getting a second chance to finish BUD/S is extremely rare. Failing to complete an exercise in pre-BUD/S is even worse in the eyes of most instructors and their superiors, as it often signals that a candidate isn't ready for the notorious rigors of BUD/S itself.

On top of it all, heatstroke was a major red flag, as most people's bodies never fully recover. Jeremy was well aware of this due to his medical school background.

Despite what he knew was a serious setback, my oldest brother was undeterred. After leaving West Point, he had resolved to never quit anything he cared about for the rest of his life, and BUD/S would most certainly not become the exception.

"I'm not going anywhere," Jeremy said shortly after waking up in the infirmary.

With a body temperature well over one hundred degrees and his brain still cooking, Jeremy failed to fully realize that after heatstroke, the chance at a Navy SEAL career he had worked so hard to obtain was no longer up to him.

While recovering, Jeremy called one of his mentors, U.S. Navy Chief Warrant Officer Bob Jordan, who had been his intelligence instructor in Virginia Beach. Jordan, who had counseled other SEAL candidates facing similar conundrums, had almost always advised his former students to seek other navy careers after a misstep in BUD/S.

Something seemed different about Jeremy, even if Jordan couldn't put his finger on exactly what it was. Jordan would later chalk it up to the time he had already spent training my oldest brother, who he could tell had an unflinching desire to not only serve in uniform but go to war as a Navy SEAL.

"Go talk to Commander [Ryan] Zinke," CWO Jordan told Jeremy. "Tell him exactly what you just told me about making the most of a second chance."

Jeremy would soon pound on the office door of Commander

Zinke, a former Oregon college football player who had climbed through the SEAL ranks since the mid-1980s. Zinke would later become the first SEAL to be elected as a U.S. congressman and subsequently serve almost two years as U.S. secretary of the interior.

"I fucked up, sir," Jeremy boldly confessed to his commander. "I didn't take care of my body."

"You had heatstroke," Zinke said. "If this happens again in a place like Afghanistan or Iraq, that's a huge problem not just for you but for the guys serving next to you."

"Sir, I know exactly what I did wrong, and it will never, ever happen again," said my nervous brother. "I just need one more shot, Commander, and I'm hoping you will give me the chance to make you proud."

Zinke would later tell my father that, like Jordan, he saw a special something in Jeremy. Kicking my brother out could wind up being a waste of an extremely driven, promising SEAL candidate who clearly had an itch to not only finish BUD/S but excel while doing so. After all, the military was fighting two wars at once. They needed guys like Jeremy.

"All right, listen, I'm going to roll you into another BUD/S class," Zinke said. "From this point forward, you answer to me."

"Thank you, sir," Jeremy said with his life's biggest-ever sigh of relief. "I will not let you down."

"I'm proud of you, Jerms," said Ben after Jeremy finished telling the story. If anyone fully appreciated what this improbable second and final chance meant to Jeremy, it was Ben.

As the phone call with Ben continued, Jeremy listened to stories about enemy gunfire, explosions, and, worst of all, what some terrorists in Iraq were doing to children.

"Jeremy, they'll kidnap families at gunpoint and tell a little kid that if he doesn't go out and plant an IED or take a shot at our convoy, they'll kill his entire family," said Ben, who was becoming increasingly anguished.

Ben had looked into the eyes of eight- and nine-year-old children as they fired upon him and his fellow soldiers. Witnessing that horror tested Ben's faith in God and humanity. Ben never shared these stories with me, as I was too young and inexperienced, but in Jeremy, he had a big brother who could understand his pain, even though Jeremy hadn't yet served in a war zone.

"Just do your job, Ben," Jeremy said. "If someone is trying to kill you—no matter how old they are—you have a responsibility to those guys on your left and right. What about their wives and children back home?"

Ben understood what Jeremy was saying, but at the same time, the thought of potentially being forced to harm a child was abhorrent to Ben's beliefs, especially after a strict Christian upbringing.

Throughout the deployment, Ben and a teammate who shared his deep faith, Sergeant Robbie Walden, spent a lot of time talking to their unit's chaplain, playing guitar, working out, and reading the Bible. While in Mosul, the chaplain even arranged for Ben, Robbie, and a few fellow soldiers to visit a ninth-century church in the ruins of ancient Nineveh.

Praying inside the underground Church of Shamoun Al-Safa on the banks of the Tigris River was a cathartic experience for Ben and Robbie, who increasingly turned to the book of Revelation as their deployment to Iraq became more and more violent.

He will wipe away every tear from their eyes, and death shall be no more, neither shall there be mourning, nor crying, nor pain anymore, for all the former things have passed away.

REVELATION 21:4

While reading scripture helped Ben cope, he quickly learned that no book—not even the Bible—could explain the horrors of war.

"Here's what you'll need to look out for over here, Jerms," said Ben, shifting the conversation back to helping prepare Jeremy for urban warfare. He went on to tell more stories about combat inside the rapidly deteriorating Sunni Triangle.

"Stay safe over there, dude," Jeremy said.

"Good luck with the rest of BUD/S, bro," Ben said. "I love you."

Boom!

Ben's vehicle had struck an IED just outside of Samarra, resulting in a deafening blast and what felt like earthquake-level shaking. Ben, who was up in the turret, stayed cool as a cucumber despite a thermos bottle full of coffee spilling all over his camouflage uniform.

"I think we just got blown up," Ben said over the radio.

While it wasn't technically allowed, Ben had figured out a way to pipe music into the armored Stryker vehicle. Right after confirming they had been hit, Ben flipped a switch and blared Metallica into everyone's ears as an intense firefight began.

With "Enter Sandman" serving as the soundtrack, bullets tore through the blowing sand as Ben began blasting away at the insurgents from the turret. The resulting dust, noise, and carnage had become the norm a few months into a deployment full of firefights.

On this particular day, the IED had been relatively small and caused little damage. Soon after Ben and his teammates launched their counterattack, the overmatched enemy fighters stopped firing and presumably ran away.

Forty-five minutes later, Ben had time to catch his breath, take a leak, and finish what was left of his coffee as another Metallica song, "Hero of the Day," played inside the armored vehicle. A highly skilled U.S. Army sniper, Chris Galka, had just gotten back into the Stryker vehicle following the firefight. With his uniform soaked in sweat, Galka grabbed a bottle of iced tea he had brought from a nearby forward operating base that would serve as one of several FOBs Ben's platoon would temporarily call home.

After taking one small sip, Galka spit what he had thought was iced tea all over the lower section of the vehicle.

"What the heck is wrong with you, Ven?" said Ben while using Galka's nickname, which was short for *Venomous*. "Did you choke on all that sand flying around out there?"

"Negative," the platoon's suddenly gagging sniper said. "My iced tea tastes fucking terrible—like a cup of warm piss!"

My brother suddenly became more scared than he had been during the preceding firefight; he realized that he had just urinated inside another bottle that looked exactly like the one used to store the sniper's iced tea.

"I don't know how to tell you this, Ven," Ben stammered. "But I actually think you just drank my piss."

As four American soldiers drove away from their latest firefight, their laughter pierced the Stryker vehicle's armor and echoed through Samarra's narrow, war-ravaged streets. Galka, who would later be nominated for the Medal of Honor for heroism he displayed during a July 2004 firefight, joined the laughter despite carrying the awful aftertaste of my brother's urine for the rest of the day's missions.

The scout platoon's camaraderie was an asset throughout the seemingly endless deployment. Ben was a big part of that, whether it was by hosting impromptu guitar jam sessions or inviting teammates to his temporary living quarters to watch comedies like *Super Troopers* and *Joe Dirt* or his favorite TV show at the time, *The Shield*. If Ben wasn't in his room, you could usually find him at whatever gym was available to the men and women serving on a given FOB or air base. He always tried to stay in shape.

Even as a young, relatively inexperienced soldier, Ben was quickly and quietly becoming the heart and soul of his unit.

"I respect how much so many of the people here care about their religion. What I can't respect is how we keep getting shot at from mosques."

Ben had called Jeremy to vent a rare level of frustration after coming under attack from insurgent snipers in Mosul. The Christmastime 2003 ambush was Ben's closest call to date in Iraq.

Securing Mosul, a city of almost two million people, would be a huge challenge for Ben's unit and the entire U.S. military. "The wide expanse of the city's complex urban environment, however, required a higher concentration of troops," Reardon wrote in his book.

"When each Stryker battalion arrived in Mosul, it paired up with an element from Major General David Petraeus' 101st Airborne Division," Reardon added. This operation was taking place more than three years before Petraeus took command of all U.S. troops in Iraq.

By the time Ben's scout platoon arrived, Mosul was such a hotbed that his armored vehicle could barely drive around the city without being targeted by enemy fighters. They were under fire all day and every day they were in the northern Iraqi city, which had become gripped by bloodshed, tension, and fear.

As Ben explained to Jeremy on the phone, the mosque attack began like most engagements in Mosul and Iraq in general. It started with a bang.

"IED?" a soldier in Ben's vehicle said after the first explosion. The question mark would vanish after a second, even more deafening roadside bomb explosion shook the vehicle a few moments later.

Ben was once again manning the vehicle's turret hatch, which his helmet-covered head slammed into during the second explosion. Moments later, Ben heard three or four additional bangs followed by the smell of more smoke.

"I'm taking fire up here," Ben, whom fellow soldiers admired for his ability to almost always stay calm, said over the radio without the slightest indication of panic. "Can someone please find out where it's coming from?"

As the clanging sound of bullets landing just inches from Ben's head became increasingly rapid, my brother was told that the gunfire was almost certainly coming from a nearby mosque. Snipers who appeared to be operating from the mosque's tower were hitting everything from sandbags lining the road—referred to as Route Tampa by coalition forces—to armored vehicles and carts pushed around by Iraqi civilians who were now running for cover.

After immediately turning the heavy turret gun and aiming it squarely at the mosque tower, Ben hesitated before pulling the trigger. He fully appreciated the significance of firing on a Muslim holy site, while also knowing he was allowed to return fire if fired upon. When dealing with a place of worship, however, my brother knew he had to be as close to 100 percent sure as one could be in such a hectic urban combat zone.

With more and more rounds hitting the hatch, numerous shadowy figures were spotted hurriedly moving around the tower's openings. Upon surmising that his vehicle and all four soldiers inside it were in grave danger, Ben opened fire. He and the scout platoon sniper, Galka, helped lead an American counterattack that was fast, furious, and almost certainly deadly. It culminated with a TOW missile being fired at the enemy hideout.

"We tore part of the dome off the mosque, Jerms," Ben told our older brother. "It's just really sad that I had to spend an afternoon firing on a place where people are supposed to be praying instead of shooting."

"Again, you did what you had to do," Jeremy said in his firmest possible tone. "What were you supposed to do, let them kill you and your friends?"

"I hear ya, bro," Ben said. "But that doesn't make things any less messed up over here."

BUD/S training was going well for Jeremy, who was exhausted but devoid of any tangible aftereffects from the heatstroke incident. He had survived Hell Week and the swimming- and diving-focused Phase 2, which resulted in more freedom, especially on weekends.

Navy SEAL training wasn't easy for Jeremy or anyone else, particularly when it came to being continually sprayed by freezing cold water during frequent surf torture, but overall, he was doing as well as Commander Zinke, CWO Jordan, or any SEAL instructor could have imagined.

"I absolutely love it, dude," Jeremy told Ben. "I'm so close to getting over there and joining you guys—I can feel it. Stay strong," he continued. "I love you."

"Love you too, bro," Ben said before mimicking the customary end to his letters. "Benny out."

Iraq had descended into full-blown chaos by April 2004, and once again, Ben was right in the middle of it all. What had largely been a U.S.-led coalition versus Saddam Hussein had evolved into a lethal combination of America versus al Qaeda and Shiite versus Sunni.

One hundred forty American service members were killed in Iraq that April, which wound up being the second-deadliest month of the entire war for U.S. troops.

Ben and his fellow soldiers departed their FOB at midnight local time on April 7, 2004, to join a resupply mission. As attacks on American-led convoys reached unprecedented levels that spring, essential supplies like water, food, and toilet paper were becoming scarce on numerous FOBs and other makeshift U.S. military bases in Iraq.

Ben's platoon had already been forced to start rationing water and food. Combined with searing desert heat and the stark reality of seeing fellow Americans killed and wounded in combat, a growing sense of frustration was boiling inside my brother's unit. On that particular night, in fact, the platoon was on the back end of a two-week stretch of constant patrols and street fights with a shadowy enemy they were struggling to identify during battles.

Lack of rest, food, and sleep added to the sense of dread during what the soldiers knew would be a perilous mission in the narrow, pitch-black nighttime streets of Samarra. Intensifying the aggravation was the fact that they had been ordered not to engage with anyone—even suspected terrorists—on this resupply mission unless American lives were in danger.

Considering that Ben's group of grunts had been getting blown up and shot at while riding around Iraq for more than five months, being ordered out on what was supposed to be a midnight noncombat mission elicited several eye rolls and cusswords. In addition, all of Ben's soldiers were now experienced enough to know that the likelihood of not being fired upon anywhere in the Sunni Triangle—and particularly Samarra—was remote.

The relative calm was eerie for Ben, Robbie, and their fellow soldiers as the armored vehicle methodically crept down a quiet street. They had been ambushed and attacked several times in virtually the same spot, but it was nevertheless tempting to glance at the moonlight reflecting off the Tigris River and onto the battered buildings of the prehistoric city. Samarra had seen battles before, such as a key 1733 battle during the Ottoman-Persian War, but had never been such a hotbed of turmoil and brutality in the modern age.

As palm trees gently swayed in the nighttime wind, Ben and his brothers-in-arms hoped—against their better judgment—for a quiet ride through the heart of the Sunni Triangle. That's when the bullets began ricocheting off the armored vehicle.

To Ben, it sounded like a hailstorm, albeit much louder and far more frightening. Within a few moments, his Stryker vehicle lost power and went almost completely dark.

While it was impossible to know the exact number, especially in the dead of night, approximately fifty insurgents had surrounded the American-led convoy of armored trucks and other vehicles. Three separate RPGs quickly blasted the side of Ben and Robbie's vehicle, which was also manned by the sniper, Galka, and their squad leader, Staff Sergeant Matt Hudgeons. An IED had also hit the Stryker vehicle next to them.

Ben's close friend Robbie was in the most precarious position when the firefight erupted, given that he was exposed to the enemy from an open hatch next to the driver.

Not only was it pitch-black outside other than brief illuminations from fiery explosions and whizzing bullets, but the vehicle's interior was almost as dark as Ben frantically worked to restore its power.

Using his lips to hold a small flashlight pointed toward the fuse box, two words screamed by Robbie startled Ben even more than the pulsating blasts of RPGs and IEDs.

"I'm hit!"

Robbie had been almost immediately shot when the battle erupted. The enemy bullet had ricocheted off his bulletproof vest and plunged deep into his left shoulder. Pinned behind his weapon as blood ran down his side and flooded the inside of his uniform, Robbie was now a sitting duck. His eardrum had also been blown out during the already frantic firefight.

"I've got you!" Ben said as he helped Robbie out of the turret and back inside the Stryker vehicle, which was still powerless and under siege.

Robbie had a hard time hearing Ben's exact words as my brother bandaged his bleeding shoulder without the benefit of light or—at that time—formal medical training. But it wouldn't have surprised him if Ben was quoting the book of Revelation, which they had been reading together and discussing for the past several months.

Ben helped stop Robbie's bleeding, which ultimately saved his life. As of 2019—more than fifteen years after the shooting—Robbie was still having surgeries performed on his shoulder. The wound was profound, complicated, and life-threatening.

After Ben bandaged him up, Robbie somehow mustered the strength to return to the turret gun. Despite a throbbing shoulder and ringing ears, the wounded soldier joined Ben, Galka, Hudgeons, and the rest of the armored convoy in lighting up Samarra's night skies with American firepower. The insurgents were quickly and absolutely annihilated.

Robbie returned to Camp Anaconda for treatment before being medically evacuated to Landstuhl Regional Medical Center in Germany and ultimately being sent home. Even though his deployment was cut short, Robbie and Ben had already become best friends for life.

As he strummed his guitar while recovering and waiting for his brothers-in-arms to come home, Robbie pondered the fitting nature of Ben being the soldier who had saved him from bleeding to death on the streets of Samarra.

Robbie went on to become a successful musician. His feelings of gratitude toward my brother would inspire him to write and record with the same spirit he and Ben had brought to their jam sessions on FOBs all over war-torn Iraq.

Back in Southern California, Jeremy had gotten only about four hours of sleep in the past three days. His entire BUD/S class was presumably just as cold, hungry, and exhausted when their instructor issued a challenge to my oldest brother.

"All right, Wise, if you answer this question correctly, you and your classmates get forty-five minutes of sleep," the instructor said. "Are you ready?"

"Yes, sir," Jeremy said, soaking wet and standing at attention.

"What was the name of the motorcycle Bruce Willis rode away on toward the end of *Pulp Fiction*?" he said.

There was an audible sigh of relief from the SEAL trainees, who knew Jeremy and his propensity for quoting movie lines.

"Senior Chief!" Jeremy shouted. "It's not a motorcycle, baby, it's a chopper. And its name was Grace."

"Out-fucking-standing!" the instructor said with an extremely rare smile. "Go get some sleep, gentlemen."

Ben, on the other end of the line in the Sunni Triangle, heartily laughed as Jeremy recounted how he had endeared himself to his entire BUD/S class by quoting a movie and earning them a valuable nap.

"Zed's dead, baby," my brothers, quoting another line from the same scene, said in unison while separated by more than seventy-five hundred miles. "Zed's dead."

As their phone conversation continued, Ben was struck by Jeremy's lack of sleep. While he obviously wasn't getting much shut-eye himself inside a war zone, Ben wondered how Jeremy could function at such a high level, both physically and mentally, while experiencing the fog of extreme fatigue.

"You're on autopilot for the most part," Jeremy explained, adding that he didn't even remember the events of most days. "Your brain starts shutting down, and short-term memories stop turning into long-term memories."

Ben's army training was tough, but after not making it into Ranger School, he hadn't yet experienced the kind of punishment that special operations warriors are routinely subjected to during training and top-secret missions. He was fascinated by Jeremy's BUD/S stories, which he found even more interesting than what he was doing in Iraq. Jeremy felt the opposite since he hadn't experienced combat, which made for an interesting dynamic when he and Ben talked.

"What can I say at this point, Jerms?" Ben said. "Iraq is a freaking disaster right now. It's a powder keg, and the guys and I have a front-row seat to watch it explode."

Jeremy wasn't able to watch much news while trying to get through BUD/S, but it was on this particular phone call that he began really worrying about Ben's safety. Rather than get sappy, however, Jeremy returned to *Pulp Fiction*. This time, he quoted Ezekiel 25:17, the loosely quoted Bible verse one of the movie's gangsters, Jules, would recite before carrying out an execution.

The path of the righteous man is beset on all sides by the inequities of the selfish and the tyranny of evil men.

Blessed is he who, in the name of charity and goodwill, shepherds the weak through the valley of the darkness. For he is truly his brother's keeper and the finder of lost children. And I will strike down upon thee with great vengeance and furious anger those who attempt to poison and destroy my brothers. And you will know I am the Lord when I lay my vengeance upon you.

Once again, Ben could be heard laughing on his FOB in Iraq as Jeremy quoted the verse with the same vigor as Samuel L. Jackson.

"You're something, Jerms," Ben said. "Benny out."

Black Hawk Down, based on the book by Mark Bowden, was one of the most popular war films released in the immediate aftermath of 9/11. Jeremy and I saw it together, while Ben had gone out to see it while stationed at Fort Lewis. Ben was the kind of guy who liked going to the movies by himself, especially when the film had a serious subject.

Ben knew he was going to war by the time *Black Hawk Down* was released, but he couldn't have predicted how similar a dilemma he and his fellow soldiers would face on a different battlefield in the fall of 2004.

"The fighting that day invited comparison to a similar event during October 1993 in Mogadishu, Somalia, when U.S. personnel rescued the crews of two downed Black Hawk helicopters," Reardon wrote.

Indeed, September 4, 2004, in Tal Afar, Iraq, was Ben's *Black Hawk Down* moment.

Ben hadn't slept in about three days when he was sent out on a dangerous assignment about sixty miles west of Mosul. Tal Afar, which would become the epicenter of a major battle with al Qaeda in Iraq almost exactly one year later, was already gripped by fierce fighting and sectarian violence. Ben leaned on Jeremy's advice on how to operate on little or no sleep while embarking on his latest mission.

Ben was busy helping arrest four suspected terrorists when insurgents started firing RPGs from a house in the same vicinity. That set off a massive firefight, which included a truckful of Iraqi soldiers being hit by an RPG as Ben's unit also came under fire.

"The increasing enemy activity prompted the two Kiowa Warriors [helicopters] accompanying the operation to fly low to better see the narrow alleys crisscrossing the area," Reardon wrote.

Soon after, an enemy RPG downed one of the two American choppers. Much like in Somalia a decade earlier, the enemy fighters on the ground erupted in jubilation as the helicopter lay burning on the ground.

"The insurgents celebrated their success in bringing down the aircraft with a gale of steadily mounting fire," Reardon wrote.

Ben knew that from that moment forward, every second would count. The unit commander, Lieutenant Colonel Karl Reed, ordered the Kiowa pilots to take cover and stay put while he and Ben's scouts rushed toward the crash site to rescue them.

Braving enemy gunfire and explosions, Ben and his fellow soldiers quickly reached the pilots, both of whom had been injured, one seriously, according to Reardon. Not only did Ben help save both men's lives, he and the other scouts also recovered several sensitive items—presumably maps, intelligence reports, and weapons—that the terrorists could have used to target American soldiers.

Securing the crash site was no easy task. "The scouts were receiving small-arms fire down every alleyway, making it impossible for them to secure good positions without suffering losses," Reardon wrote. As Ben's unit waited for reinforcements, "sustained bursts of enemy assault rifle and machine-gun fire were erupting from the west."

Ben and his fellow soldiers responded by unleashing hell on the insurgents. "The dismounted scouts returned burst for burst, using so much ammunition that for the first time in ten months they found themselves sending back to their Strykers for more," according to Reardon.

The fighting became so heavy—and the situation so precarious for American forces—that Lieutenant Colonel Reed eventually called in an air strike by two U.S. Air Force F-16 fighter jets. Ben and his unit had just three minutes to take cover before a suspected insurgent about three hundred yards from where he was standing was leveled by American airpower.

"Within seconds of the bomb's release, a wall of dark smoke and dirt rose well above the skyline," Reardon wrote.

Covered in debris, sand, and the blood of injured American pilots, Ben experienced a momentary thrill of victory. More than one hundred insurgents had been killed in the battle, according to Ben's commanding officer, compared with seven U.S. troops injured. Ben was relieved and extremely proud that no Americans had died that day, largely because he and his teammates were able to reach the downed pilots before the enemy could.

"I couldn't believe how prepared they were to recover this aircraft," Lieutenant Colonel Reed later told Reardon. "It looked as if they had rehearsed the task beforehand."

Ben was involved in several more firefights before coming home, including a September 30, 2004, ambush that resulted in five Americans being wounded by a roadside bomb and the ensuing firefight. Ben's scouts killed at least six insurgents during the battle.

By Thanksgiving, Ben was home from Iraq after surviving and excelling under the most difficult and grueling urban fighting conditions a modern soldier could experience. Because of food rationing and many other missed meals while out in the field, he had lost a huge amount of weight—probably more than fifty pounds—while deployed. It's safe to say that Thanksgiving dinner in 2004 was the best meal of Ben's life.

When it was all said and done, Benjamin Brian Wise had been part of a historic deployment that army officers and leaders would study for years to come.

"They performed remarkably well in Samarra and Mosul, quelled the violent streets of Baghdad, fought and won in Tal Afar," Reardon wrote. "In the process, they earned the nickname Ghost Soldiers from the enemy, a tribute to the relative silence that accompanied their rubber-tired Stryker on the battlefield."

Thirteen U.S. Army soldiers were killed in action on the deployment, according to Reardon's book, including an additional thirteen noncombat deaths and "some three hundred casualties." Seeing friends like Robbie leave Iraq with serious wounds as other soldiers departed the war zone in flag-draped caskets had a huge impact on Ben, who also never fully shook the harrowing images of AK-47s being fired by kidnapped children.

Ben called Jeremy as soon as he was stateside to let him know he had survived the war in Iraq. He was thrilled to learn that at the same time, Jeremy had finished BUD/S training and would soon become a Navy SEAL.

"You did it, Jerms," Ben said before cracking a joke. "And it only took about ten years."

"Thanks, dude," Jeremy said. "Now it's on to Jump School. What's next for you?"

Ben, who didn't want Jeremy to think he was trying to steal any of his thunder, paused before sharing his plans.

"I want to go special ops . . . just like my big brother," he said. "I want to be a Green Beret."

5

BACK TO IRAQ

Just as Ben started the lengthy training regimen required for any U.S. Army soldier who wants to become a Green Beret, Jeremy arrived in Baghdad for his first combat deployment as one of the newest members of SEAL Team 4.

"I cannot believe I'm being paid to do this, Beau," Jeremy told me shortly after arriving in Iraq. "This is amazing."

Based on his wide-ranging combat experiences in Iraq, Ben had warned Jeremy that in early 2005, Navy SEALs weren't getting the majority of high-leverage missions due to the U.S. Army being in command of combat operations in Iraq. The hairiest assignments, which were coveted by SEALs, would often go to Rangers and sometimes Green Berets.

That didn't sit well with Jeremy, who joked that the early part of his deployment resembled being left with blue balls. Like his teammates, my oldest brother wanted to spend every single day in the fight.

"I don't get it, Beau," Jeremy said. "We're all ready to go to hell and back, yet most of the time they want us sitting here doing next to nothing. I just don't understand it."

Jeremy's occasional frustrations were far outweighed by his

pride in having earned the coveted SEAL trident and for finally getting the chance at deploying to a war zone. He was in the best shape of his life, both mentally and physically, and embraced the chance to learn from a tight-knit group of Virginia Beach–based special operations warriors.

The first thing many of the SEAL Team 4 guys noticed about Jeremy was the exact same hobby Ben was known for inside his infantry unit: playing the guitar. For the second time in as many years, the sounds coming from a Wise brother's amplifier could be heard echoing through part of a U.S. military base during an especially violent chapter of the war in Iraq.

There was one big difference, however: Ben was a much better guitar player than Jeremy.

"For Christ's sake, Wise, that sounds like a bunch of dying cats!" one of the SEALs yelled at Jeremy from his bunk. "Knock it off!"

To put it mildly, many of the SEALs were not pleased with the new guy's repeated attempts to play Van Halen and AC/DC inside their makeshift living quarters at Baghdad International Airport. It got so bad that Jeremy was eventually kicked out of the barracks and then another common area for annoying the other guys with his electric guitar's errant shrieks.

"What the fuck is that?" one of the SEALs asked a few days later while walking by a medium-size wooden box with a cord running inside it. "Is there an animal in there?"

Instead of finding a dying cat, the SEAL discovered Jeremy strumming his guitar inside the insulated crate. Like Ben, he loved music so much that nothing—not even a bunch of tough Navy SEALs—would stop him from trying to play his favorite instrument.

There had been several landmark events in Iraq since Ben left and Jeremy arrived. The historic, bloody Second Battle of Fallujah had concluded just before Christmas in 2004 with nearly one hundred Americans killed and more than five hundred wounded, with much bigger losses for the enemy.

While the massive urban clash was a hard-earned victory for coalition forces, it most certainly did not end the violence in Al-Anbar Province or the country as a whole. In fact, Ben was deployed to Iraq for the two deadliest months of the entire war, April and November 2004, while Jeremy arrived in the third-worst month: January 2005.

On January 26, 2005, thirty-one U.S. troops were killed when a CH-53E Super Stallion helicopter carrying U.S. Marines assigned to secure a polling site for the upcoming parliamentary elections crashed in Al-Anbar Province. It was the deadliest incident and overall day—with thirty-seven U.S. service members killed around the country—of the entire Iraq war.

"The story today is going to be very discouraging to the American people. I understand that," President Bush, who had just started his second term as commander in chief, said at the White House on that tragic day. "We value life and we weep and mourn when soldiers lose their life. And—but it is the long-term objective that is vital, and that is to spread freedom."

As the polarizing debate over the Iraq war continued at home, Jeremy focused on nothing but becoming the best special operator that he could possibly be. Early on, Jeremy's primary job was not to "kick down doors, blow shit up, and shoot people in the face," which had always been his ultimate goal. Instead, he was mostly assigned to be a driver in convoys protecting Iraqi and coalition VIPs.

While it wasn't Jeremy's first choice, he had completed an evasive driver course—essentially special driving school—as part of his SEAL training. Like you might see in *The Fast and the Furious* and another favorite car-chase movie of Jeremy's, *Ronin*, he had learned how to drive like a Hollywood stuntman in real life. The difference, of course, was that my oldest brother wasn't standing in for an action movie star but preventing terrorists from reaching their targets in the middle of combat zones.

Jeremy sometimes served as a gunner in a trail vehicle, but most often, he was driving the "takeout vehicle" that would confront any enemy car, pickup truck, or SUV that was trying to penetrate the cone that would surround the vehicles carrying Iraqi and foreign dignitaries. After the circle of U.S. and coalition vehicles collapsed around the VIP, Jeremy's Suburban or Crown Victoria would come roaring in while using any means necessary to incapacitate a vehicle that posed a threat.

Basically, Jeremy was riding around Baghdad smashing into vehicles full of insurgents and terrorists. It was intense, exhilarating stuff.

Ayad Allawi was the first prime minister of Iraq after the fall of Saddam Hussein's government. In power since mid-2004, when the U.S.-led coalition officially transferred the country's sovereignty back to Iraq, Allawi was put squarely in the middle of a burgeoning Sunni-Shiite civil war as coalition troops battled foreign and domestic terrorists throughout the country's deserts and city streets. Even though he was widely regarded as a moderate Shiite, the prime minister was nevertheless targeted by would-be assassins shortly before Jeremy had arrived in Iraq.

After a few weeks in Baghdad, Jeremy was assigned to Allawi's protection team. Much like U.S. Secret Service agents, Jeremy and his fellow SEALs were tasked with keeping Iraq's interim leader safe at all costs, including their own lives.

Ben had already battled al Qaeda in Iraq during his first deployment. Now it was Jeremy's turn to confront al-Zarqawi's growing group of vicious killers.

It was nighttime in western Baghdad on April 20, 2005, when a pickup truck packed with TNT and mortar rounds tried to ram into Allawi's convoy at a roundabout near Al-Zawraa Park, according to Al Jazeera. The network's April 20, 2005, report said the attacker blew himself up after "security guards"—most likely Navy SEALs—started shooting at him.

The subsequent explosion "was a massive blast and many homes in the area were badly damaged." Two Iraqi police officers were killed, but Allawi escaped with no injuries. Al Qaeda in Iraq later claimed responsibility for the terrorist attack and assassination attempt.

Jeremy never told me whether he was part of that specific convoy, but given his assignment to Allawi's protection team, I would be willing to bet that he was. Additionally, Jeremy later showed me an Armani suit and an expensive watch, both of which he said were given to him by Allawi as expressions of gratitude. While it's only an educated guess based on several conversations with former SEALs, I have a strong feeling that Jeremy played some sort of role in saving the Iraqi prime minister's life on that harrowing night.

Allawi wound up serving less than a year as prime minister after his party lost the parliamentary elections, but if it weren't for Jeremy and his SEAL platoon, Iraq's fledgling post-Saddam leadership would have almost certainly faced even greater turmoil. Allawi later wound up serving as the country's vice president from 2014 to 2015 and again starting in 2016.

Shortly after Jeremy returned from Baghdad, Ben, who was in North Carolina for Green Beret–related training, went to Virginia

Beach to welcome his big brother home. They had gone out to a local sports bar to relax and have a few drinks when Jeremy noticed an attractive waitress.

"You need to talk to her," Ben told Jeremy. "There's something different about her."

Jeremy did just that. The friendly, pretty brunette's name was Dana, and after a few subsequent dates, Jeremy knew he had found the love of his life. My oldest brother became quickly and fully devoted to Dana and her young son, Ethan, whom Jeremy would always treat like his own little boy.

As Ben continued to excel during the many challenging phases of Special Forces training, Jeremy was probably the happiest he had ever been. He had found his purpose in life as a Navy SEAL, a devoted boyfriend to Dana, and a father figure to Ethan.

Unlike the first deployment, leaving for Iraq in late 2006 was difficult for Jeremy. Several SEALs in his platoon had wives, fiancées, or girlfriends and a few had children, but it was impossible to understand what it was like to leave significant others behind until you actually did it.

The only solace Jeremy could take was that SEAL combat tours were almost always much shorter than standard military deployments. If everything went as planned, which was far from a certainty in the middle of unprecedented levels of terrorist activity and sectarian violence, Jeremy would be back from Iraq in early 2007.

When my oldest brother landed at Baghdad International Airport in late 2006, it marked the third straight calendar year that a Wise brother had served in Iraq. That ominous streak, which was enormously stressful for my parents back home in Arkansas as they prayed for the safety of my brothers, would continue until a new annual streak of Afghanistan deployments began in 2009.

One Navy SEAL who served on Jeremy's second tour of duty called it "the greatest deployment ever." Another referred to Baghdad at the time as "the Wild West." It was during these violent months that Jeremy finally got his chance to go head-to-head with the enemy on a regular basis.

It was nighttime as Jeremy's Delta platoon—made up of SEALs, Green Berets, and Iraqi Special Forces troops the Americans were tasked with training—approached a relatively large house in Baghdad. It was almost completely quiet except for the sound of slowing rotor blades of the helicopter from which the U.S. and Iraqi special operations warriors had dismounted.

While the target location was technically within city limits, it didn't feel to Jeremy like he was still in the Iraqi capital. The home was in an uncharacteristically rural neighborhood on Baghdad's outskirts, with a large backyard and a stream running behind it. It was a good thing the SEALs always had their night vision equipment, because the only light was coming from the moon.

Jeremy wasn't one of the breachers that night, which—knowing my oldest brother—was a disappointment. Instead, Jeremy was on the assault team behind the SEALs who were assigned to bust down the door and immediately secure the home's interior.

Right as the breacher ignited a small explosion to bust open the door lock, Jeremy looked up and saw a shadow moving rapidly through the house's second-story window. Given the intelligence reports indicating that the structure was full of insurgents, Jeremy and the assault team had been authorized to fire if they sensed a threat to the breachers or anyone else.

With years of training in his back pocket, Jeremy knew it was time for him to act. Judging by the radio silence, nobody else had even seen the shadow, which meant my brother had to make a split-second decision to protect his fellow SEALs. With no time to spare, Jeremy took off running through the darkness and toward the house.

Pop! Pop!

Jeremy fired what's known as a *hammered pair,* or two shots fired in swift succession, at the window. Without the luxury of a warning, the breachers were suddenly covered with shattered glass as smells of gunpowder and smoke filled the previously calm nighttime air.

Before the armed suspect could fire a shot, the man Jeremy had fired upon jumped from the window and started limping toward the backyard, presumably hoping to make it to the stream and escape. He only made it a few steps before being tackled and manhandled. Jeremy kind of felt bad for the guy, knowing that he had absolutely no chance against America's elite.

When the bad guy was handcuffed, the platoon medic was called in to render aid after one of the SEALs who'd tackled him realized the suspect had suffered multiple gunshot wounds.

After the assault team finished clearing the building and rounding up more suspected insurgents, Jeremy saw the man he had shot at lying in the grass before being put on a stretcher. One of the gunshots had almost completely shattered his forearm.

"Wise, didn't you fire a couple of rounds at this guy?" one of the SEALs said as he and Jeremy made their way back to their helicopter.

"Yeah, that was me," my brother said.

"Why's he's still alive, then?" Jeremy's SEAL buddy said with a chuckle.

While it may seem cold or even heartless, Navy SEALs are trained to kill. If someone in the platoon fired a nonfatal shot or missed his target, he would sometimes be subjected to some friendly mockery from his teammates. These were men of war, and when you're in a red-hot combat zone getting shot at almost every single night, the brand of humor was much different from the jokes Jay Leno and David Letterman were telling on TV back home.

Despite gentle ribbing from the other SEALs, Jeremy knew he had almost certainly helped spare the breachers from being wounded or even killed. It was a good feeling and precisely the reason my brother loved his job.

Just before Christmas in 2006, Jeremy and a fellow SEAL were coming back to their base—Camp Dublin at Baghdad International Airport—from another mission. As my brother went through a checkpoint, he and the other SEAL noticed a boxful of puppies shivering in the nighttime air. Baghdad got a lot colder that time of year than most Americans realized.

"We had about ten of them," one of the U.S. Army soldiers guarding the base told Jeremy. "The mom wasn't healthy, and a few of them died."

When the soldier asked Jeremy and his buddy to take a couple of puppies back to Camp Dublin, they were forced to decline due to protocol, as a senior officer was watching from inside the guard station. Later that night, however, Jeremy and his fellow SEAL changed out of their uniforms, jumped in a Suburban, and snuck back over to the checkpoint carrying only their military IDs.

Jeremy and his friend then discreetly found the army veterinarian responsible for the base's military working dogs and convinced him to vaccinate the little puppies, who would become the unofficial pets of Camp Dublin. The SEALs named them Hooley and Sledge, after two of the tools used during breaching operations.

As the puppies wandered around Camp Dublin, which the

SEALs had built with their own tools and bare hands, Jeremy passed the time between missions mostly by calling or emailing Dana, playing his guitar, and reading. This was not typical among the SEALs, as most could be found sneaking beer onto the base, playing pool, watching football, or "reading" adult magazines.

While Jeremy joined in most of those activities and was generally one of the guys, he was probably the only SEAL on the base regularly reading William Shakespeare, Friedrich Nietzsche, and the Bible. Along with Jeremy's frequent tardiness, which started when he was late to his own SEAL graduation ceremony, my brother's bookworm-like habits occasionally rubbed his teammates the wrong way. Some thought Jeremy was trying to show off his intellect, when in reality, my oldest brother—much like Ben during his Iraq deployment—was just being himself.

Jeremy helped counter the nerd narrative by becoming a contributing editor of an on-base newsletter called *The Horse's Ass*. Like an offline, militarized version of *The Onion*, which was just starting to gain online popularity back home around that time, the entirely unofficial SEAL publication poked fun at a special operator's life while deployed and almost always at the decisions being made by commanding officers. That made the newsletter a closely guarded secret among those serving in the Baghdad platoons.

"It's so shitty over here that all I have to look forward to is this newsletter," a SEAL on base told one of Jeremy's buddies.

As the calendar flipped to 2007, Jeremy was in firefights approximately three out of every five nights. The roadside bombs that Ben had frequently encountered in his Stryker vehicle were becoming even more commonplace, as were the ambushes that usually accompanied the explosions. In 2007, the definition of a U.S. service member facing death was simply getting in a vehicle and driving around Iraq for a few hours—or even minutes. Baghdad, like so many areas of the ancient, war-torn land, was incredibly kinetic and dangerous.

From al-Zarqawi's terrorists and al-Sadr's militia to Iranian-backed fighters pouring in from places like Syria, the country had become a nightmare, particularly in the west. The only hope seemed to be the new commander of multinational forces in Iraq, General Petraeus, who would soon implement several innovative counter-insurgency methods. Petraeus didn't take over until late January, however, which meant the impact of his new strategy wasn't really tangible until Jeremy's SEAL platoon went home.

The rest of Jeremy's time was spent training the Iraqi special operations guys, a duty that the SEALs and Green Berets mostly dreaded, since some of their foreign counterparts were lazy and wouldn't listen. Jeremy's platoon had been trained to kill terrorists, not teach a ragtag group of foreign troops how to execute tasks the SEALs had learned long before BUD/S. While politicians back home loved giving speeches about "training the Iraqis," it was viewed as a distraction by Jeremy, his teammates, and presumably many other U.S. troops risking their lives in Iraq during the height of the insurgency.

For Jeremy, the worst firefights were the ones he wasn't allowed to participate in. One particular night, a close friend of his serving in the partner platoon was sent on a mission several hours from Baghdad. The SEALs and Green Berets stumbled on a massive camp full of insurgents, resulting in a huge twenty-four-hour battle. Instead of being in the fight, Jeremy and his Delta platoon teammates were stuck listening to the frantic voices of their friends on the camp's radio.

When they heard a SEAL say that several had already been wounded, Jeremy asked his commanding officer for authorization to be a QRF (quick reaction force) for their Team 4 brothers. The request was denied.

Cursing as they packed up their gear, Jeremy and a close friend decided to defy orders and drive toward the danger. They made it as far as turning on a Humvee's engine before being emphatically directed to stand down. The SEAL officer in charge had to stand in front of the vehicle to prevent my brother and his buddy from disobeying orders.

Backed by air support, the pinned-down SEALs and Green Berets courageously captured, wounded, and killed countless insurgents before being airlifted out of the exhausting, costly battle. While it was seen as a victory, Jeremy, his friend, and others were furious at being ordered to stay away from the fight. The fact that several SEALs were wounded only added to Jeremy's frustration, even though he ultimately wasn't disciplined for attempting to circumvent orders.

By the time Jeremy and several teammates were eventually ordered to leave the Baghdad deployment early for an operation in Central America, my oldest brother was ready to get out of Iraq. Not only was he pissed off by what he believed was bureaucratic red tape getting in the way of accomplishing the mission he was trained for—killing terrorists—he missed Dana and Ethan. After a few months serving just north of the equator, Jeremy returned home in time to share in the joys of summer on Virginia Beach's beautiful boardwalk.

Shortly after my oldest brother got home, I moved into his and Dana's town house to spend time running, working out, and training by his side. I had tried pursuing a career as a percussionist by studying music on scholarship at Southern Arkansas University but quickly dropped out. Like Jeremy in medical school, my heart was elsewhere.

While I hadn't signed any enlistment papers yet, the fascinating stories from Ben's and Jeremy's deployments had only solidified my resolve to eventually serve in uniform. I wanted to do exactly what my big brothers had been doing in Iraq.

One evening, Jeremy and Dana asked me to come out with them and watch Ethan while they dined at their favorite Mexican restaurant. They hadn't been alone in a while, and I wanted to give them some time to themselves. Since the restaurant was located in a shopping center, I took Ethan, then four years old, to an ice cream parlor next door.

Jeremy and Dana's dinner was taking longer than anticipated, but rather than interrupt their romantic evening, I took Ethan back to the car to hang out. There were no iPads to entertain children in those days, so I put on the radio and tried to teach him some Led Zeppelin and Van Halen songs. Jeremy (and Ben) would have been proud.

When Jeremy emerged from El Tapatio, I noticed that Dana was crying. A few moments later, they told Ethan and me that they had just gotten engaged.

True to form, Jeremy had said nothing to me about his plans. As I extended both my right hand and my deepest congratulations, Jeremy was sporting the same mischievous grin as the night I had initially gotten in trouble for stealing our sister's Halloween candy. Just like when we were kids, being able to fool his little brother had made Jeremy's special evening even more memorable.

The next day, Jeremy and Dana were gone when I woke up early to start my morning workout routine. There was a note on the table asking me to watch Ethan after he woke up, so I figured the newly engaged couple had gone out to breakfast to celebrate.

After a few hours, I called Jeremy on his cell phone. I asked if he and Dana would mind me taking Ethan to the nearby Virginia Aquarium for a few hours.

"I'm getting married, dude," Jeremy said.

"Yeah, I know. I was there last night, remember?" I said rather incredulously. "Congratulations . . ."

"No, you don't understand," Jeremy said. "I'm getting married *right now*. I have to call you back."

Before I could react, Jeremy hung up. I later found out that they had gone straight to the county courthouse. My brother and his new fiancée were ready to tie the knot, and to put it mildly, they didn't want to wait another minute.

The next year, 2008, was full of similarly memorable moments. The first was Ben's Special Forces graduation at Fort Bragg. It would also mark the last time that all three Wise brothers were together.

Newly married and preparing for his third SEAL deployment to Iraq, Jeremy was exceptionally proud of Ben. As a special operations warrior himself, Jeremy knew the many years of hard work Ben had completed to reach this important moment, from their fight when he'd first enlisted in the infantry to Ben finishing the exhaustive fifth and final Green Beret training phase, which is known as Robin Sage.

Joining Jeremy, Dana, my mom, my dad, Heather, and me was Traci, whom Ben had met about a year prior while stationed at Fort Lewis. By coincidence, she was the next-door neighbor of Staff Sergeant Joe McCarty, with whom Ben had served on his first deployment to Iraq. Ben and Traci had quickly fallen in love and wound up getting engaged about a month after his July 2008 Green Beret graduation ceremony.

Like the first time Jeremy showed us his Navy SEAL trident, getting our first look at Ben in his green beret was a proud moment for the entire Wise family. My parents had been praying for all their children and especially me, since they were worried I was about to follow in Ben and Jeremy's footsteps. At the same time, they knew what my two brothers had endured to earn their respective places in the special operations community. Both accomplishments were tremendous.

As the booze started to flow following the graduation ceremony's pomp and circumstance, Ben pulled out his brand-new Yarborough knife. Since a few months after 9/11, every new Green Beret had been presented with a special version of the expensive stainless steel knife, complete with an individualized serial number. I had never seen a weapon so shiny and majestic looking. Combined with the Green Beret headgear, the knife was evidence that Ben had just done something extremely important.

True to form, Ben held up the knife in one hand and his beer in the other and started quoting lines from *Three Kings*, a 1999 movie about Operation Desert Storm starring George Clooney, Mark Wahlberg, and Ice Cube.

"Hey, Jeremy, is it true that to be in Special Forces, you have to cut off somebody's ear?" Ben yelled.

As his fellow special operator nodded and laughed, Ben and I posed together in a parking lot for a picture as we smiled and drank.

"Ben, pretend that you're cutting off Beau's ear," Jeremy said between gulps of beer. "Beau, you pretend to scream."

Just as we started to pose, Jeremy stumbled after spilling part of his beer. My oldest brother was bigger and more muscular than ever, so when he bumped into Ben, it was the worst possible outcome for the guy with the blade being held up against his ear. Seconds later, there was blood all over my (thankfully) dark dress shirt.

"You assholes!" I yelled.

Traci, Dana, and Heather were horrified, but all the military men watching were almost immediately howling with laughter.

That included Jeremy after he checked to make sure Ben hadn't cut off my ear, much like the gruesome scene in *Reservoir Dogs*.

Upon realizing that I would be fine, Jeremy shouted out another line from *Three Kings* that just about put every military man in the room on the floor.

"Well, Ben, you did it!" Jeremy said. "You actually cut off a guy's ear!"

Ben was mortified and apologized even more profusely than the blood gushing from my ear. Traci, whom I barely knew but could already tell was a great match for Ben, then rushed outside with a pile of paper towels. As it turned out, patching up my wounded ear wound up being Ben's first official act as one of the U.S. Army's newest Green Beret medics.

By the time Jeremy received his orders to return to Baghdad International Airport toward the end of 2008, Ben—who had asked an overjoyed Traci to marry him right before deploying—was already in Iraq.

I had enlisted in the Marine Corps that September, much to the chagrin of my parents and especially my mother, who didn't speak to me for two weeks after I informed her of my decision. Considering that my mom was about to have two sons serving in Iraq at the same time, her reaction was entirely understandable. Even at the seven-year mark of America's post-9/11 wars, very few military moms had experienced the anxiety that Mary Wise would soon be forced to endure as one son after another left home to join the fight.

In a strange way, Jeremy's third deployment seemed more like his first. Even though he had already fought in Iraq twice, he didn't have a wife or little boy during his initial rodeos. On top of everything, the war—at least in the Iraqi capital—had reached a relative lull by the time Jeremy's SEAL Team 4 platoon returned in late 2008. In addition to what seemed to be a constantly evolving military strategy in Iraq, a new commander in chief—President-elect Barack Obama—was about to move into the Oval Office.

One of Jeremy's teammates described their previous Baghdad deployment as "like living in a video game." Using that analogy, my oldest brother's third and final stint in Iraq was more like reading *War and Peace*. There was combat, to be sure, but compared to Jeremy's first two tours, things were slow, drawn out, and rather boring.

Once again, Jeremy passed the time by calling and Skyping with Dana, playing the guitar, reading his nerdy books, and writing humorous pieces for *The Horse's Ass*. His articles were funny but also getting a bit edgier this time around as Jeremy and some of his teammates grew more and more frustrated with some of the daily decisions being made by leadership.

On this deployment, Jeremy's SEAL platoon was working with U.S. Army Rangers in addition to Green Berets. Some in command probably viewed these units like all-star teams, but they functioned more like a group of highly paid free agents who never fully found their team chemistry. In pro football terms, the joint platoon should have had an undefeated 16–0 season on paper. In reality, they were more like a 9–7 team that barely made the playoffs. Simply put, there were too many egos to fit in one locker room.

For Jeremy, the bright side of this Baghdad deployment was finally being able to fulfill his dream of being a breacher. While the nature of the enemy he was facing sometimes prevented Jeremy from doing the job as he had always pictured, the skills my brother had carefully developed over the last few years became invaluable to SEAL Team 4.

While al Qaeda in Iraq was still a factor on his third tour, Jeremy was usually going up against Iranian-backed militias. They would often hide in three-story structures, which made Jeremy responsible for getting inside without alerting everyone in the building to his presence. Instead of kicking down doors, blowing shit up, and shooting people in the face, Jeremy would often use his hydraulic tools to quietly and carefully penetrate a lock. Once the door flung open, however, my war paint–faced brother would join the assault team in battling the Iranian-financed insurgents and terrorists up close.

Jeremy also went out of his way to make sure the younger SEALs were not only doing their jobs but doing them as safely as possible. Even during frantic house-to-house combat, Jeremy would have one eye peeled to the newer guys to make sure they weren't putting themselves or others in unnecessary danger. While Jeremy could fire a split-second shot as well as anyone, he would often be the only SEAL taking an extra moment to ensure those around him were in the safest possible positions first.

As good as Jeremy felt after his platoon cleared a house full of bad guys, he was angry and anguished when he believed those in charge were holding his platoon back as they risked their lives during each and every mission.

While I don't know if one particular night was the last straw for Jeremy, it certainly had a big impact on his outlook and overall morale. For weeks, Jeremy and his fellow SEALs were keeping a close eye on an Iranian-funded terror cell.

After U.S. troops were targeted there in several attacks, Jeremy's platoon formally asked the U.S. Army, which was in control of the area, for permission to break up the cell with the purpose of saving American and Iraqi lives.

With military leaders (and the politicians they answered to) presumably not wanting any more violence ahead of the upcoming Iraqi elections, the platoon's request was denied.

Jeremy saw the incident not only as an intelligence failure but one of leadership and a classic example of bureaucracy getting in the way of a war fighter's duty to defend the brave men and women serving next to him. In addition to another run-in with commanding officers during the deployment, Jeremy decided at some point during his final months in Baghdad that he would turn down the opportunity to reenlist.

Over three tours in Iraq, Jeremy had finally gotten an opportunity to live his dream as a Navy SEAL at war, but things were different now. In addition to his deeply held concerns about how the Iraq war was being waged, my oldest brother had a wife and a son to think about.

By the time Jeremy embraced Dana and surprised Ethan on a Virginia Beach playground while still donning his battle fatigues, he was at peace with his decision. Hearing Ethan yell, "Daddy's home!" to the other kids on the playground almost certainly solidified what had been a very difficult choice.

There would unfortunately be no rest for the weary, as Jeremy soon took a job with Xe Services, which was known as Blackwater until a bloody, controversial 2007 incident involving the deaths of Iraqi civilians. As far as Jeremy knew, the company had changed its ways and would give him the chance to provide for his new family. The job would require travel to war zones, however, including his first trip to Afghanistan.

By the middle of 2009, Jeremy was a married ex–Navy SEAL and Iraq war veteran. Ben was a soon-to-be married Green Beret still at war in Iraq, while I was a young, single U.S. marine hoping for the chance to follow my brothers' footsteps into war. While all three Wise brothers were doing what we wanted, the pressure it put on our parents, Dana, Traci, Heather, and others was sometimes lost in the fog of war. To me, all members of military families are heroes, too.

Even as a new marine, I didn't fully understand how dangerous Jeremy's new job would be. I definitely wasn't aware that his duties would include top-secret work for the CIA, either.

As for Ben, his Green Beret deployments wound up being more perilous than I ever could have imagined. It wasn't until later that I realized that my middle brother was known for being highly skilled not only as a combat medic but as an elite Special Forces sniper.

6

U-TURN

Four and a half years after first patrolling Mosul as a U.S. Army infantry soldier, Ben returned to the war-ravaged northern Iraqi city
in September 2008. His first Green Beret deployment was nearly
simultaneous with Jeremy's third and final SEAL deployment.
Overall, my two brothers deployed five times to Iraq between 2003
and 2009.

As Jeremy had witnessed in Baghdad, much had changed in
Iraq since 2004, from the rise of the Islamic State of Iraq (ISI) terrorist group to President Bush's mostly successful 2007 troop surge
led by General Petraeus. In Mosul, a lengthy operation, known
as the Nineveh campaign, began in January 2008 with a goal of
pushing ISI out of northwestern Iraq. The heaviest fighting had
occurred in May during an Iraqi-led offensive dubbed Operation
Lion's Roar. While there were victories along the way—most nota-
bly U.S. forces killing Abu Khalaf, the al Qaeda leader in Mosul—
overall results were mixed. By the time Ben arrived in Mosul, the
coalition offensive had unofficially concluded.

Like Jeremy's SEAL team, Ben and his fellow Green Berets
also had to grapple with rapidly tightening rules of engagement for
U.S. service members in Iraq. In some cases, pursuing a suspected

terrorist would require the U.S. military first going before a judge and obtaining a court order. Both my brothers were trained to find and kill terrorists, but due to decisions well above their pay grades, they were starting to feel more like police officers.

One would think Ben's prior experience riding around Mosul as part of the army's inaugural Stryker deployment would be valuable to his new Special Forces team. In reality, no one really cared. In the eyes of most of the Green Berets in A Company, Third Battalion, First Special Forces Group (Airborne), Ben was just another new guy who would have to earn his place on the elite combat squad. Because of his training schedule, Ben also joined the team midway through its Iraq deployment, which made his first few weeks there even more challenging.

When Ben arrived at FOB Marez, which was adjacent to another coalition military base known as Camp Diamondback, he was informed that there wasn't enough space for him to live among his teammates. Instead of bunking with his fellow Special Forces soldiers, my brother was sent to live with contractors in a small trailer. Being separated from the guys only added to the sense that Ben was some sort of outsider. While the Green Berets bunked and laughed together at night, Ben would lie on a cot listening to the sounds of the Mosul highway that separated the two U.S. military bases.

After getting his last good night's sleep for about five months, Ben called his new fiancée to tell her he had safely arrived in Iraq. Traci was nervous, but Ben tried to keep her emotions at bay by telling her he was mostly sitting inside a trailer on a heavily fortified base. The less Traci knew, Ben surmised, the less she would worry.

When Ben showed up at the firing range to greet his fellow Green Berets, he was met by a few cautious nods, but mostly looks of skepticism. Instead of talking up his previous Mosul deployment to the more experienced Special Forces soldiers, however, Ben decided on a different strategy to earn their respect. He started by picking up an M24 bolt-action sniper rifle.

Ben's new teammates were immediately impressed by my brother's skills as a marksman. Many were also surprised—and jealous—that a brand-new junior medic could shoot with such precision, even if it was only at paper targets. Ben would frequently score twenty out of twenty in sniper exercises while no one else would even reach nineteen. Simply put, my brother was the best shot on the team from the moment he joined them in Iraq.

As is often the case in the military and especially inside tight-knit Special Forces teams, all new guys would eventually be cut down to size. Ben's prolific shooting skills only accelerated the need for a reality check in the eyes of the elite soldiers who outranked him.

It started one scorching September day on the firing range, when one of the team leaders suddenly grabbed two Green Berets and ordered them to lie motionless in the hot desert sand.

"Hey, you're a casualty!" he yelled. "So are you!"

Ben was busy examining one of the team's new mine-resistant RG-33s, which were among the biggest armored vehicles he had ever seen. Ben and his senior medic were trying to figure out how to load casualties on and off the massive truck, which was high off the ground and would require a giant ladder, when all the commotion started.

Before Ben could figure out what was going on, the team sergeant was in his face screaming a series of orders.

"This guy has a gunshot wound to the chest!" the sergeant yelled, pointing to the soldiers he had handpicked. "This guy has lacerations on his arms and stomach!"

"Yes, Sergeant," Ben stammered, fumbling around for his medical kit.

"What are you waiting for?" the sergeant said. "You're the medic on scene—*get to work!*"

For the next fifteen minutes, everything that could go wrong went completely wrong for Ben. When he finally found his medical bag, he opened it with such authority that the kit's contents essentially exploded, leaving tools and bandages scattered all over the sandy terrain.

With sweat starting to soak his uniform as he panicked in front of the new teammates he had been so eager to impress, Ben let out a shriek of frustration.

"Fuck me!" Ben yelled as several onlookers couldn't help but shake their heads and laugh.

After a brief pause and a very deep breath, Ben let his many years of training kick in. My brother gathered his tools, composed himself, and got to work.

There were several more mishaps along the way, from Ben accidentally tearing open an IV bag to errantly ripping off the handle of his tactical combat tourniquet. Instead of going back into panic mode, though, Ben improvised. He found another IV bag and tore off part of a fellow soldier's uniform to replace the damaged tourniquet. His initial freak-out notwithstanding, Ben's creativity under pressure made a positive impression on the Green Berets in charge.

After successfully treating both casualties, Ben took a big gulp of water and smiled at the soldier who had originally barked the orders.

"Well, it could have been worse, I guess," said my smirking brother, who was still sweating profusely in the one-hundred-plus-degree desert heat.

Instead of complimenting Ben's efforts, the sergeant got right back in his face. "You're a new guy!" he screamed. "You're not allowed to have an opinion about anything!"

"Well, okay, Sergeant," Ben replied with a clear hint of sarcasm. "Whatever you say."

As the sergeant walked away, Ben turned to a few of his new teammates, all of whom had been entertained by the new guy's frenetic casualty drill.

"Why is that dude such an asshole?" Ben quipped.

Several of Ben's fellow Green Berets erupted in laughter. They not only admired Ben's ability to improvise under pressure but his sense of humor. In fact, the sergeant would later tell Ben that he was only kidding when he'd yelled at him the second time. He just wanted to see how my brother would react.

While Ben still had a lot to prove, he gradually blended into the culture of his new company. Jeremy's SEAL career might have been simultaneously coming to an end in a different part of Iraq, but for Ben, his special operations journey was just getting under way.

Ben wasn't as frustrated by Iraq's changing political climate and strict rules of engagement as Jeremy, mostly due to the fact that Ben hadn't been to war in nearly five years. His overwhelming interest was learning the ropes as part of a new team. In fact, Ben's first Special Forces deployment wound up being more like an extended training exercise rather than the almost daily firefights that served as the hallmark of his previous infantry stint.

Ben's team did occasionally get shot at, but mostly by nervous Iraqi soldiers who mistook them for the enemy. Night reconnaissance missions, during which Ben and his teammates would either drive or walk around an area of Mosul looking for threats, often posed the biggest risks. They were fired upon several times by Iraqi troops near checkpoints, but thankfully, no Green Berets were wounded. Even after more than five years of war, the Iraqi military simply didn't have the technological capabilities necessary to significantly lower the risk of friendly-fire incidents. It was just another challenge that Ben and his fellow soldiers had to deal with.

Ben also learned that for Green Berets, the most successful missions were those that prevented firefights rather than caused them. While many terrorist safe houses would be cleared during those five-plus months in Mosul, Ben's company prided itself on getting the jump on the bad guys to lower the risk of a violent encounter.

Whenever Ben went out on a mission, he and the senior medic would be tasked with bringing what was essentially a fully stocked hospital along with them. From severe trauma to the most annoying, widespread, day-to-day problem for U.S. troops in Iraq—mosquito bites—Ben had to be prepared for all possibilities at all times.

In addition to his responsibility to care for the wounded, Ben was still a Special Forces soldier in his own right. If a battle erupted, he was expected to fight.

Many civilians might think that deployments mostly devoid of hellacious firefights are boring for U.S. troops. While there is occasionally some downtime depending on where you are stationed, most combat tours are nevertheless hectic and exhausting. Between intelligence gathering, training, going out on missions, and mountains of paperwork, Ben and his teammates probably worked twenty-hour days in the blazing desert heat. Imagine doing that job thirty days in a row, let alone for five straight months.

Using breaching tools, shotguns, and other weapons, Ben's Green Beret team cleared dozens of suspected terrorist safe houses in Mosul. The problem, as Ben soon realized, was that the best ISI operatives—the ones who would cause the most problems for U.S. and Iraqi forces—knew to never keep bomb-making materials where they ate or slept. Most of those top terrorists would be transported to and from abandoned buildings to build their IEDs and suicide vests.

The result was that when Ben's team captured a suspected terrorist, he would usually spend a few weeks in the military prison system before eventually being released due to a lack of evidence. Risking their lives to capture bad guys who would subsequently be granted the privilege of using legal loopholes to escape justice was exasperating to any war fighter and especially to those in the special operations community.

Still, Ben did his job with quiet confidence that grew by the hour. He helped several fellow soldiers recover from shrapnel wounds, broken bones, sprained ankles, illnesses, and nasty bug bites. At the same time, he got a whole new perspective on war from some of the world's most elite warriors. Even if the action wasn't as frequent as his infantry deployment, it was every bit as interesting. The experience also helped prepare Ben for the combat missions he knew were almost certainly in his future.

When it was all said and done, Ben and his new Special Forces team made it all the way to the end of the deployment without firing a single shot. More importantly, no Green Berets were wounded or killed in action.

Despite the everyday frustrations they experienced, the men in Ben's company did their job and came home safely, which was almost unthinkable during the period of bloodshed Ben saw up close in Iraq less than five years earlier. It was a tremendous accomplishment for my brother and his new teammates.

Sitting inside a car outside Seattle-Tacoma International Airport on a chilly, gray January 2009 day was Traci, who nervously twirled her long blond hair as she waited for her fiancé to return from Iraq.

Ben was flying home commercial, which seemed strange to the

soon-to-be army wife. There were no American flags, WELCOME HOME banners, or red, white, and blue balloons. *Is this really what it's like?*

Without fanfare, Traci would see Ben for the first time in nearly six months at Sea-Tac's curbside check-in area. As they hugged and kissed, Traci was relieved to see no bumps or bruises on Ben's face. My brother also seemed calm and happy to be home, which was another relief, as Traci had also been worried about post-traumatic stress.

"I love you," Ben said. "I told you I'd be home soon."

To Traci, everything seemed fine. At long last, it was time for her and Ben to get on with their lives.

On March 29, 2009, Traci stood in a sparkling white dress inside a chapel on tiny Fox Island in Washington State's picturesque Puget Sound. It was her wedding day.

Unfortunately, I wasn't able to witness Ben and Traci exchange vows. After finishing basic training at South Carolina's Parris Island, I was training for my first deployment to Afghanistan somewhere in the Southern California desert. The Marine Corps had denied my leave request to attend my brother's wedding. Jeremy, who was making the transition from the navy to his new job as a contractor, was thankfully able to be part of the festivities, along with Dana, Heather, and my parents.

Traci was missing her own father, who had recently passed away, when Ben suddenly appeared in the chapel area before their wedding ceremony. For reasons only known to my middle brother, Ben had been charging around the small building as if he were clearing a safe house. Instead, he was looking for his soon-to-be wife.

When he found Traci, however, Ben quickly lost his power

of speech. Whatever he had planned to tell her was suddenly less important than admiring the beauty of his bride.

"Ben, what are you doing?" Traci said in a hushed tone of voice after noticing him standing there. "You're staring at me!"

My brother didn't say anything in response. Perhaps he was still too stunned to speak.

"You're not supposed to see me right before the wedding," Traci said. "Go back upstairs!"

A few minutes later, Traci and Ben once again locked eyes as they joined hands in front of their family and friends. Behind the altar was a large window facing out to Puget Sound. The only thing obstructing the breathtaking view was the happy couple, the pastor, and the bridal party, including Jeremy, who towered over just about everyone.

After hugging her oldest son, Ryan, Traci tried to compose herself as the ceremony began but quickly realized she was every bit as emotional as Ben seemed to be a few moments earlier. While Ben assumed that she was still thinking about her father, that wasn't it. Without any warning, Traci was overcome with gratitude that she and Ben had found each other a few short years earlier.

Tears filled Traci's eyes as she looked at Ben and became consumed by one singular thought: *This man would do anything for me.* Some people go their entire lives without finding a partner who embodies all their hopes and dreams. In that moment, Traci knew she was marrying a man she would always love and trust.

When it was time to recite their vows, Traci could hardly speak. Ben, who still thought she was emotional over her father's passing, tried to help Traci along as the audience gently laughed and cried along with her. Everyone in the chapel knew they were witnessing something special. This wasn't just another wedding.

Sure enough, the groom and the pastor helped Ben's bride

verbalize the rest of her vows, and just like that, Traci Wise was America's newest military wife.

The only surprise for some in attendance was that when they looked toward the altar, their field of vision wasn't full of shiny military uniforms. Not only was Jeremy officially out of the navy, but Ben had made a point not to wear his majestic Green Beret uniform while marrying Traci. As a gesture to his wife and everyone watching them tie the knot, Ben chose to wear a tuxedo like one would see a groom wearing at any other civilian wedding.

In that special moment, my brother didn't think of himself as an elite U.S. Army Special Forces soldier. He was, first and foremost, Traci's husband.

"To a long marriage, a happy life, and a wonderful family," Jeremy said at the reception while toasting the new couple. "Cheers."

Ben nodded in appreciation as he looked into the eyes of his big brother and took a sip of champagne. He and Jeremy had embarked on a long journey since their big fight back in Arkansas. Not only had the oldest Wise brothers become special operations warriors, but much more importantly in the eyes of my parents, they were good men who loved their wives.

There was no way Ben and Jeremy could have known that night was the last time they would ever see each other. I would give anything to have been there with them.

Shortly after the wedding, Ben found out that his Green Beret team would be deploying to northern Afghanistan in early January 2010. In an unlikely coincidence, Jeremy was scheduled to be in eastern Afghanistan at the same time for his first overseas assignment as a contractor for Xe.

To cap it all off, my first Marine Corps deployment was set to begin in November 2009. I was headed to southern Afghanistan to participate in the historic invasion of Marjah in the war-torn country's volatile Helmand Province.

Instead of looking forward to the holidays, Jean and Mary Wise were dreading having three sons in Afghanistan as soon as the calendar flipped to 2010. To this day, I cannot imagine what that looming sense of dread would feel like for any parent, including my own.

Fortunately, Ben had some big news that brought some much-needed joy to our mom and dad. He and Traci were expecting their first child—a son who would be born right around Christmastime. The timing would hopefully give Ben an opportunity to meet his baby boy before heading to Afghanistan.

As luck would have it, Luke Benjamin Wise was born at 1:30 p.m. Pacific time on December 15, 2009. The army had agreed to let Ben join his Green Beret team a few weeks late, which meant he wouldn't have to leave Washington State for Afghanistan until January 2, 2010.

Traci made a point to let Ben help out as much as possible during Luke's first two weeks on earth. Knowing that he would soon be stationed on a remote FOB largely without internet access for the next six months, Ben tried to pack the most into every single day, whether it was bottle feedings or simply lying beside Luke's crib.

During those two weeks, Ben took changing a diaper just as seriously as treating a wound on the battlefield. Nothing meant more to either of my brothers than being good fathers.

In the middle of one cold December night, Traci awoke to find nobody lying beside her. Guided by the dimly shining Christmas lights, she crept over to Luke's bedroom to check on her new baby. It was there that she found Ben sitting on a chair in the corner as Luke slept silently in his crib.

Ben had his Bible open but wasn't reading scripture. He was thanking God for his little boy.

"Please help me be the best dad that I can be, Lord," Ben said. "Amen."

When Ben and Traci woke up from another mostly sleepless night caring for their baby on December 30, 2009, Jeremy and I were already in Afghanistan. In just three days, Ben was set to board a plane and join us there.

It was a Wednesday, and my parents had just arrived in Washington State to meet their new grandson. There were no big plans that day other than driving over to Fort Lewis to pick up some baby diapers and groceries at the base's post exchange, or PX.

While Ben's upcoming deployment had cast a shadow over that entire week, including New Year's festivities, it was an otherwise normal, happy day for the Wise family. It was chilly, but the sun was shining when Ben, Traci, the kids, and my parents pulled out of the driveway in two separate vehicles. Ben was behind the wheel of one car, while Traci was driving the other.

A few minutes later, Ben's military-issued cell phone rang. In a panic, he quickly flagged down Traci and told her to make a U-turn and go straight home.

From that moment forward, life would never be the same.

7

THE BIG PUSH

In the fall of 2009, a few months before Ben received that fateful phone call, my fellow marines and I had gathered for our predeployment briefing at Marine Corps Base Hawaii. It was almost time for us to leave for southern Afghanistan.

"Gentlemen, Helmand Province has just been declared the most dangerous place in the entire world," Major Stubbs told my company.

"Ooh-goddamn-*rah!*" yelled my U.S. marine buddy, Sergeant St. John. His chant swiftly ignited the rest of us to join in our company-wide battle cry.

"*Ooh-rah!*"

Instead of being annoyed by the interruption, a smirk emerged on the major's usually grim, battle-hardened face. I could tell he was not expecting to hear such a thundering response to his sobering assessment, especially since he had just taken command of our weapons company.

Our screams were mixed with anger at the enemy and enthusiasm for doing our duty as United States Marines, which seemed to warm the heart of our new commanding officer (CO). After all, the last thing any CO wants to do is to lead a bunch of marines into combat who don't want to be in a hazardous area of operations (AO) in the first place.

"My bad, sir," St. John said to Stubbs, indicating that he was sorry for interrupting the major's briefing.

"Please don't apologize, Sergeant," said Stubbs, affirming his appreciation for the boisterous unanimity of our collective gusto.

Now smiling ear to ear, our combat leader resumed his briefing. "As I was saying, Helmand is the Wild West," Stubbs began.

Once again, the major was interrupted, but this time in my thoughts, which immediately flashed back to a recent conversation with Ben.

"Helmand Province is the Wild West," Ben, who was preparing for his own Afghanistan deployment, had just told me. "Keep your head on a swivel, brother."

Since I had far less military experience than Jeremy or Ben, my reply was predictably naive.

"I'm not worried, brother—" I started to tell Ben.

"Beau," Ben interjected in a tone that was growing louder by the word. "You should be! Fuck that Marine Corps invincibility bullshit. This is not a fucking video game."

Jeremy, who was (unbeknownst to me at the time) doing top-secret contracting work for the CIA, had started to look up to Ben over the last few years, even though they were both special ops warriors.

"Ben is one salty motherfucker," Jeremy, who would soon be stationed in a different part of Afghanistan, told me before we both headed off to war. "But make sure you listen to him."

With Jeremy's advice in mind, I apologized to Ben.

"It's okay," said Ben, whose tone had shifted from heated to one of genuine concern. "My mindset before my first deployment was exactly where yours is now."

After Ben made sure I had the correct set of tourniquets ready for what could be a bloody deployment (which was extremely important advice), he started to sound like our mother.

"Don't forget to wear your sunscreen," Ben said.

Even though I wanted to crack a joke at his expense, I resisted the urge. Ben was just looking out for his little brother.

"Got it," I said with an eye roll.

Ben's U.S. Army Special Operations Command (SOCOM) classification was 18 Delta, which meant he was more advanced than ordinary medics. In fact, SOCOM is said to be the second-most academically challenging military training program, next to nuclear chemistry. Like Jeremy said, Ben knew his stuff.

Still, as Ben told me what to be ready for in Helmand Province, I couldn't help but remember that even though he was preparing for a deployment there, he hadn't actually been to Afghanistan yet.

Once Ben finished the motherly advice, he started quoting from military intelligence reports about southern Afghanistan. Since Ben's team was heading to the war zone's vastly different northern sector, I realized that he didn't get this information from his team's briefings. Ben had used his special ops clout to obtain these reports because—as I had sensed in his voice—he was worried about me.

"I don't know exactly who is in Helmand right now, Beau, but you can bet your ass there are more of them coming," Ben warned.

Did he think I wasn't ready? Maybe it was just the dangers of Helmand—by far the most violent province in Afghanistan at the time—that concerned him, I thought. Perhaps he was just being a big brother, or maybe it was a little of both.

"All right, brother, I gotta go," Ben said as he pulled up to his house in Puyallup, Washington, where he was still preparing for Luke's birth and his Afghanistan deployment. "Remember: keep your head on a swivel."

"I will, Ben," I said. "Love you."

"Love you, too, brother," he said. "I'm praying for you. Good luck. Benny out."

Back in Kaneohe Bay, Hawaii, my attention shifted to my CO's pre-deployment briefing.

"First Battalion, Third Marines is inheriting part of an AO that is responsible for 60 percent of the world's supply of opium," Stubbs said. "The poppy trade is the only economic base and the only source of income that Helmand really has. The Taliban owns it all, gents. Opium is the Taliban's bank, and we're gonna shut it down."

Ben was right. This really was the Wild West.

"Pashtun culture is the most conservative of all Islamic tribes," the major continued. "It's also the oldest and most primitive in Afghanistan, especially in the south. Do not underestimate them. They've been fighting for the last century, fighting each other and the best the East and West could throw at them."

The hooting and hollering that once filled the room had turned to silence as each marine began to fully appreciate our mission's very real and daunting challenges.

"The good news is that these guys haven't faced the Marine Corps yet," our CO said.

Suddenly, the room's sagging chins began tilting upward.

"Gentlemen, about one in one hundred Americans will enlist in their lifetime," Stubbs said. "One-seventh of those will join the Marine Corps, and one-tenth of those will go marine infantry. This is just like Operation Phantom Fury in Fallujah. If you want to invade a fucking city, who do you call?"

"Marine Corps!"

"I'm sorry, who?" Stubbs said.

"Marine Corps, sir!"

"Damn right," the major said with a nod.

Our pre-deployment briefing might have been over, but as my fellow marines and I prepared to trade Hawaii's beaches for Afghanistan's mountains, Ben's "keep your head on a swivel" advice was still stuck in my head.

The Marine Corps was about to make America's biggest push into the world's most dangerous place. Even though I lacked the battlefield experience of my two brothers, I was poised—and ready, I hoped—to take part in a historic military campaign.

Less than a week later, we arrived at Camp Bastion (the British side of the base conjoined with Camp Leatherneck, then the largest U.S. Marine Corps base in southwest Afghanistan) for five to six days of orientation, briefing, and climatization, which was a fancy word for getting used to being thousands of miles from home. Next, we would push out to our battalion AO, FOB Geronimo.

From Geronimo, we would head to our respective company FOBs and/or patrol bases. Second Combined Anti-Armor Team was to have our own AO colocated with Bravo Company in the northernmost section of Nawa District, which was east of the notorious Taliban stronghold of Marjah.

Camp Bastion/Leatherneck was so much bigger than anything I had ever expected. It was a city packed to the brim with coalition forces: U.S. Marines, British troops, Afghan National Army soldiers, and Afghan police. U.S. Marines staged there before the Helmand invasion to take full advantage of the PX (which is basically the military's version of Walmart) and stock up on American tobacco, energy drinks, snacks, and canned goods.

We "meatheads," as marine infantry grunts are commonly referred to inside the military, also tried to take every advantage of the last opportunity to work out in a decent gym for the next seven months. As an 0331 infantry machine gunner, I took great pride in our meathead reputation as the original gangsters of the Marine Corps.

One morning, my buddy Daehlbacka and I decided to sign out for a workout break. After changing to our "green on green" PT (physical training) gear, we went to the closest "prison gym," as we called them. We decided on a dead lift leg routine and started our workout.

My marine buddy and I spoke very little, which gave my mind the only chance it needed to wander. I thought about my two brothers and the coincidental alignment of our deployment timelines.

Since I was unfamiliar with how things worked in a twenty-first-century war zone, I started to daydream about the remote possibility of running into one or both my brothers as we served "together" in Afghanistan. In reality, there was little to no chance of that happening. Because of the impending arrival of Ben and Traci's first child, who I wouldn't get to meet for another seven months (or so I thought at the time), Ben's arrival in Afghanistan had been delayed for another three weeks.

Then I thought specifically about Jeremy, who had told me even less than Ben about where he was going and what he would be doing. Through Xe, his new employer, Jeremy was hired by a Global Response Staff (GRS) team, which would be working directly for the CIA at FOB Chapman (also known as Camp Chapman) in Afghanistan's mountainous Khost Province near the border with Pakistan.

All I knew about Jeremy was that he would be working on a base somewhere to my north. At the time, I knew nothing about the CIA's involvement and what I would later find out was the top-secret, highly classified nature of his work in Afghanistan.

For some reason, all the unanswered questions about Jeremy's deployment began stacking up inside my head, but nevertheless, I wasn't truly worried about him. Since I was a child, my image of Jeremy was one of infallibility. In my mind, *Jeremy knew everything.*

Now almost completely lost in thought, I continued contemplating the possibilities of Jeremy's deployment. That's when another marine buddy, Greene, walked in with a baffled look on his face.

"Guys, what the fuck are you doing?" he said. "Inspections started ten minutes ago."

What?

Daehlbacka and I exchanged stunned looks before my eyes wandered down to my watch and then upward to the gym clock. That's when I realized it was set to the wrong time zone.

Shit!

We grabbed our rifles and made a mad dash for the weapons company tent, where we were supposed to already be in platoon formation for inspection. I grabbed my various weapons and threw on my flak jacket, Kevlar helmet, and protective eye pro goggles. When I sprinted outside and fell into formation, however, I realized I had forgotten my tactical belt, which would be considered a serious offense if a higher-ranking marine noticed.

From my POA (position of attention), I could hear my buddy Johnson and our TL (team leader), Lopez (everyone called him Lo-Lo), whisper the same exact thing: "Where the fuck have you been?"

"The gym," I whispered back. "I never reset my watch! Sorry."

Gearbomb is a putdown inside the Marine Corps for a grunt who can't get his gear straight. That's exactly what I was during my first PCI (pre-combat inspection), and by showing up late, all I had done was drawn unwanted attention to my accidental incompetence.

When the formation was released, I saw our lieutenant, Barnes, shaking his head before starting to whisper into Lo-Lo's ear.

"Tell Lance Corporal Wise to get his head out of his ass," I pictured him saying, even though I couldn't hear his exact words.

This was Lo-Lo's third deployment after being busted down from corporal at his previous unit due to a drunken driving charge. DUI notwithstanding, Lo-Lo knew he was squad leader material but nevertheless took his punishment like a man. He was a good marine who made a big mistake and took complete responsibility for it. I was grateful to have him as my TL.

For that reason, the look of disappointment on Lo-Lo's face was probably the worst punishment I could have received. As we started walking briskly back to the tent, he turned and gave me a brief shrug.

"Come on, bro," Lo-Lo said. "You're better than that."

"I know," I said. "I'm sorry."

"Take all that shit off, man," he said with a smile. "You look like a gearbomb."

As I sat down on my cot and began properly reassembling my gear, I was mad at myself for not being prepared like I knew Ben and Jeremy would have been. For the next hour, I obsessively organized my gear until it was perfect. If they sent us out on a mission right then and there, I would have been 100 percent ready to draw ammunition.

Still, I felt like crap for making Lo-Lo look bad to the lieutenant. Hat in hand, I walked over to his cot.

"It won't happen again," I told him.

"I know," Lo-Lo said with a grin.

By our third day stationed at Camp Leatherneck, my fellow marines and I were getting antsy. Despite our initial briefing about the dangers of Helmand Province, we still knew very little about the district we were going to and next to nothing about the job.

That's when our first sergeant walked into our company tent.

"Attention on deck!" his booming voice yelled.

The marine expeditionary battalion (MEB) commander, General Nichols, then strode like a giant into our company tent to deliver a significant proclamation.

"You're going to Marjah, gents!" he hollered.

Like our CO previously telling us we were deploying to the world's most dangerous place, the MEB commander's news was well received, to say the least. The invasion of Marjah was to be the biggest coalition invasion of a city since the Iraq war's bloody battles of Fallujah. This was supposed to be the deployment that every grunt dreams about and thinks he truly wants.

About five weeks later, we had already settled into to Patrol Base (PB) Casa Bonita, affectionately named after a *South Park* episode, as were the rest of our forward positions, much to the hesitant consent of our battalion commander (BC). The other positions within our immediate AO were Man Bear Pig, OP Junkyard, Castle Sunshine, and, finally, Combat Outpost (COP) Spingher.

We were colocated with Bravo Company and our PB was less than four klicks from their company COP (Spingher) and Man Bear Pig, which had been taking harassing fire from Taliban fighters nearly every day and whose immediate AO was riddled with antipersonnel mines. Because they had already sustained multiple casualties, several of the marines who would be playing key roles on the upcoming mission were rightfully stressed out and pissed off.

That's when our next set of orders came. Second Anti-Armor Team / Section One was ordered to Spingher, where we would soon be among the first marines in history to knock on the gates of Marjah. We took everything with us there—from TOW (tube-launched, optically tracked, wire-guided) missile trucks to AT4 rocket launchers—and enough ammo to sustain a company-size element.

When we arrived at the COP, we were initially denied entry due to a funeral procession for a fallen marine whose name I didn't recognize. The mood there was angry and tensions were high, as the marines were wound tight and worn out at the same time. Hopefully, by working together, we could find a resolution and give those guys a breather before the big push into the Taliban-dominated city.

In our briefing that night, we were told that we would need to reveille (wake up) at 0300 to start the invasion. With that, my fellow marines and I forced ourselves to sleep. I'm surprised I got any sleep at all.

I awoke in a panic at 0700, thinking that perhaps my watch was still set to the wrong time zone and everyone left without me. Yet as I looked around, I realized we were all still there, undisturbed. Nobody knew what was going on.

That's when Lieutenant Barnes walked in.

"Mount up!" the lieutenant yelled. "OP Junkyard got conked [attacked], so we're heading south to Geronimo [the battalion FOB]. Battalion's got something else for us to do."

Mount up and go? This was not the ever-thorough Lieutenant Barnes we knew.

Everyone felt angry, robbed, and even lied to that our historic set of orders had been changed. I never could have imagined why it actually happened.

Upon arrival at the battalion FOB, I sank into my turret before removing my Kevlar to avoid drawing attention to the screaming war hawk my buddy Nibbles had shaved into my head the night before what was supposed to be the big push. Through my turret window, I saw the lieutenant looking up toward my vehicle.

"Wise, can you hop out for a second?" he said.

Convinced that I was about to get in more trouble for having an unauthorized symbol shaved into my head, I tried to quickly look around the vehicle for any available headgear to cover it up. Having no luck, I sheepishly jumped out of the turret.

"Where are we headed, sir?" I said.

"COC," said the lieutenant, referring to the command operations center.

Fuck my life, I thought.

"We just gotta run up there and grab something," he said.

Wait a second, why did he pick me just to grab something? He passed the entire team before asking for me, which didn't make any sense. My mind started jogging. *Why me?*

I didn't know, but I started prepping myself for worst-case scenarios. I was trying to recall the date Ben was supposed to arrive in Afghanistan. I had spoken with Jeremy just a few days prior on my PB when I'd received a call from him from Camp Chapman, and I had been concerned about his stressed tone, which I could sense through the broken connection relayed from sat phone to sat phone.

As the conversation ended, we had been saying our goodbyes when Jeremy said, "I love you, Beau," which was jarring.

"I love you too, bro," I replied. "When will you be home?"

"Sooner than you," he said.

Those were the last words I had heard my oldest brother speak before our satellite connection went out. Speaking with another service member or contractor (even if it was your brother) via sat phone was extremely rare inside a war zone, as military and intelligence officials had become increasingly concerned about calls and locations being intercepted. For that reason alone, I had already felt extremely grateful for the chance we had somehow been given to talk.

The conversation with Jeremy was haunting me as I tried to reassure myself during our walk to the COC. *You're overreacting! It could be any number of things.* Plus, this was my indestructible oldest brother, who was far too tough, experienced, and savvy to get in trouble, injured, or worse. *Jeremy knew everything.*

Our formation of two started veering away from the main entrance and toward a lone, unmarked office not connected to the main corridor. Very swiftly, Barnes and I stepped inside what was essentially an eight-by-eight wooden box, where we were greeted by a man I immediately recognized as the battalion chaplain.

"Good morning, Lance Corporal. I'm Chaplain Rhoades. Please have a seat," he said. "There's never a good way to go about this, so we'll just get right to it. Is your brother Jeremy Jason Wise?"

My airway seized.

"Y-yes," I said.

"It's my unfortunate duty to inform you that your brother has been killed near Khost. There was some kind of explosion," the chaplain said. "I'm sorry, but that's all we know right now."

I exhaled fully for the first time in what seemed to be minutes. With that breath came some emotional release but also pure devastation.

I began to weep before punching through the sheet of five-eighths plywood that made up the front wall of the chaplain's desk.

I was about to apologize before I realized neither officer had

budged from my display of anger. It was expected and perhaps understandable in their eyes, even to the chaplain.

"We have a contact number provided by your family if you'd
like to call," he said.

"No," I interjected. "Not yet."

I don't know why, but I didn't want my parents to hear me cry.
I allowed myself to feel the worst pain I had ever felt for a minute
or two.

"Okay, take your time," the chaplain said after the awkward
period of silence. "Whenever you are ready."

Right then, I turned my emotions off.

"I'm ready," I said as firmly as I could. "I'd like to speak to my
family now."

The chaplain dialed and handed me the phone, which I pointed
to the spot I thought would probably have the best reception. As I
walked to a berm near the landing zone (LZ), Jeremy's wife, Dana,
answered the phone. She seemed fragile, yet unbroken.

"We need you home, Beau," she said.

"I don't know if I can, Dana," I replied.

"We already talked to your command," she said with increasing desperation. "You have to come home!"

"I'll talk to my boss," I said.

After hanging up with my brother's wife, who had suddenly
become a widow, I approached Lieutenant Barnes.

"How does this work, sir?" I said.

"You have to go home, Wise," he answered. "Take care of your
family."

"But how long do I stay?" I said.

"How long do you want to stay?" he asked.

"Honestly, I want to bury my brother and come right back to
Afghanistan," I said.

"We'll be here, bro," said the somewhat surprised lieutenant. "Section Two is bringing your travel gear."

I called home one last time before leaving the country where my oldest brother and (as I would later find out) eight others—not including the attacker—had been killed. Seven were working for the CIA.

This time, Ben answered. Unbeknownst to me, he had received the fateful phone call while driving to the PX with Traci, the kids, and my parents just a few hours earlier. I had never been so relieved in all my life to hear his voice.

I started bombarding my only living brother with questions before he interjected.

"We're okay, Beau," he said. "Just get here safe and call us when you touch down in Europe to give us your arrival time."

"Okay," I said. "En route."

Despite my numbness, one thought was ever present. I had to bury my brother—or so I thought—and then fly back before I missed the big push through Marjah. I knew going home was the right thing to do, but what if the show here in Afghanistan started early? What if one of my fellow marines got hurt or killed because I wasn't there to have his back?

Out of guilt for not prioritizing my grief for Jeremy and concern for our parents and the entire family, I dismissed those thoughts. There would be a time for all that military stuff, but not now.

It was time to go home. For at least one U.S. marine, the invasion of Marjah would have to wait.

8

INTERSECTION

I hadn't slept in thirty-six hours by the time I arrived at Norfolk International Airport. I was sitting at the baggage claim after flying from Afghanistan to Kuwait to Amsterdam to Germany to Newark and—finally—to the Virginia Beach area.

After pondering the possibility of trying to take a quick nap while waiting for Ben to pick me up, I realized I was too tired to sleep. I decided to grab a cup of coffee and a newspaper instead.

When I opened up *The Virginian-Pilot*, I instinctively flipped to the sports section to catch up on college football. Being mostly disconnected from reality in Afghanistan other than learning of my brother's death, I had no idea if our beloved Arkansas Razorbacks had won their bowl game. As it turned out, the Hogs had just beaten East Carolina in overtime to win the Liberty Bowl in Memphis. *Woooooo, Pig! Sooie!* Jeremy would have been so happy.

The smile that had briefly lit up my face vanished when I flipped to the obituary section. Since Jeremy's passing still didn't feel real to me, I was shocked when I saw his face in black-and-white newsprint. A few moments later, my tears began dotting the page.

Jeremy Jason Wise, 35, passed away unexpectedly in Khost, Afghanistan on Dec. 30, 2009. Jeremy was a former Navy SEAL, with eight years of service, who was serving with Xe Security Company in support of Operation Enduring Freedom. He graduated from Westside Christian School in El Dorado, Ark., and received a degree from Hendrix University in Conway, Ark. He was a member of the Trinity Church in Virginia Beach. Survivors include his wife, Dana Maria Wise; son, Ethan Daniel Prusinski; father, Jean Farley Wise; mother, Mary Lee Wise; sister, Mary Heather Skaleski; brothers, Benjamin Brian Wise and Matthew "Beau" Jordan Wise; and his grandmother, Mary Theresa Morgan. He was preceded in death by his grandparents, John Dale Morgan, Floy Wise and Mildred Wise. A memorial service will be held at NAB Little Creek Amphibious Base Chapel on Thursday, Jan. 7, at 1 p.m. Following the memorial service a reception will be held at the Officer's Club.

"He was preceded in death by his grandparents" was the line that hit me the hardest. It wasn't Jeremy's time to die at age thirty-five. Since nobody had told me exactly how he was killed, I still stupidly held out hope that this was all a mistake, even as I read "Jeremy Jason Wise" over and over again in the newspaper.

The only thing that comforted me was the anticipation of finally getting to see Ben. As a special operations guy who was stateside before and after Jeremy was killed, surely he would know what really happened to our brother by now.

Other than a hello and a hug when he first picked me up from the airport, Ben was stoic and mostly quiet as we started the half-hour drive to Jeremy and Dana's town house. After about five minutes, I broke the silence.

"Bro, what the fuck happened to Jerms?" I said.

"We don't know," said Ben, who was clearly expecting my question. "No bullshit, we really don't know. I think the bomb went off inside the FOB. They're not telling me one way or the other, which means it had to have gone off inside."

With the newspaper still crumpled up in my hand, Ben's news only added to my sense of confusion and burgeoning position of denial.

"How the fuck could a bomb get inside the FOB?" I said, knowing how secure the base I had just come from in Afghanistan was, or so I'd thought. "It doesn't make any sense."

At that point, Ben had a lot more time and sleep to process Jeremy's death than I had. Sensing my anger and uncertainty, Ben realized—as my big brother—that he needed to calm me down.

"Look, I really don't know anything," he said in an extremely calm, measured tone. "Let's just wait until we can actually sit down and talk to someone before we get too bent out of shape."

"Maybe he's still alive . . . ," I stammered.

Ben immediately pulled over. "*No!*" he said in his firmest possible tone. "We are not going to do that, Beau. Jeremy is gone."

I nodded in silence. I knew Ben was right, but I still hadn't reached the point of acceptance. It was still too much to process.

As if he were flipping a switch, Ben got back on the road and launched straight into some of our favorite Jeremy stories, from the Halloween candy fiasco as kids to his brilliant idea to have Ben put a knife to my ear the last time the three of us had been together. For a few minutes on that cold, winter day in early 2010, my surviving brother and I managed to share a few laughs.

Ben and I were still joking around when we walked into a town house filled with mourning relatives. I felt terrible for temporarily being in a good mood, especially when I saw the face of my oldest brother's grieving wife. I felt sick to my stomach about our crass, insensitive behavior.

After apologizing and expressing my deepest sympathies to Dana, I asked if she had any more information about Jeremy's death. She said no.

As I continued making my way around the room to hug people and see if anyone knew anything about what happened, someone pulled me aside.

"Beau, you do know that Jeremy was working with the agency, right?" the person said. The "agency" was, of course, the Central Intelligence Agency.

I knew Jeremy was doing something important in Afghanistan, but I did not know his contracting work for Xe was in concert with the CIA.

Unbeknownst to me at the time, news of the suicide bombing that took my brother's life had been reverberating around the world for several days. After I checked on young Ethan, someone handed me a copy of another newspaper.

"The suicide bomber struck the CIA's operation at Camp Chapman in eastern Khost province on Wednesday," the Associated Press had reported on New Year's Day in 2010. "The base was used to direct and coordinate CIA operations and intelligence gathering in Khost, a hotbed of insurgent activity because of its proximity to Pakistan's lawless tribal areas, former CIA officials said.

"Among the seven killed was the chief of the operation, they said," the AP article continued. "Six other people were wounded in what was one of the worst attacks in CIA history." The death toll was probably reported as seven at the time because that was the number of Americans killed. A Jordanian intelligence officer and Afghan security chief also died in the attack.

When I put down the newspaper and walked into the living room, I saw the rest of my family. Like Ben, my dad was mostly quiet. Dana, my mom, and Heather were tearful. Ethan, like almost any child would be in that situation, was worried and confused. These were just a few tragic consequences of a suicide vest that had detonated half a world away.

The air was frigid as my family and I stood outside on the tarmac at Dover Air Force Base in Delaware. We were waiting for my brother's remains to return to American soil for the first time.

The Wises were not the only family grieving that night. We were standing next to the loved ones of Dane Clark Paresi, a forty-six-year-old former U.S. Army soldier who, like Jeremy, had joined Xe after retiring from active duty. We were joined on the base by the families of fallen CIA officers Elizabeth Hanson, Harold Brown Jr., Darren LaBonte, Scott Michael Roberson, and Jennifer Lynne Matthews. The magnitude of this tragedy was staggering.

While your thoughts and prayers are always with the other families, it is nevertheless impossible not to focus on your own loved ones at an hour of such darkness. If I was shaking from the extreme cold, my parents, Dana, and Ethan, who had been given blankets during the bus ride from the hotel, were most certainly feeling the effects. I was worried about them.

I rubbed Ethan's back to help keep him warm and eventually rested my hand on his shoulder. That's when—one by one—the flag-draped coffins began coming off the massive C-17 jet that had brought the remains of seven American heroes home.

It was almost completely silent until the wife of one fallen hero cried out for her husband and collapsed onto the cold pavement. Even the most battle-hardened Green Beret or marine would have a visceral reaction to witnessing such heartbreak up close. Ben and I were no exception.

My family wasn't sure which casket was which until an army colonel walked up behind me and quietly uttered three words that instantly put a lump in my throat.

"This is Jeremy," he said.

That's when the members of my family in attendance began to break down. No one had an audible emotional outburst, but one could definitely sense our sadness through the bitterly cold air on that January night in Delaware.

When the dignified transfer ceremony was over, the families were quickly ushered out of the cold. That's when a member of another grieving family must have spotted my Marine Corps dress uniform through the darkness.

After getting my attention, she motioned for me to lean down so she could whisper something in my ear.

"Kill them all," she said, hugging me tightly. "Go over there and kill all those motherfuckers."

At Dover, the CIA held individual conferences for the seven families, all of whom had many questions about what had happened to their loved ones in Afghanistan. The informational sessions didn't contain much actual information, but my family appreciated the gesture nonetheless.

Since Ben and I were active-duty military, the CIA granted us a separate session that would presumably contain the details that couldn't yet be shared with civilians. I became even more frustrated when they failed to shed any further light on what happened to Jeremy.

The CIA officer leading the briefing was an extremely tough, rugged-looking individual. He was much bigger than I was and looked like he had spent every day since 9/11 engaged in hand-to-hand combat with terrorists hiding in caves.

When I started pressing him for information, he didn't try to intimidate me with his physical prowess. Instead, he seemed to shrink into his chair. I could tell he was nervous.

"I just need you to tell me whether my brother was killed inside the FOB or not," I said, clearly irritated.

After my multiple attempts failed, I took a deep breath and decided to speak in a much calmer tone. "Okay, let's try this," I said. "You recovered his remains, right? I mean, we just watched a flag-draped casket get pulled off a plane, we were told—"

"Yes," the agent interjected softly. "We recovered your brother's remains."

"From where?" I said. "Inside the FOB or outside the FOB?"

The agent, who once again declined to answer my question, looked almost totally defeated. To this day, I think he desperately wanted to tell us whatever he knew, but he simply wasn't allowed.

Through all of this, Ben was staring blankly with his elbows on the table and fingers interlocked. His security clearance was higher than mine, and for that reason, I think Ben knew beforehand that the CIA guys wouldn't be able to tell us much of anything. If we knew one fact for sure, it's that Jeremy was involved in a top-secret mission of the highest order. Therefore, the CIA had no choice but to stay tight-lipped.

"We're still collecting information and don't want to speculate," the nervous intelligence officer stammered. "The last thing we want to do is give you bad information."

After I asked a few more questions I knew wouldn't be answered, the CIA officer wrapped up the meeting and apologized for not being able to share more details.

"The only thing we can tell you for sure is that your brother is a hero," he said.

On January 7, 2010, the U.S. Navy held a memorial service for Jeremy at Joint Expeditionary Base–Little Creek, where SEAL Team 4 was based. Our family was still sorting out where Jeremy would be buried, which would likely take at least a few weeks, so we appreciated the military planning an event that would allow everyone to come together and celebrate Jeremy's life.

Sounds of bagpipes filled JEB–Little Creek's packed chapel as I laid a wreath donning red, white, and blue ribbons at the foot of a black-clothed table filled with flowers and a SEAL trident–framed photograph of Jeremy sporting his trademark grin. I felt like he was looking right at me as I put the wreath in place.

Ben, who was also wearing his uniform, followed by quietly placing a red rose in front of our brother's picture. Our mom, our dad, and Heather had done the same.

The chapel was packed with Jeremy's fellow SEALs, naval officers, CIA officials, Xe contractors, and family members. Several stood up and spoke about the impact Jeremy had on their lives.

"He was an extremely smart man who loved his wife, Dana, and son, Ethan," said Jeremy's emotional U.S. Navy SEAL platoon leader, whose voice was beginning to crack. "He spoke very highly of you two while at home and deployed." After composing himself, the SEAL Team 4 officer continued, "Jeremy deployed multiple times to Iraq in support of Operation Iraqi Freedom, where his calm demeanor, intelligence, and love for the job was evident in the awards listed in the bulletin but also through the jobs that do not merit awards," he said.

"He stood by me during a tough time," another SEAL said. "And he was a damn good friend."

A third Navy SEAL broke down at the podium as he recounted one of his final conversations with my brother.

"He told me that he was really worried that if something happened to him, there would be nobody there for you and Ethan," the tearful warrior said, looking directly at Dana. "I told him, 'Jeremy, look around. We're here. We'll be there.' So I'll say it one more time, Ethan and Dana," he said in conclusion. "Look around. We're all here."

Wearing a dark purple sweater and a black coat and scarf, my sister also stepped up to the podium that day.

"I'm going to try to get through this," Heather began. "I told my cousin on the way over here that if I didn't talk, I know I'd regret it my whole life."

I was immensely proud of Heather as she memorialized our brother in front of hundreds of people. She started by speaking about our childhood.

"You knew when Jeremy was in the room, because something was either broken, spilled, or you heard him laugh," she said. "He just had the greatest laugh." She continued, "Jeremy had a way of nicknaming people. My name was Biggie, because I was kind of a large child, and when I outgrew that, he said, 'Boy, I was getting scared. You were really fat there for a while.'"

As the chapel suddenly filled with laughter, my mind flashed back to the day we dropped Jeremy off at West Point when I was still a kid. I could still hear his words that day: "Goodbye, Skello!"

If he could have seen how much weight I had lost during the first half of my Afghanistan deployment, I guarantee Jeremy would have resurrected my childhood nickname. I would have given anything to hear him call me Skello one last time.

"Here he was this man—this awesome father, brother, friend— just an awesome man," Heather said. "There was part of him that just didn't get past the age of ten. And I told him this, 'Jeremy, you're just a big kid,' and he said, 'You know what? I plan to always be . . . life is a lot more fun.'" Heather, to her infinite credit, kept her emotions in check until the very end. "Jeremy, I love you so much, and I am a much better person for having you as a brother," she said.

Soon after finishing her remarks, Biggie got a great big hug from Skello. I hoped Jeremy could see us.

Ben asked me to accompany him to the podium to eulogize Jeremy. I did not want to speak, but I promised my big brother that if he couldn't continue, I would jump in and finish.

While I might have looked like Skello, even in my Marine Corps blues, Ben most certainly looked like the Special Forces warrior he had become.

For whatever reason, probably due to my ongoing numbness, I wasn't that emotional at the memorial service until my now oldest brother started to speak. Ben's voice was quiet, almost to the point of whispering. I could tell he was in a lot of pain.

"My brother's passing exemplified the way he lived every day, whether it was for his country or his family or his brothers in the teams," Ben said. "Jeremy always put the needs of others before his own. In our community, it's easy to talk about camaraderie and brotherhood. But I'll tell you, it's so much more meaningful when you live it every day."

Ben started to cry as he recalled an instant message conversation he'd had with Jeremy during his most recent deployment to Iraq.

"I'll never forget this: he said, 'Ben, almost everyone in this community would take a bullet for you, but not everyone will sacrifice their personal lives for you,'" my brother recounted before looking up and toward the audience. "That's probably the truest quality of friendship and definitely leadership."

I was standing right behind Ben but could barely hear him as he reached the halfway point of his remarks.

"Jeremy wasn't just proud to be a SEAL or to be with Xe because of what he did," he said, pointing toward our brother's navy and contracting teammates. "It wasn't his job; it was the company he kept. It was you guys. And I heard that all the time."

Ben's voice got a little louder as he kept talking about how much it meant for Jeremy to finally experience the brotherhood of combat after so many years of chasing his dream of becoming a SEAL.

"Whether he was sharing some cheese and sausage with one of the guys from the platoon on a cold, miserable night or trying to adopt every puppy he came across downrange, Jeremy never slighted anyone with the love he shared," Ben said. "His ability to be a top-notch warrior one minute and a loving husband, friend, and family member the next is a constant inspiration to me to always be a better man."

The conclusion of Ben's speech—starting with "I can't imagine my life without my big brother"—is a moment that I would instantly recall two short years later.

"Jeremy, I miss you, and I love you, brother," U.S. Army Sergeant First Class Ben Wise said, looking up toward the heavens. "I'll see you again."

After my oldest brother's pastor offered his gratitude for the massive turnout and said a closing prayer, Jeremy's platoon leader came back up to the podium and called on every Navy SEAL in the chapel to follow his lead.

"Jeremy Wise," he said.

"Hooyah, Jeremy Wise!" the SEALs screamed back.

Ben and I both flinched as their booming voices caused the

walls of the chapel to shake. The SEALs shouting in unison sounded a lot like artillery fire on the battlefield.

SEAL Team 4's moving tribute also reminded us that it was time to rejoin our other brothers and sisters in Afghanistan. To Ben and me, it was the only way to truly honor Jeremy and everything he stood for.

A few weeks later, the two surviving Wise brothers were at war with both the terrorists and our own demons in the country where Jeremy had just made the ultimate sacrifice. We were grieving, angry and ready to go after any al Qaeda or Taliban fighter who dared cross our path.

"Where are you headed?" someone said to Ben during the long journey to finally join his Special Forces team, which had arrived in Afghanistan right around the day Ben spoke at Jeremy's memorial service.

"Kunduz," my brother replied.

"Oh, you'll be safe there," the service member said. "All the action is in Helmand right now."

Ben might have said "thanks" while sipping a Captain Morgan and Coke on the plane, but from the intelligence reports he'd been reading, my brother knew the idea that he was going to a safe place was nonsense. There was definitely more action in Helmand, where I had just returned to rejoin my platoon during the invasion of Marjah, but at the time, the Taliban was beginning to reestablish its foothold to the north. It was only logical that as U.S. and British forces swarmed into the south, Taliban fighters would relocate to an area where fewer coalition troops were stationed. That was exactly was happening in early 2010, and Ben knew it.

My only living brother drank heavily between his speech at Jeremy's funeral and arriving in Afghanistan, which was understandable given what he had just been through. In addition to the shock of losing Jeremy, Ben was missing his newborn son and Traci, who was left alone to care for a baby and two older children.

The fact that Ben was still searching for answers about how his big brother died while on a plane bound for the very war zone where the explosion had taken place only added to the enormous stress he was feeling. Not only did he feel guilty for leaving his wife and child behind, he was operating under the impossible burden of avenging Jeremy's death. It was the most difficult few weeks Ben had ever experienced.

As soon as Ben arrived in Kunduz, he demanded to know the plans for the next day's anti-terrorism operation. The other Green Berets not only surmised that Ben probably had a few drinks during his flight but that his trademark, good-natured sense of humor hadn't made the trip over to Afghanistan with him. He was full of fury and out for revenge.

"Who is this guy, Sergeant?" Ben said, looking at a terror suspect's file on his team sergeant's desk. "What did he do?"

"Hey, Ben, you had a long flight," the sergeant responded. "You need to calm down."

Ben never calmed down in the early part of that deployment. In his mind, it was only a matter of weeks (it wound up being more than two months) before he would have to fly home again for Jeremy's burial, which was still tied up in bureaucratic red tape.

To Ben, every moment he wasn't outside the wire hunting terrorists was wasted time. While the Green Berets were on their base, a former Soviet outpost that was falling apart more than two decades later, Ben's suddenly high-strung personality and reluctance to spend more than a few minutes on required tasks like paperwork added to an already pressure-filled combat environment. Several of

Ben's fellow soldiers also became deeply concerned about his emotional well-being.

As his Green Beret teammates would soon find out, the best way to see the old Ben was to go out on missions. That was when Ben was often able to flip a switch—just like he had done in the car with me in Virginia Beach—and perform at an even higher level than he had in Iraq.

The primary objective for Ben and his team was training Afghan commandos in both Kunduz and Mazar-e Sharif, which had been the site of one of the war's first major battles in November 2001. In Ben's eyes, however, their most important function was essentially being a hammer that would crush any terrorist who dared emerge from the caves of Faryab Province all the way to the mountainous northeast. Whenever another unit called to say they were having a problem with insurgents or terrorists, Ben would be the first one rushing toward an armored vehicle to go and help.

Ben was doing two full-time jobs at once, which only added to his stress level. He would spend several hours a day training the Afghan medics before going out on missions, where he essentially acted as a platoon sergeant. A four-hour night of sleep was a luxury inside a decaying "base"—if you could call it that—without heat or refrigeration units, let alone television or a reliable internet connection.

My living conditions in Helmand were similarly deplorable, which meant that Ben and I had no communication whatsoever until Jeremy's funeral. My brother also had a hard time staying in touch with Traci and seeing pictures of his little boy.

In addition to the lousy setup, Ben's team had virtually zero air support while responsible for controlling hundreds of miles of some of the world's most unforgiving terrain. The team often felt abandoned in northern Afghanistan while many military assets went south, and they even turned down shipments of care packages from home since they knew there would be a long, treacherous drive to go pick everything up. Some teammates laughed when they were offered a shipment of beer and steaks for the Super Bowl since their base didn't even have a refrigerator.

Most nights on that deployment, twelve Green Berets would sleep in a fifteen-by-twenty room. That meant whenever Ben was particularly grouchy, everyone would see his anger up close. It was an impossible situation, but somehow, the team stuck together, with Ben ultimately becoming a big part of its success.

"This place is bad," one of Ben's teammates repeated as they rode through a particularly dangerous area of Kunduz. "This place is bad."

It was a frigid February night, and Ben was tired and still a little hungover from some booze he had managed to sneak on base. Liquor did serve a purpose other than continuing to help him mourn Jeremy, though. It helped keep my brother and many of his teammates warm.

It was about five o'clock in the morning. The sun was finally starting to rise when Ben's convoy was on its way down a hill at the front of a plateau just beneath their shitty old base. The Special Forces soldiers then passed by a group of trees that looked beautiful even with the slightest hint of daylight before turning right down a dirt road.

About three dirt roads later, the U.S. Army Special Forces soldiers reached the Kunduz Province village of Nahr-e Sufi.

Boom!

An RPG had landed right in front of the convoy. The next sound was a collective gasp as the soldiers simultaneously took a deep breath.

Boom!

It was probably mortar fire this time.

Pop! Pop! Pop!

Now the machine-gun fire had started.

As Ben and the other Green Berets snapped back to reality, they knew it was a larger-than-usual enemy ambush that would take time to put down. Ben immediately dismounted with his M4 rifle and started running behind the convoy's various trucks to get the benefit of some cover while engaging the enemy.

For the next five hours, the American soldiers laid the hammer down on the Taliban, which was what Ben wished he could be doing every moment for the next seven months. It was intensely gratifying to spend that morning exchanging gunfire with the people who—in Ben's foggy mind—had just murdered our brother.

"Sun's out, guns out" had a different meaning on that particular day in northern Afghanistan. The sunrise had been mostly obscured by smoke and flying sand, but by the time the dust had settled, it had become a fairly nice morning in the otherwise quiet village.

Everyone would go on to have a relatively pleasant day except the fifty or so ragtag Taliban foot soldiers who made the mistake of ambushing my brother and his team of highly trained Green Berets. There's no way of knowing exactly how many enemy fighters were killed, but you can be sure that Ben got his best licks in.

By the time Ben got back to his crumbling Russian base, which didn't even have electricity on most days, the awesome sensation of defeating the enemy suddenly morphed into feelings of panic and terror.

Ben had never been scared of dying when he'd fought in Iraq, but in Afghanistan, everything was suddenly different. For the first time in quite a while, Ben got down on his knees and started to pray.

"Lord, please keep me safe," he said. "Not for me but for the people who care about me. What happened to Jeremy can never happen to my family again."

To the south in Helmand Province, I received a warmer reception than I ever could have imagined upon returning from my brother's memorial service that January. From my buddies Johnson and Lo-Lo to Lieutenant Barnes and Chaplain Rhoades, who had broken the terrible news about Jeremy a few weeks earlier, everyone seemed to be patting me on the back those first few weeks. After being forced to say goodbye to my only living brother as we went our separate ways in Afghanistan, it was heartwarming to know that the Marine Corps had indeed become my second family.

That is not to say the next few months of my deployment were easy—they weren't. While I was finally getting my first taste of going head-to-head with the Taliban, I hated them and al Qaeda every bit as much as Ben did, which at times clouded my judgment out in the field. Just as the Green Berets tried to help keep Ben's emotions in check a few hundred miles away, my fellow marines occasionally had to step in and calm me down.

I was assigned to Section Two of my platoon, which was ordered to the outskirts of Marjah during the invasion. Dubbed Operation Moshtarak, the Marine Corps–led assault would officially begin on February 13, 2010.

During the early stages of the invasion, our vehicle was assigned to patrol Route Olympia, which took an east-west path into the heart of the Taliban-controlled city. One intersection we were responsible for, which was known as Five Points, was considered extremely dangerous due to the overwhelming prevalence of IEDs.

As marines rode through the area on their way to fight and also to build COP Riley, which would give coalition forces an even closer staging point when completed, Section Two's job seemed relatively simple in the beginning. We were ordered to stand guard and make sure no IEDs were planted in Five Points or the surrounding area. This meant leaving our shitty base and essentially living inside an armored vehicle for more than a week. If memory serves me correctly, we stayed outside the wire for eleven straight days.

One particular overnight shift stands out. Just before sunrise, I was in the vehicle's turret with my eyes glued to a pair of binoculars when I saw a strange, almost unbelievable sight. After throwing some water on my face and squinting through my rifle combat optic (RCO), I was almost certain that I was looking at three Afghan men digging a hole squarely in the middle of the road.

The Marine Corps was in the process of invading Marjah. Would the Taliban really have the audacity to attempt to plant an IED in plain sight? The enemy knew the Americans had the heavily traveled intersection under constant surveillance, so the move made almost no tactical sense. Still, it was my job to report anything suspicious, so I called out to my teammate, who was down below taking a nap.

"Lo-Lo!" I said before leaning down from the turret and give him a wake-up nudge with my boot. "I've got three guys out in the fucking road."

"How far away are they?" my groggy fellow marine said.

"One mile tops," I said. "Pass me the vectors."

Lo-Lo rubbed his eyes before quickly scrambling to find the vector binoculars equipped with a laser range finder before Johnson called out with a thick Alabama accent, "I got you, dog." He grabbed the vectors just out of Lo-Lo's reach and handed them to me.

"Marking the range?" Lo-Lo asked.

"Yeah," I said.

I rested the binoculars on the wall of the turret shield and focused the reticule on a berm that was concealing most of the three men's silhouettes from the moonlight.

There were several farms off to our right, which led Lo-Lo to surmise that the three men were probably Afghan contractors digging irrigation ditches.

"We still need to call it in," I said as the target's range popped up in my binocular screen.

"Sixteen hundred, Lo-Lo," I said, referring to the number of meters.

Lo-Lo agreed and reported the strange activity to battalion command, which told us to keep watch but stay put until the sun came up. Despite my desire to dismount and confront the bad guys, the powers that be probably didn't want the Taliban to know anyone had seen them. Firing up our loud diesel motors was out of the question.

The higher-ups were also probably checking to see if the activity had something to do with irrigation, as Lo-Lo had suspected. Unbeknownst to me, however, there were marines in my line of fire, about a kilometer beyond what would have been my intended target. The marines had been sent out to establish a defensive position at the future site of COP Riley. Since my M2 .50-caliber machine gun was the only weapon capable of reaching the three men, pulling the trigger was simply not an option given the friendly-fire risks.

What about the bombs? I thought. *Are we really going to let a bunch of IEDs get planted?* It wasn't ultimately my decision, but I still worried about what could happen as a result.

Less than an hour after sunrise, Lo-Lo was once again asleep when I saw another armored U.S. military vehicle about to drive past us and straight through Five Points. Within seconds of me starting to yell in the vehicle's direction, an even groggier Lo-Lo had dismounted and frantically jumped in front as I stood completely out of the turret while waving my hands in the air.

"*Stop!*" I yelled. "There's an IED in the road!"

We soon learned that the vehicle in question was full of combat engineers about to start a long day of construction work on COP Riley. Lo-Lo sat in the back seat of the vic (vehicle) with the door open as we shared our intel with the gunner, who was relaying everything down to his vic commander.

"I saw them digging about sixteen hundred meters ahead," I said. "Whatever you do, dismount no more than a klick out, start sweeping, and don't stop until you get to Five Points. I couldn't get an eye on any tools, explosives, or weapons, but trust me, there's a fucking bomb in the road," I continued, looking straight into my fellow machine gunner's eyes. "Bank on it."

When they reached one thousand meters, the engineers did exactly what I had told them and started sweeping with their metal detectors and other anti-IED equipment. I breathed a sigh of relief knowing that Lo-Lo and I had probably just spared the engineers the horror of driving directly over an enemy roadside bomb.

I was relaxing and hydrating when—at around the fifteen-hundred-meter mark—I suddenly saw the engineers getting back into their vic. *What the fuck are they doing?*

To my complete shock, the vehicle started rolling forward. They were now less than a hundred meters from the spot where I had seen the suspects digging. In a panic, I grabbed Lo-Lo, who jumped right on the radio.

"Misfits . . . Misfits . . . this is CA-AT 2-2," Lo-Lo sternly said. "You did not reach the dig site. I say again, you—"

Just as Lo-Lo began speaking, I noticed what looked like an Afghan boy atop an embankment not far from the intersection. His hands were in the air with a fresh dust cloud hovering above his head, which was a hallmark of how Taliban spotters would often signal an IED's trigger man once an American vehicle reached the kill zone.

Boom.

Before I could yell out again to Lo-Lo, the engineers' vehicle was engulfed in a giant cloud of dust. While it was thankfully equipped with a protective mine roller, the IED was so large and powerful that it sent the vehicle's plates, which probably weighed two hundred pounds apiece, flying up into the smoky morning air.

"Motherfucker!" Lo-Lo and I shouted in unison.

We couldn't believe this had happened, even after passing everything we'd witnessed up the proper chain of command and warning the engineers. Our teammate Johnson then emerged from the back of our vic, where he had been resting before being awoken by the earthshaking blast.

"What the fuck was that?" he said.

I grabbed my vectors to see if the spotter kid was still standing on the embankment. Just as my eyes reached him, I saw what seemed to be a large-caliber bullet go straight through his chest and fly out through his back. An ugly cloud of pink mist left no doubt that he had just been taken out by one of our snipers, but for reasons I don't understand to this day, I said nothing. I just watched his body collapse while simultaneously experiencing feelings of horror and relief.

I was glad a threat was eliminated, but at the same time, I had just witnessed the death of someone who looked like a teenager. Like Ben had first experienced more than six years earlier in Iraq, it was a difficult sight to come to terms with, even though my primary concern was the marines who had just been struck by an IED.

Lo-Lo was the first to break the silence. "Let's just pray the mine roller took the worst of it, ya know?" he said of our fellow marines.

"Why didn't they fucking listen?" I shouted, pounding the inside walls of my vehicle. I would later learn that each engineer had lived, although one was badly injured.

Another marine in our vic, Greene, then reached back from the driver's seat and grabbed my ankle while calling out to me.

"It's not your fault, brother. You saw it, reported it, called it in, told the fucking lead gunner," Greene said. "You did all you can do, man. This isn't on you."

Johnson and Lo-Lo tried to reinforce Greene's efforts to calm me down. All three marines had become increasingly concerned about my mental state in the wake of Jeremy's death, and they were clearly worried I might blame myself for what had just happened.

Maybe an hour later, I was astonished to see a large crowd of what looked like Afghan civilians marching straight toward our vehicle. Without having time to think, my fellow marines and I grabbed our rifles and stood our ground.

Never in my life had I been more ready to take someone else's. If anyone in that mob so much as raised a hand toward me or one of my marines, I was fully prepared to blow him away.

"Wise, what is this?" Lo-Lo said after realizing that the biggest guys in the group were carrying a large object above their heads.

It didn't take long for me to realize what it was: the body of the Taliban signal boy who had just been taken out by an American sniper. He was lying on his back, draped in white, atop what appeared to be a large rectangular table. In keeping with Islamic tradition, the villagers wanted to bury him as soon as possible. To my amazement, they planned to angrily march through our area of operations in a picket line. The boy's funeral had essentially become a hastily organized protest.

When the loud, heated group of about fifty Afghans reached us, our interpreter—a very nice Afghan of Arab-Farsi descent named Wally, who had grown up in Minnesota—stepped in. I was having none of it.

"This isn't fucking happening—tell them to turn the fuck around and go back to their village," I said. "This kid was a fucking spotter."

I was foaming at the mouth with unbridled rage. Not only did I want to take my anger about the IED out on these people, but like Ben, I wanted to get revenge for Jeremy.

"Okay, Lance Corporal, you need to calm down," said my interpreter, to his credit. "Take a deep breath."

At the time, I was unmoved by his entirely appropriate comments. "You want me to give them sympathy?" I said to Wally, intentionally speaking loudly enough so that the mob could hear me. "He was Taliban!"

By this point, I had completely made my way out of the turret and was standing on the roof our vehicle, gripping my M4. I continued ranting toward the crowd until I was suddenly interrupted.

"Wise, you've got to back the fuck off," Lo-Lo said as Wally shot me a look of disgust. "Get back in the damn turret and cool off."

Lo-Lo was not known as the disciplinarian among his peers or mine, but he also didn't have to be. We might have been the same rank, but that was only because of his DUI. This was his third combat deployment, which meant he had earned the respect of every single marine in our platoon.

Sensing the disappointment in Lo-Lo's voice, it finally registered that I was way out of line. By now, he had climbed the side of the vehicle and locked eyes with me, letting me know it was time to let him handle the situation.

Lo-Lo knew why I was mad, but Wally didn't. I would later apologize and explain to him that my oldest brother had just been killed by a suicide bomber in Khost. I had absolutely no patience for the Taliban, al Qaeda, or any Afghan civilian who condoned their murderous actions.

In reality, the dead teenager had almost certainly been forced by the Taliban to serve as a spotter. When the caravan of mourners was allowed to pass, I saw through the white shroud that he was probably no more than thirteen years old. What a senseless waste of a promising young life.

The emotions that had spilled out into the streets of Marjah that day haunted me throughout my first deployment, as did Jeremy's death. It was also bothering me that I wasn't able to hear from Ben, nor was I given any updates about where or when our big brother would be buried. The thought of Jeremy's body being stored somewhere for weeks after he'd made the ultimate sacrifice while Taliban fighters often got the privilege of being buried within a few hours made me sick to my stomach.

At the same time, I was having horrible nightmares. To say the least, it was an extremely dark period in my life.

When I finally received word from back home that Jeremy would be laid to rest on April 1, 2010, at the veterans' cemetery near Virginia Beach, I asked my commanding officer for permission to attend. To my complete dismay, the request was initially denied. It wasn't until family members intervened and managed to reach a senior Marine Corps officer that the decision was overturned. I was granted two weeks of leave to go home and help bury my brother.

As Ben similarly experienced inside his Green Beret platoon, some of the guys we served with were not happy about us being permitted to leave Afghanistan. In my case, some marines thought there had already been a funeral and didn't understand why I was getting another two weeks off. In the case of my brother, some Green Berets were actually jealous that Ben would get to "enjoy" the luxuries of electricity, home-cooked meals, and clean sheets for two weeks, even though they presumably knew their fellow soldier was going home for his brother's funeral.

Spending several months on a remote combat outpost does all kinds of funny things to your mind and overall perspective on life. At least one of the Green Berets who was initially upset with Ben wound up feeling horrible about it a few years later, as did several of the marines who gave me a hard time about leaving. The "fog of war" is not a cliché—it's a very real phenomenon.

By the time I boarded the flight from Kandahar to Kuwait, where I would hop on yet another plane, I really had become Skello. I had lost so much weight by that point that I doubted several family members would even recognize me. I could only imagine how much my drastically altered appearance would concern my already grieving mother.

After speaking to an extremely professional and courteous master sergeant who had been informed that I was flying home from Afghanistan for my fallen brother's funeral, he directed me to what was essentially a supply shed where airline tickets and other items were given out to traveling U.S. service members.

When I went inside, I noticed a guy who looked like a civilian contractor standing in line. As I walked over and stood behind him, I noticed that he was wearing a dark blue Boston Red Sox hat and ragged black polo shirt while sporting a long goatee. He reminded me of a pirate, which made me chuckle to myself as I pictured Johnny Depp in *Pirates of the Caribbean*.

When he turned around after getting his plane ticket, the pirate-looking dude accidentally bumped into me.

"Sorry, bro," he said.

I was about to say "No problem" when—to my complete shock—I realized I was looking at my brother.

"Ben!" I said, brimming with excitement.

"Beau!" he said, immediately opening his arms to give me a huge bear hug. "Whoa, you're thin as shit."

After joking around about my rapid weight loss, I tried to discern how Ben and I had ended up bumping into each other at a random airport in the Middle East. I hadn't even been sure that he would be allowed to attend the funeral, and as it turned out, he was wondering the exact same thing about me.

We then started comparing our itineraries. To my disappointment, Ben had been booked on a flight full of U.S. Army soldiers starting R & R (rest and recuperation). I was scheduled to make the next leg of my latest journey home on a different plane.

Before long, I was standing in front of the same master sergeant who had been told that I was going home to bury my brother after he was killed in action.

"This is my brother!" I told him. "He was serving up north."

The master sergeant was so surprised that tears welled up in his eyes. For the first few seconds, he thought I had found Jeremy and that the reports of his death had been a mistake. When he eventually came to understand that I had a second brother who was not only in the military but also fighting in Afghanistan, the master sergeant moved mountains to get us on the same flight. I wish I could remember his name, because I will always appreciate him convincing whoever was in charge to let Ben and me spend the next twenty-plus hours sitting next to each other.

As Ben and I flew home, we weren't deployed U.S. service members returning for our big brother's funeral. We were just two best buddies from Arkansas who were absolutely thrilled to finally see each other again. While it felt strange to be telling jokes and laughing on a plane bound for a burial service, it was exactly what Jeremy would have wanted.

9

WAR AND GRIEF

"On behalf of the president of the United States, the United States Navy, the Central Intelligence Agency, and a grateful nation, please accept this flag as a symbol of our appreciation for your loved one's honorable and faithful service," a U.S. Navy sailor said during Jeremy's funeral with full military honors on April 1, 2010, in Suffolk, Virginia.

Usually, the folded American flag is presented to a fallen hero's spouse or parent. On this sunny yet torturously sad spring day, it was presented to Ethan.

I don't remember much else about my oldest brother's funeral. While still battling the ever-thickening twin fogs of war and grief, I spent that day almost completely numb, just like I had been while sitting next to Ben in the limousine as we drove toward the cemetery.

The sights and sounds I remember most are Ethan receiving the flag, the thunderous twenty-one-gun salute, and the palpable anguish of my mom, dad, sister, brother, and sister-in-law. While it was impossible to not be impressed by the poignant dignity of a military funeral, my thoughts kept returning to the fact that Jeremy was only thirty-five years old. He had so much more to do and so many more lives to enrich, especially when it came to both Ethan and Dana.

Navy SEAL after SEAL approached our family after the funeral service concluded. Each of Jeremy's hardened battle buddies told us how much Jeremy meant to them and what a great SEAL Team 4 teammate and leader my brother had been. One of Jeremy's best friends even gave his gold SEAL trident to Ethan. Another gave me Jeremy's knife and dive kit from BUD/S, both of which I treasure to this day.

It was all very nice, but as soon as the funeral and burial services concluded, I went straight out to a local bar with a few SEALs and proceeded to get absolutely shit-faced. Ben had been drinking a lot during that time period as well, but he went back to the hotel much earlier than I did that night. The more bourbon I drank as the SEALs and I stumbled from one Virginia Beach bar to another, the more a recurring thought surfaced in the back of my head: *Where's Jerms?* Much to Ben's chagrin, I still hadn't fully accepted that our brother was gone.

I was struggling with Jeremy's absence. My urging the agency to let Ben and me see our brother's remains months earlier was met with a resounding and unanimous, "*No!* Not a good idea!" Of course, that was a very smart decision by the CIA, but it left just enough room for doubt in the mind of a grieving brother.

After all, we *still* didn't know much about how Jeremy died, even after more than three months. The lack of concrete information made being home for the funeral even more painful for both Ben and me.

My parents and the three living Wise siblings stayed together in Virginia for a few days after the funeral before everyone had to go their separate ways. I remember sitting down for a few minutes one night with my dad, who had just finished a lengthy conversation with Ethan.

"I wish that Jeremy had been around longer for that precious young boy," my dad said.

After sharing a hug and shedding a few tears, my father's attitude changed completely. He spoke about how proud he was of Jeremy not only for serving his country but for eventually returning to his strong faith after his beliefs had been tested by war and life's other challenges.

"I raised a godly son," he repeated before correcting himself. "I raised three godly sons."

Ben and I didn't feel godly while bidding each other farewell in a Norfolk International Airport terminal a few days later. We couldn't get on the same plane this time, which made us even more depressed about having to trade time with family for Afghanistan.

Not only was Ben frustrated by being forced to leave his wife and son behind, but we were both heading back to one of the world's most dangerous and seemingly hopeless places. In a few days, neither one of us would be able to take things like hot water, electricity, TV, and internet for granted. It was also time for the Taliban's annual spring offensive, during which Ben and I would be expected to set aside our sorrows and rejoin the fight with our respective units.

"On top of everything, I'm worried about what might have happened to my guys after the Marjah invasion," I said to Ben at the airport. My brother struggled with the same concerns about his ODA (Operational Detachment Alpha) team, which was still operating a few hundred miles north of my battalion.

Ben immediately shot me a concerned look. He was already worried about something happening to him in Afghanistan because of the unthinkable consequences it would pose for our already devastated loved ones, but in that moment, we both realized the shared concern for each other that would only grow by the day in theater.

"Don't go looking for a fight over there, Beau," my big brother said. "Can you imagine what it would do to Mom and Dad if one of us got blown up or shot?"

"Dude, neither of us signed up to ride the bench," I said.

"If it happens, it happens," Ben said of seeing action upon returning to Afghanistan. "Just don't chase it, Beau—trust me on this."

I knew very well that Ben's counsel came every bit as much from a standpoint of wisdom as love, but it was difficult not to shrug it off. The terrorists had killed my brother, and I still wanted blood.

After exchanging a hug, it was time for yet another thirty-six-hour journey back to Afghanistan. Were it not for our undying motivation to avenge Jeremy's death, I'm not sure Ben or I could have mustered the energy to go back over there and fight.

I got a chilly reception from my fellow marines when I returned to Helmand Province. They weren't mad at me, but a few most definitely seemed envious of my second "vacation" of the deployment. The lack of understanding about what I was going through only added to my ferocious rage at those responsible for putting my family through this nightmare. The grieving relative at Dover had told me to go over there and "kill them all," and while I'm not proud of it, that's exactly what I wanted to do as spring turned to summer in southern Afghanistan.

One of my first missions since returning from the funeral was a resupply convoy to FOB Marjah. It was in the heart of the city, which was in much better shape than before the U.S.-led invasion but still the site of almost daily gunfights and explosions.

Since the Taliban couldn't defeat the relentless U.S. Marine Corps and knew not to fuck with a platoon like ours, which was equipped with TOW missiles and many other lethal instruments of war, they often took their frustrations out on foot patrols or civilians whom they wrongly blamed for cooperating with us. Innocent people were being targeted, tortured, and murdered almost every day in Marjah, which was probably the world's most violent place in 2010.

Many times, our mobile assault platoons, which were broken down into CA-ATs (combined anti-armor teams), responded to multiple TICs (troops in contact). We were armed to the teeth when mounted in armored trucks with .50-caliber machine guns, Mk 19s (fully automatic grenade launchers), TOW rockets, and Javelin missiles. The enemy fully appreciated the devastation of those weapons systems and largely knew how to identify platoons that carried them.

Finally, we had received this promising operation to escort a colonel's personal security detail into Marjah. I was pumped up to hopefully have a chance to cut off the head of the snake—the Helmand Province–based Taliban—on the day of our mission. Once again, however, I experienced disappointment when we encountered no resistance during the bumpy ride to FOB Marjah, which each of us had previously expected to result in an ambush, IED attack, or both.

It wasn't until our arrival that I understood why things were suddenly so quiet. As soon as I emerged from the turret, I saw what must have been at least fifty U.S. and coalition vehicles twisted and maimed in the middle of the desert. Many had struck IEDs, and several were riddled with bullet holes.

"What the fuck happened here?" I asked the first fellow marine who walked by.

"Marjah happened," the marine said in a somber, expressionless tone. "Welcome to the boneyard, brother."

Third Battalion, Sixth Marines were the primary occupants of FOB Marjah. They had been dropped into the city's center for the invasion and were having a pretty rough go at it.

My eyes widened as I continued scanning the sector and looking at all the mangled trucks. American blood had definitely been spilled here, even though I didn't know exactly how many marines had been wounded or killed. It was an unforgettable sight and a humbling experience to get an up-close look at the tremendous sacrifices of the brave warriors who had patrolled this hellhole just a few short miles to our west.

In that moment, I realized that, as usual, Ben was right. As the largest U.S. military operation since the Second Battle of Fallujah continued to unfold, there was no reason for me to go out looking for trouble. At some point, either now or in the near future, war's chaos would almost certainly find me first.

After we got back to our patrol base early the next morning, I cleared my machine gun and exited the turret. After I finished prepping the truck for the next patrol, I took a seat on the hood of our truck just outside the wire, lit a cheap Korean cigarette, and stared up at the sky. That's when I started to pray for the first time in months. Unlike Ben's, my faith had been shaken by Jeremy's death.

Unbeknownst to me, Tony Peck—one of my senior marines and mentors who had taken it upon himself to monitor my well-being—was standing mere feet away from me as I prayed in the darkness.

"Amen," Peck said with me in unison while revealing his presence, which initially startled me.

Peck was never a religious type of guy. Out of respect, he just didn't want to prevent me from connecting with my faith. As he climbed on top of the hood with me and stretched out his legs, he put up two fingers (the international signal for *cigarette*) and said, "Got a smoke?"

"Yeah, are you out?" I said.

"Nah. Yours just taste better," Peck said with a sarcastic smile.

I was trying not to wake up half the platoon with my laughter or choke on the smoke as I gladly handed over a pack of cigarettes I had just purchased from the local bazaar. After lighting up and leaning back against the windshield, Peck paused and said, "Oh, never mind. All these foreign cigarettes taste like shit."

We both laughed as he exhaled in a sigh and said, "What I would do for a Marlboro right now." This was usually the part of the conversation where Peck would say, "You doing okay?" But after a brief pause, Peck made a firm observation: "You're not okay."

"Why? Because I'm praying?" I replied.

"No, because that's the first time I've seen you pray since you got back," Peck said. "Furthermore, you're praying outside the wire on the hood of a M-ATV at three in the morning when we have a patrol in less than five hours."

"Dude, you're agnostic," I said, recalling the countless religious debates we'd had in the past. Every discussion was usually very cordial and ended in an exchange of literature, which inevitably became the next hot topic.

After leaning back against the three-inch bulletproof panes of laminated glass, I lit another cigarette and exhaled, trying to find a place to begin.

"Talk to me, Goose," Peck nudged, quoting *Top Gun*.

"My brother Ben is right, Peck. I'm gonna get myself killed carrying this shit around," I said. "I'm finally coming to the realization that I'm not invincible, but what's worse, if it can happen to

Jeremy . . ." I paused for a brief moment, trying to hide a tear before continuing. "It's one thing to deploy simultaneously with a brother, but being separated . . . I've never felt so vulnerable, so helpless," I admitted with relief for finally having revealed what was really on my mind that night. "I can't talk to Ben—I can't do shit!"

"Shit, man. I hadn't even thought about that . . . all you've been through and then watching your other brother go back hundreds of miles away?" Peck said. "Damn, I had hoped that burying Jeremy would've given you some closure, but I could tell you were somehow even more tense after you got back."

"What scares me most is that we're gonna play by the fucking rules!" I continued, now ranting. "At the same time, the Taliban is gonna do what they do—pop shots from a blind spot, drop the AK, and run away. I hate driving out the enemy. I want to *end* the enemy."

"So you're thinking the more guys we kill down here, the fewer Ben will have to deal with up there? History would suggest that logic is flawed," Peck said. "There's a reason they call this the graveyard of empires, man, but even if you're right, think about it from Ben's perspective. I'd bet almost anything that Ben is saying the opposite prayer right now—that everything pushes north toward him so you will be safe. I would."

"Damn it, Tony," I said with a laugh while wiping away a tear. "Stop making so much sense!"

It was starting to become apparent that this conversation was going to consume my entire pack of smokes, but I didn't care. I was thankful for both the company and the counsel. But as dawn started to arrive, what had started as a pretty intense conversation was suddenly interrupted by the sound of morning prayers echoing from the local mosque.

Peck swiftly looked at his watch as I turned the cigarette pack upside down. By the absence of falling cigarettes, both deployed

U.S. Marines realized we had lost track of time and also forgotten to sleep.

"Shit!" I said. "We gotta go."

As we started walking back inside the patrol base, Peck stopped me in my tracks to say one last thing.

"I know you, Beau. You're not the same without your faith," he said. "For some people, it's a weekend thing, but it's obvious from our conversations that you're not just sold on it; it's who you are." Peck concluded, "Sailors aren't tested by avoiding storms, you know? Sometimes you just have to hold fast."

"Thanks, brother," I responded with gratitude.

That night's conversation had helped pull me out of a dark place. In the coming weeks, I started taking the first baby steps toward recovering from the nightmarish ordeal of the past few months.

I knew that to start truly healing, I was going to have to take things one day at a time. It might be a cliché, but for me, it was the only way to keep putting my best foot forward in Afghanistan and beyond.

Ben's welcome back to Kunduz, where his Green Beret team was still suffering through long missions and miserable living conditions, was similarly tempered with apprehension. Everyone was tired, hungry, and fed up with the strains of a lengthy deployment to a remote area.

Feelings of jealousy had also intensified about Ben's two-week "vacation," leading my brother to ask one trusted fellow Green Beret if he had done something wrong.

"No," said the soldier, who had suddenly become embarrassed when he remembered why Ben had just gone home for a second time. "There's just been a lot going on over here."

Despite Ben's ongoing anguish paired with the trepidation he experienced upon his return, he still took the time to offer spiritual counsel to any Green Beret who was struggling to keep the faith during the deployment's closing months.

"You have to read the Bible like it's a love letter from God to you," Ben told one fellow soldier, Staff Sergeant Kevin Flike, during the deployment. "Pore over every word and search for the meaning of every sentence—every nuance."

Ben would never know it, but the spiritual guidance he provided to his Green Beret teammates helped spare at least one soldier from suicide. While Medals of Honor are rightfully handed out to war heroes who shield their teammates from bullets and bombs, it makes me equally proud to know that compassionate soldiers like Ben often protect their brothers- and sisters-in-arms from potentially harming themselves.

The stress of combat is overwhelming enough to break any American warrior. It is an ongoing issue that demands our country's constant attention.

Whenever it was time to go outside the wire, Ben could still flip that switch from a comforting man of God to a lethal man of war. Not long after returning, Ben and a fellow Green Beret found themselves in the middle of what was essentially a grenade-throwing contest with Taliban fighters in a Kunduz Province village. Thanks in part to Ben, the platoon came out on top with no one on the American side wounded or killed in the battle.

Somewhere in the neighborhood of the grenade skirmish, Ben decided that he wanted to put his elite marksmanship—which his teammates had been witnessing since that first day on the range in Iraq—to the test.

"I want a sniper kill," Ben said at the FOB on the night before a patrol. "And I'm going to get a sniper kill if the opportunity presents itself."

The next day, Ben grabbed one of his platoon's brand-new M110 semiautomatic sniper system rifles and went out into the treacherous terrain of northern Afghanistan. The M110 was much larger and heavier than the standard-issue M4, but Ben didn't realize the full extent of the new weapon's bulk until he actually brought the rifle with him out into the field. My brother was also wearing body armor, side plates, and shoulder pads while carrying grenades and the M110's much larger, heavier magazines.

Ben had gained some weight while eating more than a deployed Green Beret could dream of during the two-week trip home but was still in excellent shape. Carrying a heavy rifle plus all that gear was enough to tire out even the toughest American warrior.

Ben's knees first started to buckle when his patrol, which included several Afghan National Army commandos, trudged into an irrigation canal. For the next few hours, Ben was covered with water and mud as he continually slipped under the weight of the cumbersome equipment he was carrying on his back.

After a few hours, Ben became exhausted to the point of hallucination. When he returned to the FOB that night, he was probably the tiredest he had been since his final Green Beret training exercise at Robin Sage.

"I'll never carry that rifle again," Ben said, slamming the now unloaded M110 into a locker. "I didn't even get to shoot a single round."

From that point forward, Ben switched back to the leaner, lighter M4 rifle. It would lead to some of his finest hours in the military, especially on his subsequent Afghanistan deployment.

Before long on the latter portion of Ben's first combat tour after Jeremy's death, his uniform was covered in blood. Ben's two-vehicle dismounted mobility unit was going through another Kunduz Province village when the American soldiers soon heard the screams of gunfire and frantic orders being given over their radios.

As the Green Berets quickly surmised, their patrol, which also included Afghan soldiers, was being ambushed from three different directions.

After a minute or two, Ben, another Green Beret, and some Afghan commandos decided to run through the earsplitting, smoky chaos to flank one corner of the insurgent-formed triangle, which happened to be in the middle of a nearby town. About a half hour later, Ben, his teammate, and the Afghans had secured the area and even managed to arrest a few of the Taliban's attackers.

The reason Ben's fatigues were soaked in blood was because one of the Afghan soldiers had been shot as the joint assault team flanked the insurgents. My brother stayed calm and composed while patching up the commando's wound as both soldiers took temporary cover, presumably behind a mud hut.

Upon returning to his patrol, Ben learned that one of his fellow Green Berets had nearly been killed during the forty-five-minute firefight. It was the closest call anyone on the team had had on the deployment so far, which reminded Ben of the very real risks that he and the whole team were facing on a daily basis.

After the intense firefight and a subsequent daylong operation to clear the Afghan village of bad actors while also looking for IEDs and other hidden weapons, a familiar refrain began echoing through Ben's thoughts: *This can never happen to my family again.*

Even in the heat of battle, Ben was almost always thinking about Traci and Luke. After returning to Afghanistan from the funeral, his aggressiveness in wanting to confront the bad guys was tempered only by what he believed was a sacred obligation to his wife and son.

Ben frequently changed the wallpaper of almost every computer in the FOB's makeshift operations center to photos of Traci and Luke. He also told anyone who would listen about how amazingly lucky he had been to meet Traci, let alone marry her. Ben set an example for the rest of his platoon—especially the younger, unmarried guys—about how a devoted husband and father should carry himself, even when his wife was thousands of miles away.

The internet rarely stayed connected for more than a few minutes at a time on either of our remote FOBs in different parts of Afghanistan, but for at least one night, Ben was able to have an online conversation with the woman he loved. Ben had some important news to share: he would be coming home a few weeks earlier than expected.

At 9:09 a.m. Pacific time on May 21, 2010—a Friday—Traci was overjoyed to see Ben's screen name pop up on her AOL Instant Messenger (remember AIM?) buddy list.

Traci: BABY!!
Ben: Hey there love!
Traci: Hi Love
Traci: I miss you so much

Ben: mmmmm . . . miss you too

Ben: need some kisses right now

Traci: me too

Traci: just thinking what I wouldn't do for 5 minutes in
your arms

Ben: me too. soooooo . . . got some new info

Traci: what info

Ben: it's looking more like the [deployment] extension is
not going to happen

Traci: oh Thank God

Ben: and . . .

Ben: for the bad part

Traci: my heart is racing

Ben: I'm getting taken off of combat ops

Traci: why is that bad

Ben: well yeah, bad for me

Ben: it sucks

Ben: so I don't get to go play from now until I leave

Traci: oh, that does suck . . . for you

Traci: but for me

Traci: maybe not

Ben: my return date got changed too

Traci: ugh

Traci: great

Traci: to what

Ben: 1st week of July

Traci: yay!!!!!

Traci: OMG good news—I can't believe it

Traci: yay!!!!!!

Traci: yippee!!!!

Traci: why have you been taken off combat

Ben: because the sergeant major wants our team sergeant
to send different people to [Mazar-e Sharif].

Ben: so that means, one of the B team medics will cover
down on my position in Kunduz

Traci: I thought you were in Kunduz

Ben: no baby,

Ben: I'm in Mazar-e Sharif right now; normally I work in
Kunduz. The flight I got on last night was to come
here

Ben: I will be working here soon

Traci: got it

Traci: sorry :-/

Traci: confusing

Ben: sorry for the lousy typing

Traci would go on to type that she felt "like I have to put pieces
of a puzzle together" to figure out where Ben was and whether he
was safe. That's what life is often like for a military spouse, particularly inside the special operations community. There were times, as
Dana almost certainly experienced with Jeremy, when Ben couldn't
share his location or return date at all.

Ben: I've been looking at the pics of Luke you sent

Traci: I am missing you [being] with him, Love,
so much

Ben: me too

Traci: he's becoming a little person

Traci: changing

Ben: I can see you a little more in him now

Ben: his eyes don't look like quite like mine

Traci: I love it but it makes me sad too

Ben: and I think I can see a little more of you in the shape
    of his face now
Traci: I still see you
Traci: he's so fun when he's not sleepy
Traci: this morning he was looking at me and I didn't
    know it
Traci: and when I did look at him he gave me the biggest
    smile
Ben: haha . . . that's sweet

Separated by thousands of miles, Traci and Ben's conversation
then shifted to Ethan, whom they both knew was probably having
a very difficult time now that he was suddenly without a father figure in the house.

Traci: I got ethan's b'day present yesterday
Traci: trying to mail it today
Traci: got him a mid-size nerf gun that I didn't remember
    seeing in his room
Traci: with some extra foamy bullets
Ben: Crap
Ben: I need to call him
Traci: b'day isn't until next tuesday
Traci: you're ok
Ben: cool

Ben and Traci's AIM chat then focused on problems around
the house, from fixing the lawn mower to getting an estimate for
air-conditioning repairs. Many civilians don't realize how stressful it is for spouses to suddenly find themselves on different conti-

nents, even if only for a few months, especially when children are involved. The husband or wife left behind sacrifices so much on a daily basis during almost any overseas deployment.

After getting on the same page about how to handle the home repairs, Ben began to wrap up the chat as his base's internet connection began to falter.

Ben: baby, I'm not feeling very good
Traci: i thought you were better?
Ben: not sick but my stomach is kind of sour after eating dinner
Traci: uh oh
Traci: ok
Ben: I need to lay down for a few mins
Ben: little nauseated
Ben: sorry
Traci: lost you for a minute
Traci: you there?
Ben: yes, I'm here
Traci: ok, I guess I'll talk to you later
Traci: hope you feel better
Traci: ok Love
Traci: get some rest
Traci: I'll miss you . . .
Ben: I miss you too
Traci: ok, bye Love
Ben: bye love
Traci: <3
Ben: <3
Traci: love you

Down in Helmand Province, I was finally able to jump online one day for the first time in what felt like forever. Upon logging into my Facebook account, I was greeted with a message left on my timeline from a nice girl I had gone to high school with back in Arkansas.

"Hey, Beau. I just wanted to make sure you were okay," Amber Buck wrote. "There's been a lot of talk back home. Some said it was your brother. Others said it was you. All I heard was that 'Dr. Wise's son' was killed. I just wanted to say that I hope you're safe. I'm praying for your family. If you ever need to talk to someone, let me know."

"Hi Amber, this is Beau," I replied. "I am currently still in Afghanistan. I'm okay, but unfortunately my oldest brother Jeremy was killed. Please help me stop whatever rumors might be going around. My page is flooded with 'RIP Beau' messages."

"I'm so sorry, Beau! I will. I'll pray for your family. Please stay safe!" she wrote.

"I'll do my best," I replied.

Over the next few months, Amber and I exchanged Facebook messages and emails while also having a few AIM chats of our own. Before long, we planned out our first date. While I had no idea where the new relationship would ultimately go, I suddenly began to experience a small fraction of what Ben was feeling to my north. The stakes of serving in a combat zone are that much higher when you have a compelling reason to make it home in one piece. For me, it was going on that first date with Amber.

Despite all the violence during Operation Moshtarak, which started in February 2010 and ended that same December, I was only shot at once more during the deployment before I flew home for the third and final time in June.

We were conducting a raid in Marjah when bullets started ricocheting off the roof of a nearby small building and pounding the sandy area surrounding our convoy. After my fellow marines and I took cover and cleared the sand out of our burning eyes, I settled into the turret, ready to unleash the biggest imaginable onslaught of machine-gun fire when our commanding officer's voice came over the radio.

The CO told Lo-Lo that we actually weren't experiencing an enemy ambush but errant gunfire from a nearby Afghan National Army patrol. While I am not trying to insult the ANA, some of their soldiers were such terrible shots that they were known to sometimes miss their targets by several feet instead of a few inches.

While relieved that no one was hit, my frustration with not being able to directly engage the Taliban only rose with the temperatures in the deserts of southern Afghanistan. With revenge for Jeremy always at the front of my mind, I sometimes felt like the large machine gun I was manning had been reduced to a bow and arrow. All I wanted was a chance to take the fight to the enemy, but other than a few isolated incidents, it never really came on that deployment.

Ben left Mazar-e Sharif to begin his long journey home a few weeks before most of his fellow Green Berets finished the deployment. He had been ordered to take a required medical refresher course back at Fort Lewis. Ben then started Afghan Dari language training, which came in handy during what he soon found out would be his third combat tour as a Special Forces soldier.

When he departed from his second Green Beret deployment, my brother did not want to leave his brothers-in-arms behind—again—especially to sit in a classroom. While suddenly grieving

Jeremy without the daily distraction of combat, Ben also began to drink heavily upon realizing that a hellacious ten-hour firefight had occurred in the mountains only days after his departure. Ben felt guilty for missing the battle and personally apologized to at least one Green Beret for not being there to have his back.

Were it not for Traci and the vast sense of responsibility they both felt for Luke, Ben might have completely unraveled when he received even more unwelcome news a few days after the rest of his unit returned in July 2010. In about seven months, Ben and his Green Beret unit would be going back to Afghanistan.

All in all, Ben and his exhausted teammates would get to spend only about three months out of those two years at home with their families. These are the sacrifices our nation's heroes and their loved ones are often forced to make in wartime.

While my post-deployment stress and grief were similarly intense at times, Ben's faith was tested like never before during those few months between Afghanistan deployments. Both of us became even more unsettled when our parents told us that Jeremy's name had been added to the CIA's Book of Honor. Our brother had also received a star on the famous Memorial Wall at CIA headquarters in Langley, Virginia.

Don't get me wrong: Jeremy being honored by the CIA was a great source of pride for Ben, me, and our entire family, but we still didn't know much of anything about how he had died. After finding out that my own second tour to Afghanistan was on the horizon, Ben's and my attention became divided between vigorous pre-deployment training exercises and trying to find out exactly what happened to Jeremy—and precisely who was responsible for ending his life.

10

CIA STAR

"Death will come to you through unexpected ways," an al Qaeda terrorist said in a propaganda video recorded in late 2009. "We will get you, CIA team. *Inshallah,* we will get you down."

Inshallah means "God-willing" in Arabic. While sitting inside a vehicle, the operative then showed off something hidden under a sleeve of his heavy, baggy, greenish-brown cloak to the camera.

"Look, this is for you," he said. "It's not [a] watch. It's [a] detonator to kill as much as I can."

The man, whose bloodshot eyes appeared to be as empty as his soul, was holding a crutch after suffering a recent leg injury.

He proceeded to threaten not only Americans but an agent in Jordan's General Intelligence Department (GID), which is widely known as the Mukhabarat. The terrorist had spent months convincing Captain Sharif Ali bin Zeid that he was working on behalf of not only the GID but the American CIA.

"This is my goal: to kill you, to kill your partner . . . Jordanian partner," the mysterious-looking bearded man said.

In the tape, the would-be killer went on to make an unmistakable reference to recent CIA drone strikes targeting the Taliban and al Qaeda in Afghanistan and its tribal region near the border with Pakistan.

"Don't think that just by pressing a button and killing mujahideen you are safe," he said.

There had been hundreds of terrorist propaganda videos released in the more than eight years since 9/11, including several from al Qaeda's number-two terrorist, Ayman al-Zawahiri, as well as Osama bin Laden himself. Americans had been particularly shocked by several gruesome recordings that showed beheadings like the murders of *Wall Street Journal* reporter Daniel Pearl in Pakistan in 2002 and American contractor Nicholas Berg in Iraq in 2004.

The killings were believed to be carried out by two of al Qaeda's most notorious terrorists: Khalid Sheikh Mohammed, who helped plan the 9/11 attacks before being captured by the CIA in Pakistan in 2003, and Abu Musab al-Zarqawi, who was killed by U.S. forces in Iraq in 2006.

There was a key distinction between prior terrorist tapes and the aforementioned late-2009 recording, however. The man holding up a suicide bomb trigger and threatening to kill American spies wasn't just an al Qaeda operative. For nearly a full year, Humam Khalil Abu-Mulal al-Balawi—a Jordanian doctor—had been posing as a CIA informant.

On December 21, 2009, Jeremy—who had been working directly with CIA agents as a Xe contractor stationed at FOB Chapman in Khost, Afghanistan, for the preceding three weeks—sent an email to one his fellow ex–Navy SEALs. He was deeply troubled by recent events he had witnessed in eastern Afghanistan, including plans for a December 30 meeting inside FOB Chapman's heavily guarded perimeter with the CIA informant, who had asked not to be frisked.

"Sometimes it's your job to say something—'Sir, I don't think you should do that. It's not a good idea,'" Jeremy wrote nine days before the meeting, according to Pulitzer Prize–winning *Washington Post* reporter Joby Warrick's 2011 book, *The Triple Agent.*

According to Warrick's meticulous research, Jeremy's concerns were the same as fellow Xe contractor Dane Paresi, a former Green Beret. Army Ranger turned CIA case officer Darren LaBonte shared Paresi's and my brother's concerns about the perceived lack of security for the upcoming meeting, which prompted an aggressive appeal to the agency's station chief in Amman, Jordan. LaBonte's email was received and read by the station chief, but after a subsequent, classified chain of events that remains unclear to this day, the request for tighter security was ultimately denied.

Scott Roberson, a former police officer who was now the eastern Afghanistan CIA team's security chief, recognized and concurred with the red flags being raised by LaBonte, Paresi, and Jeremy.

"Later, as final arrangements for [al-Balawi's] visit were being made, Khost's security chief offered a word of advice for a colleague who was planning to go to the meeting to see the informant who had generated such excitement," Warrick wrote. "Roberson cautioned the officer, *Stay far away from this.*"

Why were some top CIA officials, including Khost base chief Jennifer Matthews, willing to take substantial security risks that ex–special operations warriors and police officers could seemingly spot from miles away? The reason was because they thought their informant, al-Balawi, had penetrated the innermost circle of the terrorist organization responsible for murdering thousands of Americans on 9/11 and many other attacks like the 2000 bombing of the USS *Cole*.

Through disinformation al-Balawi had given to his CIA handler and several staged videos, the CIA believed their informant was providing medical treatment to al-Zawahiri, who was then the world's second most wanted terrorist and had the same bounty on his head—twenty-five million dollars—as bin Laden himself.

"But unlike bin Laden, [al-Zawahiri] continued to personally direct numerous terrorist operations, including an alleged 2003 plot to attack New York City's subway system using chemical weapons," Warrick wrote. "Zawahiri himself called off the attack for reasons that remain unclear."

Warrick noted that the CIA tried and failed to kill al-Zawahiri with a missile strike in Pakistan in 2006. After he escaped, he released a video taunting the U.S. military's then commander in chief.

"Bush, do you know where I am?" al-Zawahiri said. "I am among the masses."

Al-Balawi's purported proximity to al Qaeda's number two was the closest the CIA believed it had gotten to al-Zawahiri since the futile 2006 missile attack. Top agency officials also wondered if al-Balawi's role as an al Qaeda doctor could eventually lead to bin Laden himself.

The CIA's collective excitement reached a new high when al-Balawi sent a tape showing him sitting in a tent with senior al Qaeda commanders. Warrick later discussed the significance of the recording in a July 19, 2011, interview with WBUR news radio.

"You cannot imagine anything that would provoke more interest and attention at the CIA than videotapes showing this guy had actually gone into the tent of al Qaeda," Warrick said. "It was incontrovertible evidence, the kind that just grabbed everybody by the throat, [leading them to think,] 'Wow, we've really got an amazing asset here.'"

The CIA carried out several subsequent tests to verify the authenticity of al-Balawi's messages. He passed with flying colors. Having a mole deep inside the heart of America's archenemy was seemingly the break every top national security official in the U.S. government had been waiting for since the moment hijacked airplanes crashed into the World Trade Center, the Pentagon, and a Pennsylvania field.

What the CIA didn't know was the tent video was not only staged by al Qaeda, but al-Balawi was taking direct orders from the very terrorists they hoped to capture or kill. Al-Balawi's ongoing success in fooling the agency was one of the biggest brewing disasters in the history of American intelligence-gathering.

As a contractor, Jeremy almost certainly didn't know the exact nature of the planned December 30 meeting with al-Balawi, but knowing my oldest brother, he wouldn't have cared any more or less if he was informed of his involvement in a top-secret operation directly related to the hunt for al-Zawahiri and bin Laden. From the moment Jeremy received his Navy SEAL trident to nearly five years later as a CIA contractor stationed in Khost, Jeremy cared about one thing and one thing only: the safety of the men and women serving next to him. Nothing else mattered.

I could hear the agony in my oldest brother's voice when he made that last satellite phone call to me from FOB Chapman. Even though I was coping with my own stress while preparing for the invasion of Marjah south of Jeremy, I could immediately sense that my brother's anguish was on an entirely different level. Everyone Jeremy was responsible for protecting was at high risk of being wounded or killed in an entirely preventable attack, and his December 21 email made clear that he knew something was off about the planned meeting from the start.

December 30, 2009, was a Wednesday. It was also one of the most significant days of the entire war on terrorism. Agent Matthews and other top CIA officials couldn't wait to finally meet their "golden source"—al-Balawi—and evaluate not only his demeanor and overall truthfulness but whether he might be the key to defeating al Qaeda once and for all.

"The pressure had been exquisite. Perhaps two dozen people in the world knew about the pending visit by Humam al-Balawi, but one of them happened to reside at 1600 Pennsylvania Avenue in Washington," Warrick wrote. "President Barack Obama, in his second briefing about Jordan's 'golden source,' had been told of CIA plans to meet with the informant in Afghanistan."

Warrick underscored just how high the stakes were on that December day on a remote forward operating base near Afghanistan's border with Pakistan.

"The president of the United States would be awaiting news of the extraordinary events at Khost," he wrote.

The subsequent moments are portrayed not only in *The Triple Agent* but the 2012 Hollywood blockbuster film *Zero Dark Thirty* starring Jessica Chastain.

Of the portrayals, nothing meant more to me than a paragraph on page 6 of Warrick's book. It is the only known written account of a phone call my brother made to Dana on the afternoon of December 30 as he and the other CIA contractors and agents stood under a camouflaged awning on the cold, windy FOB Chapman grounds while waiting for al-Balawi's vehicle to arrive.

My brother was "speaking slowly" while "feeling strangely anxious," according to Warrick, who added that Jeremy "hesitated" while leaving a message for Dana on their home's answering machine.

"I'm not doing very well," my big brother said. "Tell Ethan I love him."

Jordan's Captain bin Zeid and fourteen Americans, including Jeremy, were eagerly awaiting the Subaru Outback's arrival at the checkpoint located at FOB Chapman's outer gate, where guards had been ordered to allow the small red station wagon to proceed unchecked. Matthews and other CIA leaders were worried that any aggressive actions by guards, especially ex–special ops guys like my oldest brother, would spook their golden source and lead to one of the biggest missed opportunities of the war on terror.

As the vehicle drove through the desert on its way to Camp Chapman, al-Balawi was almost certainly saying prayers to Allah, judging by what he said in the video. A powerful bomb was strapped to his chest as the car he was riding in slowly made a bumpy ride through the rugged terrain of Pakistan and ultimately eastern Afghanistan. Al-Balawi had fooled everyone, including some of the world's foremost intelligence analysts and experts. Unbeknownst to my brother and Dane Paresi, they represented America's last line of defense against al Qaeda.

After a lengthy wait, the CIA agents and contractors standing out in the cold finally saw dust kicking up on the horizon. Indeed, it was the Subaru Outback carrying Dr. Humam Khalil Abu-Mulal al-Balawi.

There had been a rehearsal for this exact moment conducted a few days before the meeting, according to *The Triple Agent*. CIA agent Darren LaBonte was not impressed with the results.

"This is a gaggle," LaBonte had said during the training exercise, according to Warrick's book. "It's a clown show."

"LaBonte's chief complaint: too many people," Warrick continued. "Fourteen intelligence operatives and a driver were about a dozen too many, by his way of thinking."

It was twenty-three degrees when Jeremy woke up and petted his latest adopted war zone dog, "a white, lop-earned mongrel he named Charlie that slept in the guards' quarters and liked chewing on the men's beards when they sat on the sofa," according to Warrick's book. I'm glad the dog was able to comfort Jeremy during what would be his final morning on earth.

As the Americans anxiously watched the vehicle get closer and closer through Khost's frigid late December air, bin Zeid's cell phone rang. The voice on the other end of the line was none other than al-Balawi's.

"You'll treat me like a friend, right?" he said, according to Warrick.

After bin Zeid gave him his word that he would not be manhandled by the guards, the vehicle carrying an al Qaeda terrorist operative was permitted to drive right past an American .50-caliber machine gun and into FOB Chapman's grounds.

The day's first and most inexcusable intelligence failure had just occurred. As Jeremy's brother and a U.S. marine with experience in securing American forward operating bases in Afghanistan, I'm sickened by the next paragraph of Warrick's book.

"Balawi sat low in his seat, the weight of the heavy vest pressing against his gut, but as bin Zeid had promised, there was no search," he wrote. "Arghawan [an Afghan security officer who had been sent to pick up al-Balawi] turned left into the main entrance, and the car barely slowed as it zigzagged around a final series of HESCO barriers and into the open expanse of the Khost airfield."

I can't imagine what was going through Jeremy's mind during

the next minute or two before the red Subaru Outback pulled up in front of him. Knowing my oldest brother, he wasn't thinking about himself or even his family. He was rigidly following his many years of training, which had started several years earlier on the SEAL beach during those torturous opening weeks of BUD/S.

With the car now a stone's throw away from Jeremy, I strongly believe that my brother was focused on shielding those around him from the peril I could tell he sensed during our last conversation. As U.S. Marine Corps General James Mattis once said, "Be polite, be professional, but have a plan to kill everybody you meet." That's exactly how Jeremy operated in a war zone, and this high-stakes meeting with al-Balawi would be no different.

Finally, the Subaru Outback pulled up to the fourteen Americans and bin Zeid, who was smiling as he unknowingly welcomed an enemy fighter onto a U.S. military base. At that moment, my brother was looking into the glassy eyes of a heavily armed terrorist.

"Balawi was staring blankly at the group when the car door opened and he was suddenly face-to-face with a bear of a man with a close-cropped beard and piercing blue eyes," wrote Warrick, who was clearly referencing Jeremy. "One gloved hand reached for Balawi, and the other clutched an assault rifle, its barrel pointed down."

If one thing was for sure that day, al-Balawi was a lot more scared than Jeremy. I can tell just by watching the suicide bomber's sad, rather pathetic farewell video. Plus, I knew my brother. A guy like al-Balawi didn't concern him—unless he couldn't see what was under his cloak.

"Balawi froze," Warrick continued. "Then, slowly, he began backing away, pushing himself along the seat's edge away from the figure with the gun."

Moments before his death, Jeremy had made his presence felt

deep in al-Balawi's vacant soul. I have no doubt that Jeremy did everything in his power to disarm the terrorist during those frantic final seconds, during which al-Balawi initially slid to the other side of the back seat and limped out of the car.

"Men were shouting at him now, agitated, guns drawn," Warrick wrote of the moment al-Balawi "began walking in a slow-motion hobble as his right hand felt for the detonator."

By this point, both my brother and Dane Paresi undoubtedly knew al-Balawi was a suicide bomber. This was the scenario they had spent most of their adult lives training for.

"Now [Paresi] and Wise were shouting almost in unison, guns at the ready.

"'Hands up!' they yelled. 'Get your hand out of your clothing!'"

A split second later, al-Balawi flipped the switch, which triggered the detonator.

"*La ilaha illa Allah!*" he shouted, which means "There is no God but God" in Arabic.

I can picture Jeremy standing alone on the dimly lit Navy SEAL beach as the massive bomb engulfed everything around him with fire, pressure, and dust, precisely where he had stared out at the city lights and noticed that lone ship out at sea. As he gazed from Coronado Island out to San Diego, Jeremy's worst fear wasn't dying in war but not getting the chance to serve his country.

While he would surely miss Ethan, Dana, my parents, Ben, Heather, and me, Jeremy Jason Wise had died doing exactly what he'd wanted with his life. After a job well done on earth, he was now finally aboard that sailing ship, which was bound for a beautiful place.

The last words my brother heard were spoken by a terrorist who had twisted one of Islam's most sacred creeds into a perverted justification for murder. I believe the next words heard by Jeremy were spoken by God himself, who instantly transformed those feelings of panic and pain into overwhelming sensations of caring and calm.

I love you, Jeremy.

Back in the United States, Leon Panetta awoke to a loud bang on his door in the early hours of December 30, 2009. The director of the Central Intelligence Agency was told that he needed to get out of bed to take an important phone call.

"It was Amy, my former briefer and now one of the senior aides in my office, on the line," Panetta wrote in his 2014 autobiography, *Worthy Fights*. "Her voice was trembling."

"I need to talk on a secure line," she said. "There's been an attack in Afghanistan, and some of our officers have been hit."

After a few seconds of initial confusion, "it became clear that Balawi, whom we'd imagined as our double agent, in fact had been working with al Qaeda," Panetta wrote. "We had been so excited by the prospect of inserting an agent into the highest ranks of our enemy that we let down our guard."

Seven Americans had been killed, as well as bin Zeid, the Jordanian intelligence officer, and Arghawan, the Afghan security officer. It was the deadliest day for the Central Intelligence Agency since April 18, 1983, when terrorists attacked the U.S. embassy in Beirut, killing eight CIA employees.

Upon realizing he was suddenly leading the CIA during one of the darkest hours in its storied history, Panetta's next phone calls were to Director of National Intelligence Dennis Blair, Vice President Joe Biden, Joint Chiefs chairman Admiral Mike Mullen, and, finally, President Barack Obama. Panetta recounted part of his conversation with his boss, who was also Ben's and my commander in chief.

"This guy turned out to be a double agent," Panetta said of al-Balawi. "We lost seven people."

"Obama was quiet at first," Panetta wrote of the forty-fourth president's reaction. "He expressed his sorrow, offered to help any way he could."

Both President Obama and Director Panetta followed through on their promises to be there for all seven families, including mine. Unbeknownst to Ben or me through the fog of grief, the CIA director attended my brother's memorial service that day in Virginia Beach, which meant he personally witnessed the impassioned eulogies delivered by Ben, Heather, and some of Jeremy's closest friends. Even though I didn't realize it until starting work on this book, my family and I deeply appreciate Panetta taking the time to be there.

Just over a month later, after Ben and I had already returned to Afghanistan following Jeremy's navy memorial, Obama and Panetta hosted all seven families of the fallen at CIA headquarters in Langley, Virginia. More than a thousand guests were in attendance, which meant the event had to be held outside in a tent instead of in the famous foyer, which you've probably seen portrayed in countless movies and TV shows. Guests included Speaker of the House Nancy Pelosi, Senate Minority Leader Mitch McConnell, and many top military and intelligence leaders. Sitting in the same tent were my parents, along with Dana and Ethan.

"America's intelligence agencies are a community, and the CIA is a family. That is how we gather here today," said President Obama, whose breath was visible in the crisp, cold air. "I speak as a grateful commander in chief who relies on you. There are members of Congress here who support you. Leaders—Leon Panetta, Steve Kappes—who guide you. And most of all, family, friends, and colleagues who love you and grieve with you.

"For more than sixty years, the security of our nation has de-manded that the work of this agency remain largely unknown," the president continued. "But today, our gratitude as citizens demands that we speak of seven American patriots who loved their country and gave their lives to defend it."

After a short pause, President Obama solemnly spoke all seven names, presumably in alphabetical order.

Harold Brown Jr.
Elizabeth Hanson
Darren LaBonte
Jennifer Lynne Matthews
Dane Clark Paresi
Scott Michael Roberson
Jeremy Wise

When the president spoke my brother's name, he almost cer-tainly wasn't aware that both of Jeremy's brothers were currently fighting in the same country where seven American heroes had just been killed. The president paused before continuing his February 5, 2010, remarks.

They came from different corners of our country—men and women—and each walked their own path to that rug-ged base in the mountains. Some had come to this work after a lifetime of protecting others—in law enforcement, in the military; one was just a few years out of college.

Some had devoted years, decades, even, to unravel-ing the dark web of terrorists that threatened us; others, like so many of you, joined these ranks when 9/11 called a new generation to service. Some had spent years on dangerous tours around the globe; others had just arrived in harm's way.

But there, at the remote outpost, they were bound by a common spirit. They heard their country's call and answered it. They served in the shadows and took pride in it. They were doing their job and they loved it. They saw the danger and accepted it. They knew that the price of freedom is high and, in an awful instant, they paid that price.

There are no words that can ease the ache in your hearts. But to their colleagues and all who served with them—those here today, those still recovering, those watching around the world—I say: Let their sacrifice be a summons. To carry on their work. To complete this mission. To win this war, and to keep our country safe.

To their parents—it is against the natural order of life for parents to lay their children to rest. Yet these weeks of solemn tribute have revealed for all to see—that you raised remarkable sons and daughters. Everything you instilled in them—the virtues of service and decency and duty—were on display that December day. That is what you gave them. That is what you gave to America. And our nation will be forever in your debt.

To the spouses—your husbands and wives raised their hand and took an oath to protect and defend the country that they loved. They fulfilled that oath with their life. But they also took your hand and made a vow to you. And that bond of love endures, from this world to the next. Amidst grief that is sometimes unbearable, may you find some comfort in our vow to you—that this agency, and this country, will stand with you and support you always.

Next, President Obama spoke directly to the kids who trag-
ically lost their moms and dads on that terrible December day in
Khost, Afghanistan.

And to the beautiful children—I know that this must
be so hard and confusing, but please, always remember
this. It wasn't always easy for your mom or dad to leave
home. But they went to another country to defend our
country. And they gave their lives to protect yours. And as
you grow, the best way to keep their memory alive and the
highest tribute you can pay to them is to live as they lived,
with honor and dignity and integrity.

Every day, Ethan does exactly what the president asked of him.
Jeremy would be so proud.

They served in secrecy, but today every American can
see their legacy. For the record of their service—and of
this generation of intelligence professionals—is written all
around us. It's written in the extremists who no longer
threaten our country—because you eliminated them. It's
written in the attacks that never occurred—because you
thwarted them. And it's written in the Americans, across
this country and around the world, who are alive today—
because you saved them.

And should anyone here ever wonder whether your
fellow citizens truly appreciate that service, you need only
remember the extraordinary tributes of recent weeks: the
thousands of Americans who have sat down at their computers and posted messages to seven heroes they never

knew; in the outpouring of generosity to the memorial foundation that will help support these proud families.

And along a funeral procession in Massachusetts, in the freezing cold, mile after mile, friends and total strangers paying their respects, small children holding signs saying, "thank you." And a woman holding up a large American flag because, she said simply, "He died for me and my family."

As a nation, we pledge to be there for you and your families. We need you more than ever. In an ever-changing world where new dangers emerge suddenly, we need you to be one step ahead of nimble adversaries. In this information age, we need you to sift through vast universes of data to find intelligence that can be acted upon swiftly. And in an era of technology and unmanned systems, we still need men and women like these seven—professionals of skill and talent and courage who are willing to make the ultimate sacrifice to protect our nation.

Because of them, because of you, a child born in America today is welcomed into a country that is proud and confident, strong and hopeful—just as Molly Roberson welcomed her daughter Piper this week, both of whom join us today. Piper will never know her dad, Scott. But thanks to Molly, she will know what her father stood for—a man who served his country, who did his duty, and who gave his life to keep her safe.

And on some distant day, years from now, when she is grown, if Piper—or any of these children—seeks to understand for themselves, they'll need only come here—to Langley, through these doors, and stand before that proud Memorial Wall that honors the fallen.

And perhaps they'll run their fingers over the stars that recall their parent's service. Perhaps they'll walk over to that Book of Honor, turn the pages, and see their parent's name. And at that moment of quiet reflection, they will see what we all know today—that our nation is blessed to have men and women such as these. That we are humbled by their service, that we give thanks for every day that you keep us safe.

May God bless these seven patriots, may he watch over their families. And may God bless the United States of America.

President Obama kept his word to all seven families. A few months later, the CIA once again invited loved ones of fallen CIA officers and contractors to Langley, where twelve stars—including seven honoring those killed at Khost—were added to the agency's iconic white marble Memorial Wall. At the time, Jeremy was one of just 102 fallen heroes honored with a bold star on the legendary wall.

"No matter when or where they served, or whether their names are known to the world or only to us, each cherished colleague remains a constant source of inspiration and courage," Panetta said on June 7, 2010. "We take strength from their powerful example as we carry on their vital work and the vital work of this Agency."

Between the American and CIA flags, a U.S. military officer laid a wreath and saluted as Panetta stood at attention.

"Every day, throughout the world, the CIA is answering that call as a sacred commitment," the director said. "It is a mission without break. It is a mission without pause—one that must, and will, end in victory over hatred, ignorance and oppression. That triumph, when it comes—and it will come—will be the product of the many who draw strength from the seven who died at Khost."

Leon Panetta was right. Less than a year later, U.S. Navy SEALs who trained at the same military base Jeremy once called his own stunned the world by killing Osama bin Laden. The CIA, which Jeremy had also briefly been a part of, had been instrumental in finding the elusive terrorist who bore the highest level of responsibility for the 9/11 attacks.

"The two shots that ended bin Laden's life did not vanquish the threats of terrorism or even al Qaeda," Panetta wrote in *Worthy Fights*. "They did not ensure this country's safety, nothing can. But they denied al Qaeda its founder, its functional leader, and its mythological figurehead. More important, his death proved that America was resolute."

Ben and I had both just started new deployments to Afghanistan when we respectively learned that bin Laden had been brought to justice. When we heard it had been the handiwork of SEALs, it was impossible not to immediately think of Jeremy. He would have been so proud of his U.S. Navy brothers-in-arms.

"It took years of work and a brave call by the president of the United States. But the end of bin Laden firmly proclaimed that no matter how long it takes or how much risk is involved, this country will not let others do violence to us without repercussions," Panetta wrote. "To the victims of 9/11, the victims of Khost, the victims of terrorism anywhere, we proved that we will fight until justice is done."

On July 1, 2011, Leon Panetta became secretary of defense. He couldn't have imagined that less than six months later, the last name Wise would once again cross his desk.

11

THE CAVE

"I am an American soldier," Ben said in Afghan Dari to a group of terrified women and children huddled together in a cave on January 9, 2012. "You are safe."

On a foggy, eerily quiet winter morning in northern Afghanistan, my brother had unknowingly just saved the lives of several innocent Afghan civilians. The fact that he had spent several preceding months refining his mastery of their language presumably made Ben's voice even more soothing to the petrified locals, all of whom Ben and his fellow Green Berets thought were hiding from al Qaeda fighters holed up somewhere in those godforsaken mountains.

As the mothers and their kids filed out of the cave one by one, Ben briefly tilted his head backward in the hopes of catching a brief glimpse of the morning sky. He saw nothing but dense fog and a pair of towering cliffs, where he knew his fellow Green Berets and also Delta Force warriors were hunched over in fighting positions on each side. While their presence was comforting, Ben was disappointed by his inability to catch a fleeting glimpse at what he hoped was the beautiful blue morning sky.

After all the civilians were out of the cave, they were whisked away to a nearby mosque by Afghan National Army commandos who had joined Ben for the dangerous mission.

With the women and children safe, it was time for my brother to turn his attention to another cave. It was the last of five openings that his Special Forces team was busy searching in the hopes of discovering the source of several recent rocket attacks aimed at nearby Mazar-e Sharif, the fourth-largest city in Afghanistan.

Another set of Afghan commandos was supposed to enter the cave before Ben or his fellow Americans. After all, securing the village and the country as a whole was supposed to be their fight, not just ours.

So far, the only disturbance to the early-morning silence had been the Muslim prayer calls from a nearby village, the sounds of a river flowing nearby, and the gravel beneath the soldiers' boots. Yet as Ben moved closer to the cave entrance, the Afghan fighters stopped in their tracks. Even after many months of training by my brother and his fellow Green Berets, they were far too frightened to infringe on the cave's mysterious darkness.

Without hesitation, Ben stepped in front of his anxious Afghan partners.

"I'll go," Ben said over the radio to his American teammates, signaling toward the cave and pulling out a fragmentation (frag) grenade.

Like Jeremy two and a half years earlier, Ben was now inching closer to an enemy our nation had been fighting since September 11, 2001. Both of my brothers loved their families and friends, but as American warriors who had endlessly trained for the chance to go head-to-head with al Qaeda, there was nowhere they would rather be than in the middle of what both firmly believed was a fight between good and evil.

In what seemed like an instant, Ben was blinded as a bright

burst of light emanated from the cave. Faster than almost anyone could have imagined, the sound of Ben's boots slowly trudging over small rocks was overwhelmed by a deafening group of popping sounds.

That was when one of Ben's fellow soldiers heard a loud clanging noise that could only mean one thing: bullets were rapidly striking my brother's body armor.

As Ben fell backward, the fog was joined by a large plume of smoke that was now pouring out of the cave. In the dreadful moments that followed, I can only pray that Ben somehow got one last glimpse at the soaring blue skies just below heaven.

Thud. Thud. Thud.

"What the fuck is that?" an irritated Special Forces soldier said about nine months prior to the cave mission. "Are we under attack?"

Almost every Green Beret in ODA 1316 was in a bad mood during what would eventually amount to spending eighteen of the past twenty-four months in Kunduz and Mazar-e Sharif, Afghanistan. While the amenities and air support were much better this time around, the improvements didn't make the soldiers miss their families any less.

The Special Forces warriors also had an incredibly difficult time sleeping due to an almost inhuman pace of nighttime missions. Getting three hours of rest on a given night was almost universally considered a luxury.

Thud. Thud. Thud.

"Seriously, what the fuck is that?" the same Green Beret said as more of his exhausted teammates began to rustle. "I'm gonna kill whoever is making all that goddamn noise!"

That's when Staff Sergeant Kevin Flike, the fellow Special

Forces soldier who had bonded so closely with Ben over their shared faith, spoke up.

"It's Wise," said Kevin, who had been sleeping inside the same former Soviet base Ben's team had deployed to the previous year. "He got back from Bagram late last night and is probably out on the range refitting his PEQ [laser]."

Indeed, Ben had spent the first six weeks of his team's latest combat tour at the largest U.S. military base in Afghanistan. Traci had pleaded with him not to leave home so soon after Jeremy's burial, but my brother once again felt a solemn obligation to join his teammates in battle. Being initially relegated to Bagram for the deployment's opening chapter was not at all how Ben had envisioned his return to the country where our big brother had died.

While refining some of his medical skills and doing additional Dari language training, Ben had largely been sitting at a desk doing administrative work, which he absolutely hated, especially while fully aware that his teammates were risking their lives to his north. Still, orders were orders, and Ben had no choice but to do what he was told.

There was one crucial consequence of Ben's six weeks as a desk jockey. He hadn't shot a rifle in more than a month. The next morning, he was scheduled to leave Kunduz with his teammates for a seventy-two-hour field mission. Failing to practice beforehand could result in Ben missing a critical shot in battle. Many lives would be at stake, including his own.

Even though it was the middle of a chilly April night in eastern Afghanistan, it would also mark Ben's only chance to calibrate his sniper rifle and practice shooting at targets instead of real Taliban fighters.

"Hey, Wise! Shut the fuck up!" another Green Beret yelled after opening the door of his room on the still rickety base. "This could be our only chance to sleep for three fucking nights!"

Thud. Thud. Thud.

After another twenty minutes of relentless noise, even Ben's pal, Kevin, was fed up. By the time Ben cleared his weapon, came inside, and began taking off his gear, he was getting the proverbial cold shoulder from even his closest battle buddies.

"Well, I guess I might as well make you a cup of coffee," a disgusted soldier who had tried and failed to get back to sleep told Ben.

After apologizing to his teammates for the disturbance, Ben calmly retreated to his room and put on his headphones to listen to an old favorite, Filter's "Hey Man Nice Shot," which he and Jeremy used to jam out to together on their guitars. While listening to hard rock before going to bed made little sense, my brother was simultaneously getting fired up for the big mission that would start in just a few hours.

"Something's off today," Kevin said to Ben as their helicopter landed under the cover of darkness. "I can feel it in the air."

As the Green Berets dismounted and made their way toward the Faryab Province village of Wadi Guchgar, ODA 1316 started splitting up while approaching a road that basically cut a series of mud huts in half. The Green Berets were quietly moving down a valley with mountains on both sides, where ten fellow soldiers each were watching closely from above in case a firefight erupted.

On the ground that day, there were a total of eighty American and Afghan soldiers. Ben was on the forty-man team on the east side, while Kevin and the junior medic, a staff sergeant named Shane, headed west. The medics were always in separate squads in case one was wounded or killed.

The sun would be up soon, but until then, the moonlight made the shadows of the mountains seem even more ominous. Then, as if a transformer exploded above a quiet city street in the middle of the night, Ben's team was jolted by a massive boom and a shocking flash of light. One soldier who was on the mission would later say he had never been more scared in his life.

Despite all the meticulous planning that went into the three-day operation, the U.S. Special Forces and Afghan soldiers had walked right into an L-shaped ambush in the mission's opening minutes. Three Afghan commandos were immediately hit by gunfire before the other thirty-seven on the team, including Ben, had a chance to take cover and regroup.

Through the dark mist, Ben quickly realized the ambush was being led by two primary sources of gunfire. Less than a minute later, my brother had one of the Taliban leaders in his sniper scope. Without taking the time to wipe the sweat from his brow or take a deep breath, Ben had the laser he had just calibrated a few hours earlier pointed squarely at the terrorist's forehead.

There was no hesitation or remorse as my brother pulled the trigger. For whatever reason, this unidentified man was trying to kill Ben's brothers-in-arms, which meant he had to die.

In what seemed like slow motion, the first 7.62×51 mm round fired by my brother blasted right through one of the insurgent's eyes. He died instantly, which allowed Ben's teammates to immediately turn their focus to the other Taliban fighter leading the ambush. A few minutes later, he was dead, too.

After everyone caught their collective breath, a radioman up on one of the cliffs relayed a disturbing observation.

"I've got approximately fifty enemy subjects coming down the hill right toward you guys," he said. "We'll do what we can, but if we can't get them, they'll probably reach you in about three minutes. Over."

Rather than expend the massive amount of ammunition required to kill another fifty enemy fighters, the U.S. Air Force combat controller (CCT) assigned to ODA 1316 requested permission to drop a five-hundred-pound bomb right on top of their heads. That's exactly the kind of air support the Green Berets had lacked during their prior deployment. Having that added capability on their 2011/12 deployment didn't just make missions easier; it saved lives.

After Ben and his teammates took cover, a gigantic explosion thundered through the valley like nothing most soldiers on the ground had ever heard or seen. Other than the sounds of U.S. and Afghan troops checking on one another by calling out in both English and Dari, the valley was mostly silent except for a few frightened goats. Nothing could silence the sounds of a frenetic battle like a giant five-hundred-pound bomb.

The sun was coming up now, and after Ben's team secured the village following the bomb blast, my brother joined Kevin's team to go clear the west side. While walking near the mountain, Ben saw the mangled bodies of the Taliban fighters who'd probably thought they were about to surprise a bunch of stupid Americans. All told, ODA 1316 killed at least sixty enemy fighters that day while suffering just three casualties of their own—the Afghans who had been struck during the opening seconds of the ambush.

After a few more hours of doing his duty in the hot sun, Ben was worn down and exhausted. Unlike his teammates, who had been running and gunning in Afghanistan's harsh terrain on a nightly basis, my brother had been sitting behind a desk for the last six weeks. Despite his fatigue and desire to rest, though, Ben never once complained or asked for a break. My brother preferred to suffer in silence rather than risk slowing his fellow soldiers down.

Upon completing their questioning of villagers and ensuring that no threats remained, Ben, Kevin, Shane, and their dozens of teammates began walking toward the designated landing zone to finally relax, drink some water, and jump on their respective helicopters. It was during this walk that the Special Forces soldiers began discussing what had unfolded during the ambush.

Many of the guys—including the Green Beret who had been most upset about being woken up by Ben's practice shots the night before—were now marveling about his remarkable shot to take out the first terrorist.

"Hey, Wise, thank *God* you zeroed your fucking laser last night!" the soldier said, patting my brother on the back. "I was wrong."

Everyone laughed, including Ben, who quietly thanked the Green Beret for what was clearly an apology. That's when Kevin put his gloved hand on the back of Ben's neck to give his friend a grateful squeeze.

"Guys, I think Sergeant First Class Ben Wise might just be our good luck charm!" Kevin said with a smile. "It's good to have you back, brother."

Just as the teammates were sharing a few laughs and starting to relax after a long and extremely dangerous day, the CCT's voice once again echoed through the valley. He had spotted a strange light in the distance that could be another threat. As the service member responsible for calling in air strikes, the CCT quickly got on the radio to ask for another.

When the American and Afghan soldiers boarded their helicopters, with many of their legs—especially Ben's—feeling like Jell-O, another massive bomb rained down on the majestic Kunduz Province valley. As almost everyone had quickly realized once their birds (helicopters) were airborne, another twenty or so Taliban fighters had been marching right toward them before, thankfully, the CCT noticed their presence.

While Ben hydrated and began to reflect on the day's frantic series of events, including ending the life of a man he had never met, he watched in silence as he witnessed the rising fireball and plumes of smoke from below. The sights and sounds of that mission left my brother both physically and spiritually shaken, but most of all, he missed Traci and Luke. As the helicopter turned toward the day's next mission, Ben wondered what his wife and son were doing thousands of miles away at the same moment.

There had been some improvements to the old Kunduz base since last year, but mostly, Ben and his teammates were surrounded by mountains, sand, plywood, and posters of attractive models that soldiers would occasionally tack on base walls. For his part, Ben was still changing the wallpaper on computers in the operations center to photos of Traci and Luke. While my brother was not a perfect man by any measure, he was truly devoted to his wife and family.

During this deployment, Ben had a small room in a tiny separate building with a metal roof that sounded like it was about to cave in whenever it was being pelted by ice or sleet. As luck would have it, Kevin's equally small, private enclosure was right across from Ben's. Oftentimes, the soldiers got together to shoot the shit and drink "apple juice," which was actually Captain Morgan spiced rum that had been mailed over to Afghanistan by Traci. My brother's wife had successfully disguised the forbidden alcoholic beverages in Mott's apple juice bottles.

Kevin had brought a guitar over to Afghanistan with him in the hopes that Ben would have time to teach him how to play. In reality, they were rarely on the Kunduz base long enough for lessons, and when they were, Ben would show more interest in finishing a new amplifier he had first started to build at Bagram. *No worries,* Kevin thought—there would be plenty of time for Ben to teach him once they finally returned from the deployment to Fort Lewis.

Either way, both Green Berets had something bigger in mind than guitars and amplifiers. Despite planning for missions, doing mountains of required paperwork, and working out as often as possible, Ben and Kevin managed to start a Bible study group for any soldier who wanted to attend. Reading from their own Bibles, including Kevin's thick New International Version (NIV) that had been heavily notated in most margins, the two soldiers did their part to spread the word of God in a place that he had seemingly forgotten to bless.

By the summer of 2011, Ben, Kevin, and their fellow Green Berets were in the middle of what was—to that point—the longest Special Forces deployment of the entire war on terror. Most special ops deployments were seven or—in rare cases—nine months. ODA 1316 was scheduled to be in Afghanistan for almost an entire year.

Coming on the heels of a previous seven-month tour to the same treacherous theater, even the toughest, most seasoned warrior couldn't help but be somewhat bitter, homesick, and frustrated by the huge burden placed on the shoulders of the men and their families.

In addition, the eleven-plus-month timeline meant each Green Beret was entitled to mid-tour R & R. While commanders did their best to give each soldier his leave without disrupting overall operations, it was almost impossible to keep morale high and operations crisp when the full team was rarely together for a given mission. Guys would also have to fill in for those on vacation while also performing their own duties.

Like almost any worker, being asked to do two jobs at once can lead to discouragement and even anger. It's a whole different ball game when the job requires putting your life on the line while also worrying about the safety of those around you.

Ben wasn't immune from those frustrations, and neither was Traci.

"The majority of the time I feel like a robot when you are deployed," she wrote to her husband in a May 16, 2011, email.

"Yes, I am a mother and I love that and am thankful every day for the joy [the kids] bring, but when you are gone I long for the other part of me . . . the wife in me when you are home; it feels like that just disappears when you go away."

In his reply, Ben poured out his heart to the wife that missed him so much.

Baby, the only thing I have to do is give what is beyond my control to God, and focus on the things I can affect. I can't wait to work a job that doesn't require me to sacrifice so much constantly, and allows me to be there for you and the kids; I miss being a husband and father so much my heart aches every day. I pray for you probably a dozen times a day; pretty much whenever I can. I know things are very tough some days; I can hear it in your voice like I did last night, and I wish you didn't have to bear that burden alone. I love you Traci, with all of my heart.

When it was time for R & R, Ben was most certainly ready to go home, fall into the loving arms of his wife, and enjoy some precious time with their growing toddler.

The highlight of my brother's two-week visit back to Washington State might have been a trip to Safeco Field (now T-Mobile Park) with Traci and the kids for a Major League Baseball game between the hometown Seattle Mariners and the Boston Red Sox on August 12, 2011. They were belatedly celebrating the birthday of Traci's son, Ryan, whom Ben always treated as his own, just like Jeremy had with Ethan.

It was also the night before my brother was going back to Afghanistan. That made it hard for both Ben and his wife to relax, but as is the case with R & R during a combat deployment, Traci knew she had to soak up every last moment.

Given that we didn't have a home team while growing up in Arkansas, Ben had adopted the Red Sox as his favorite MLB club after getting the chance to visit historic Fenway Park while in New England for a training exercise many years earlier. More than any particular team, especially since Traci was (and is) a huge Mariners fan, Ben loved baseball and getting the chance to spend the next three hours and eight minutes with little Luke on his lap.

As he pointed out the pitcher, catcher, umpire, batter, and fielders to Luke and the kids, Ben had to feel like he was in heaven compared to those miserable, war-torn valleys in northern Afghanistan. The glorious crack of the bat and accompanying ballpark sights and sounds were eclipsed only by Traci's gentle voice and warm smile.

They had done many family activities during those two weeks, including a trip to the zoo and a weeklong visit by my parents, but for Ben, that special night at the ballpark stood out. To my brother's delight, the Red Sox won the game, 6–4.

As Traci dropped her husband off at Sea-Tac International Airport the next day for yet another tearful farewell, Ben couldn't have known he had just watched his last ball game or—much more importantly—hugged and kissed the wife and son he adored for the very last time.

Saint Michael the Archangel, defend us in battle. Be our defense against the wickedness and snares of the devil. May God rebuke him, we humbly pray, and do thou, O prince of the heavenly hosts, by the power of God, thrust into hell Satan, and all the evil spirits, who prowl about the world seeking the ruin of souls. Amen.

September 25, 2011, marked the start of another big mission.

Even though Kevin had just lost his Saint Michael pendant during a previous firefight, he and my brother nevertheless got on their knees and put their hands on Kevin's Bible after Ben's close friend led a group prayer asking the archangel for protection. They were in the final hours before what was supposed to be another consequential operation in ODA 1316's fight against al Qaeda and the Taliban.

This time, Ben, Kevin, and several of their teammates were stationed at their northernmost base in Mazar-e Sharif, where Ben had spent a significant amount of time training Afghan commandos during the previous deployment.

Ben had been back from R & R for just over a month and had been in a sour mood since returning to Afghanistan. He missed Traci and was counting the days until he could see her again. Kevin had also noticed that Ben was talking about Jeremy more often as of late, perhaps because of the risks associated with their daily missions.

While not consumed by fear, the fact that Jeremy was gone had fully sunken in by the latter stage of Ben's second deployment since our big brother's death. Over and over again, Ben stressed the importance of his loved ones—especially our parents—never getting another dreaded knock on the door.

Having spent much of the last two years living in close quarters with Ben, Kevin could sense how much this unique burden was wearing on his brother-in-arms. Everyone was scared of the unknown, but along with his sniper rifle and body armor, there was no question Ben was carrying more weight than most.

As was the case before almost every mission, Ben was intently listening to an armed forces radio that tracked the movements of all units serving in Afghanistan. Whenever he was able, Ben checked for news about my unit, which was in the closing months of our second deployment in the volatile south.

Ben had already missed my wedding in Hawaii, where my Marine Corps battalion was stationed before leaving for Afghanistan that April. In case you're wondering, yes, I wound up marrying Amber not long after she initially messaged me on Facebook thinking I was dead. On a serious note, however, Ben intensely worried that Amber would join Dana as another Wise family widow before he and Traci even got the chance to meet my new bride.

On any given day while both of us were simultaneously serving in Afghanistan from April to November 2011, Ben could have been informed that he lost another brother to combat. Or, of course, Ben could have been wounded or killed himself. It's a burden few American soldiers, sailors, airmen, and marines have carried in combat since 9/11. Speaking from experience, I would not wish that added stress on any deployed service member.

Ben checked in as often as he could, including sending messages to Amber when he couldn't reach me.

"How is he?" Ben wrote to his new sister-in-law in a Facebook message.

"Hot and tired!" Amber replied. "He just received a package full of junk food; he will be good for a while, ha ha."

"Awesome," Ben wrote back. "Where is [Beau] now?"

"He didn't say," Amber messaged. "They are out somewhere for a few days."

"I think I know where he's at," Ben wrote about a minute later.

After a few more minutes of chatting about family updates, Ben had no choice but to end the conversation.

"Hey, my time's up, I've gotta share the computer," he wrote before answering a question from Amber about the temperatures in Afghanistan. "It'll be scorching when I get where I'm going tomorrow."

"Okay, take care, Ben!" Amber replied. "I'm praying for you all!"

"Thanks," Ben wrote back. "I'm praying for you guys, too."

Ben usually started preparing for the day's mission right after getting off the computer.

"The tempo we're operating on right now is crazy," Kevin said to Ben as they put on their body armor and checked their weapons. "I don't think we can sustain it."

"Ten-four," Ben said, yawning after another virtually sleepless night. "But what choice do we have?"

Ben and Kevin had just been to Mazar-e Sharif and knew what it was like to navigate the terrain while also putting their lives largely in the hands of the Afghans they were tasked with training. The feeling of not being in control of their own fate was foreign to most in the special operations community, who tirelessly train on every detail of what could occur on the complex battlefields of modern warfare.

Another concern was the reliance on foreign commandos. Some Afghans were dedicated soldiers, and some—to put it kindly—were not. Putting their lives in the hands of Afghan National Army soldiers, especially as terrorists wearing ANA uniforms were increasingly turning their guns on American soldiers all across Afghanistan, made most of ODA 1316 extremely nervous.

Kevin, who had successfully pleaded to go on this particular mission after initially being left off the roster, sat quietly as his helicopter soared above Faryab Province, where the sun was almost ready to rise over the majestic mountains. Like Ben and the rest of his teammates, Kevin would have rather died in the field than stay on base while someone else got hurt. Despite all the difficulties of being deployed to a war zone, that's the kind of love shared by those serving together in battle.

The team was in the middle of a rather gloomy, treacherous streak of enemy encounters on several consecutive trips outside the wire. Judging by the intelligence the Green Berets had reviewed while planning for the mission, Kevin and Ben both believed this particular morning would be no different.

While Kevin's helicopter landed at the mouth of yet another valley inside an area of responsibility controlled by SEAL Team 7, Ben was assigned to a "support by fire" mission, during which he would join two U.S. Navy snipers in an overwatch position atop a nearby cliff. It calmed Kevin and the other Green Berets to know that when a firefight almost inevitably erupted in the lush green valley they would soon patrol, ODA 1316's best sniper was looking down on them with the SEALs.

Just as the sun began to rise on the lower end of the twin mountains that dominated the valley, which looked as if it had been carved in the earth for the specific purpose of soldiers fighting there, Kevin and his fellow Green Berets and Afghan commandos began walking toward the tiny village of Qullam Bulaq, which they had been ordered to clear. Moments after Kevin and his teammates started questioning locals about the Taliban's presence while simultaneously starting a search for weapons caches, a familiar echo bounced between the cliffs.

To almost no one's surprise, it was gunfire. If there was one collective thought among the soldiers and SEALs, it was probably *here we go again.*

A small offshoot led by another Green Beret, a sergeant first class named Clay, had come under fire just a few yards from where Kevin had been questioning an Afghan civilian. While Ben and the SEALs hurriedly scanned the valley with their rifle scopes, Kevin decided to move up toward the ambush, kill the bad guys, and be done with the day's fighting.

That's when the machine-gun fire got more intense. For at

least a few seconds, the soldiers closest to the firefight couldn't even tell where it was coming from.

"What's going on?" Kevin said on the radio. "Who's pinned down?"

Someone up on the mountain—perhaps Ben—then helped Kevin and the Green Berets identify the source of the shooting, which was coming from somewhere inside the village.

The next eight hours—*eight*—were nothing like most Hollywood war films. If the Green Berets just blindly fired all around the village, they would have not only risked killing civilians but running out of ammo in a matter of minutes. In fact, gunfire between U.S. forces, Afghan commandos, and the Taliban occasionally picked up before slowly dying down and eventually ceasing entirely before the cycle endlessly repeated itself.

Nobody had been wounded or killed thus far, and almost everyone on both sides of the armed conflict was tired, thirsty, and taking cover while their commanders decided what to do next. Eventually, those in charge of SEAL Team 7 decided it was time to get the civilians to safety before bombing the village sector that was the source of most enemy gunfire. Hopefully, the Americans thought, the bombing raid would force an end to a very long day.

The Taliban must have been dug in, because the gunfire actually increased after bombs were dropped and the smoke cleared. While Kevin, Clay, and another Green Beret nicknamed Deuce were subsequently pinned down on the ground, Ben and the SEAL snipers were seconds away from being on the receiving end of enemy fire up on their mountain.

"Hey man, nice shot," a SEAL sniper said to Ben after my brother struck an enemy target in the village. Even in the middle of a battle, Ben chuckled to himself that the SEAL had coincidentally just verbalized the lyrics to one of his favorite songs.

Moments later, a rock pile right in front of Ben popped up and blew apart, sending shards of rock and dust right into his eyes. Another inch or so, and Ben would have been shot in the face. Had he not been wearing protective eyewear, he could have also suffered severe eye injuries or even blindness.

As Ben and the SEALs quickly fell back to a small cemetery atop the cliff, the gunfire seemed to follow them. Without time to shoot back, Ben had no choice but to dive behind a grave until the hail of bullets stopped whizzing by.

Since Afghans in that region often buried their fallen inside large dirt mounds aboveground, Ben could hear the awful sounds of gunshots hitting a dead body that was shielding him from danger. It was the closest call Ben ever had in combat to that point.

Down in the valley, Deuce volunteered to draw gunfire to himself so Kevin, Clay, and their teammates could advance closer to the Taliban fighters. The majority of the gunfire, as Kevin discovered upon getting on top of a roof before being ordered to jump down and take cover, was now coming from a dry riverbed almost directly in front of them. Kevin and his team would either have to shoot at the enemy while running down the riverbed's slope or ponder the possibility of ending up in direct hand-to-hand combat with terrorists.

As Kevin crept forward while using one of the village's small buildings as cover, he decided to pop out for one last look before he joined his fellow Green Berets in charging down the riverbed. That's when Kevin first felt it.

Like a sledgehammer had just struck his stomach, Kevin collapsed in overwhelming pain upon realizing he had most likely just been shot. As he tried to stay conscious, the medical training he and every Green Beret had received from Ben, Shane, and past team medics immediately kicked in. While feeling around for the wound, Kevin called his teammates.

"I've been hit," he said calmly over the radio, following training procedure. "I'm behind a mud hut right in front of the dry riverbed. Clay and Deuce are still pinned down."

The gunfire that had been directed upward toward Ben and the SEALs had abruptly halted a few minutes earlier, which meant Ben would have quickly heard Kevin's call for help over the radio. Hearing the anguished voice of one of his best friends after he had just been shot had to be one of the worst moments of my brother's life.

Kevin couldn't find any blood or an exit wound, which led him to think he was probably bleeding internally. Pain like nothing he had ever felt before was also shooting up his femoral artery as the minutes it took for his teammates to reach him began to feel like hours. Kevin had no other option but to suffer and wait.

My brother never panicked in battle, but for those frantic few minutes, he felt helpless knowing his friend was lying on the ground as Ben was trapped high above on a cliff and unable to help. All Ben could do was take cover behind another rock, bow his head, and say the same, slightly modified prayer he had recited that morning with Kevin.

Saint Michael the Archangel, defend Kevin in battle. Be his defense against the wickedness and snares of the devil. May God rebuke him, we humbly pray, and do thou, O prince of the heavenly hosts, by the power of God, thrust into hell Satan, and all the evil spirits, who prowl about the world seeking the ruin of souls. Amen.

Just as Ben finished praying, Kevin came back over the radio. The calmness the wounded soldier had admirably displayed a minute or two earlier was understandably absent.

"You'd better get the fuck down here," the wounded soldier said. "It's serious."

Ben was emotionally fraught. He knew the Green Berets on the ground were doing everything they could to reach his friend, but because of the rapidly increasing enemy gunfire, Ben worried it might be too late. Even in the first few hours after Jeremy was killed, Ben—an elite U.S. Army sniper working side by side with Navy SEALs—had never felt so utterly useless.

Finally, an Afghan soldier whom Kevin had been training for the better part of two years ran through the bullets and became the first to reach the wounded American soldier. An attached platoon sergeant with the army's Eighty-Second Airborne Division was next, followed by Clay, a few others, and, most importantly, the junior medic, Shane.

When the medic went to work, he discovered both an entry wound to Kevin's stomach and a broken hip. All Ben could do was keep praying while listening to the chaos unfold over his radio.

"Hey, come here and give me some fire on this fucking tree line," one of the Green Berets said over enemy machine-gun fire while helping put Kevin on a stretcher.

"It's very painful in my left leg right now," Kevin stammered from the ground.

"All right, Kev, you're good, bro," said Shane, trying to reassure his wounded teammate, who suddenly let out a grunt of agony.

"Give me the morphine, please!" the wounded soldier said.

The Green Berets knew they had to get Kevin on a helicopter and out of the kill zone as soon as possible for what would almost certainly be the first of several lifesaving surgeries.

"You guys see anything in that tree line, you fucking kill it," said the Green Beret before adding that it was time to move Kevin. "Everybody work together and stay calm."

"*Covering fire!*" several of Kevin's teammates yelled to the Afghan commandos as the Americans lifted up Kevin's stretcher and started running through the battlefield. The frenzied moments that followed included hellacious bursts of machine-gun fire and grenades being thrown back and forth.

Fortunately, no further American or Afghan casualties were suffered before the soldiers carrying Kevin ran through greenish smoke and reached the medevac chopper.

From atop the mountain, Ben watched in silence as the helicopter ascended above the confusion and flew toward the nearest American combat hospital in Mazar-e Sharif. My brother knew it could have easily been him on that bird after nearly being shot before diving into the cemetery. Even considering the consequences to his loved ones, Ben would have gladly traded places with Kevin.

"Please, Lord, don't let my friend die," Ben prayed.

Upon arriving at the hospital, Kevin asked the surgeon on-site if he would live.

"I don't know," the doctor frankly replied.

Moments later, at Kevin's request, a Catholic priest gave the wounded soldier his last rites.

Back home in Arkansas, my sister, Heather, reacted with surprise as she looked down at her cell phone screen and saw something strange. It was a short, seemingly random phone number similar to the digits that would appear when Jeremy used to call her from Afghanistan. She would have given anything to pick up and hear her fallen brother's voice.

Instead, Heather quickly realized it was one of her two living brothers, both of whom were currently deployed to the same war zone where Jeremy had just made the ultimate sacrifice.

"Hello?" Heather said with trepidation.

After a brief moment of silence as the faint connection crackled, my sister heard an unmistakably soothing voice.

"It's me," Ben said.

Heather took a deep breath before asking her oldest living brother if he was okay.

"Is something wrong?" she continued. "What about Beau? Did something happen to Beau?"

"I haven't talked to Beau in a while, but I would have heard if something happened," Ben responded. "I'm sure he's fine. As for me, I should be dead right now, Heather."

The feeling in Heather's stomach was a mixture of sickness and sheer panic. Losing Jeremy had been her worst nightmare. Being told that the unthinkable had been that close to happening again was almost impossible for my sister to process.

"Oh, Ben," she said through tears. "I'm so glad you're okay—thank God."

"The bad news is that Kevin was shot," Ben continued without warning. "We don't know if he's going to make it."

Heather hadn't met Kevin, but she knew how much he meant to Ben as both a fellow warrior and faithful friend. For the first time, she heard fear in Ben's voice, not for his own safety but for that of his wounded teammate.

"I need you to pray for Kevin," Ben said. "And I also need you to pray for all my guys. Don't tell Traci, but things are rough over here—really rough."

Without hesitation, Heather lowered her head and recited the Lord's Prayer, with Ben doing the same from thousands of miles away in miserable Mazar-e Sharif.

"Please be careful," Heather said. "I love you, Ben."

"I love you too, Biggie," Ben said. "Remember to keep praying for us."

A few days later, Heather was doing just that in her kitchen when the same strange number once again popped up on her mobile phone screen. The connection was even worse this time, but soon after picking up, Heather was relieved to once again hear Ben's voice.

"Are you praying?" he said, barely intelligible.

"Yes," Heather responded. "I was actually praying for Kevin when you called."

"I thought so," Ben said. "I could feel it."

After telling Heather that Kevin had been flown to Germany for another round of emergency surgeries, my brother repeated his deep concerns for the perilous course his current deployment had taken.

"My men are risking their lives over here every single day," he said in a hushed tone that was difficult to discern through the crackling connection. "Like Kevin said before he was hit, I'm not sure how much longer we can sustain this pace."

"God will protect all of you, Ben," Heather said.

"Thanks, Biggie," Ben said before telling her to please tell our mom and dad that he loved them. "I hope you're right."

A few days later, Ben sat down and wrote me an email.

Dude,

I just got back from some hairy stuff; never been in a full all day knock down drag out like this one. One of our guys got shot in the stomach; he's ok, in Germany now. Me and a few others almost bought it a few times. I was up on a ridgeline with two SEALs and we started getting fire from both sides and had to fall back and get cover behind some graves. Ironic that they probably saved our lives. I schwacked at least one guy, and one of the SEALs with me got two I think.

*These [enemy fighters] weren't like the punks we've fought
in the past. They could shoot, they had excellent fighting positions
and were well disciplined and coordinated. I was really surprised.*

I don't remember exactly when I got Ben's email, but I do recall not only saying a prayer for his wounded teammate but thanking God that my last living brother had survived that harrowing
day on the cliffs.

On a cold, rainy December 2011 day, Kevin debated whether to answer his cell phone after undergoing a torturous round of physical
therapy. After doctors and nurses rallied to save his life in Afghanistan, Germany, San Antonio, and now Washington State, Kevin
was in the middle of a daily struggle to recuperate. His left leg was
paralyzed, while 20 percent of his colon had to be removed, among
other serious aftereffects.

Upon catching his breath and trying not to think about the
tremendous pain, Kevin decided to answer his phone. He never
could have imagined how important the call would be.

"Hey, Kev, it's Benny," my brother said from Afghanistan.
"How are you feeling today?"

Nothing helped Kevin during those challenging first days
back home more than talking to his still-deployed teammates, and
especially Ben, who told him he was still running the Bible study
group in his honor. Everyone in the unit who prayed was constantly
praying for Kevin to make a full recovery.

After catching up and sharing a few laughs, Ben's tone became
as serious as Kevin had ever heard it.

"I was so worried that we were going to lose you, Kev," said
my brother, whose voice was cracking even more than the satellite phone connection. "It was nothing compared to what you went

through, but I just want you to know that it was a brutal day for all of us."

After a painstaking, step-by-step recounting of what happened the day of the shooting, Ben told Kevin that it was time to share some big news.

"We got him," Ben said. "We took out the guy who shot you."

My brother explained that he had briefly seen Kevin's would-be killer through his sniper scope that day, but he wasn't able to get a clean shot before he and the Navy SEALs had been forced to take cover in the cemetery.

"When we got back to the edge of the cliff, it was quiet at first, but after a few minutes, they started shooting at us again," Ben said. "We could barely lift our heads up from behind the rocks, but when we finally did, I saw that same guy."

Ben *never* celebrated or bragged about killing someone, even in the case of the Taliban attacker during the L-shaped ambush earlier in his deployment. Given that this particular terrorist had shot one of his best friends, however, it was hard for him to mask his satisfaction.

"Let's just say that guy won't be shooting anyone else," Ben said.

After thanking my brother for the good news, Kevin asked how the rest of the deployment had been going.

"You never know, but it's colder than Alaska over here, and I think our al Qaeda and Taliban friends are packing it in for the winter," Ben said. "Three more weeks and—hopefully—we're home free."

Kevin had already seen Traci and knew how excited she and the kids were to welcome Ben home. Most of all, he missed his friend and couldn't wait until Ben was able to come hang out with him in the hospital.

"Guess what? The army just shipped my guitar," Kevin told

Ben. "I know we didn't get to jam before I got hit, but when you get back, you'd better start teaching me how to play."

"Heck yeah, brother!" Ben said with excitement. "You'll be a regular Eddie Van Halen by the time I'm done with you."

"Take care, Ben," Kevin said. "You and the boys stay safe over there."

"Ten-four," said my brother. "See you in a few weeks."

Indeed, the spring and summer fighting seasons that stretched deep into the fall of 2011 had almost completely died down. Still, Ben and his teammates were going out on occasional missions with cold weather gear covering their already cumbersome body armor. The sounds of boots on gravel had been replaced with the crunching sounds of pure white snow during ODA 1316's increasingly rare foot patrols.

Most of the time, Ben and his teammates were busy packing up their belongings for the journey home while dreaming of their wives, fiancées, or significant others. Remember: it wasn't just one eleven-month deployment for these guys. Minus R & R, almost everyone on the team had been in Afghanistan eighteen of the past twenty-four months, with several having spent additional time in Thailand or—in Ben's case—doing administrative work at Bagram and other bases. I think I can safely speak for these rough-and-tumble Green Berets by saying it was the most difficult two-year stretch of their military careers.

I got home from my second Afghanistan deployment, which had been relatively uneventful, in November 2011. Like Kevin, Traci, Heather, and our parents, I was anxiously awaiting my brother's return and felt guilty enjoying the beaches of Hawaii with Amber while Ben was trudging through the snowy cliffs of northern Afghanistan. All I wanted was to introduce Ben and

Traci to my new wife while we kicked back and had a few beers in the picturesque sands of Waikiki. In a few short months, it was supposed to happen.

"Yo dude, how's the 'Stan?" I wrote to my brother on Christmas Eve 2011, using a common military nickname for Afghanistan. "I miss you very much [and] I was furious when I missed your call the other day. Please call again soon and Merry Christmas, brother," I continued. "I called Traci but no one was home. I'll try again today. Love, Skello."

"I'm doing alright, Beau," Ben replied on Christmas Day. "I'm just ready to get back and see my family. I'll try and call you later tonight. Love you, Beau. Benny out."

After spending another Christmas and New Year's Day in the cold and desolate mountains, things stayed mostly quiet for the men of ODA 1316 until January 8, 2012.

Later that morning, Ben's team was called out on a mission to support the storied Delta Force, with whom they had been secretly operating for several months. If there was any doubt about the importance of many of the missions ODA 1316 was being sent outside the wire to perform, the mere presence of Delta operators speaks for itself. Like Jeremy, Ben was involved in some of the most crucial counterterrorism operations undertaken since 9/11.

This particular mountain mission was hairier than Ben, Shane, Deuce, Clay, and their teammates would have hoped given that they were now just two weeks from going home. The thought of their families being notified of a loved one being wounded or killed that close to their welcome home ceremony was almost too much for many of the Green Berets to bear. They were ever so close to the finish line.

For Ben, those emotions were privately multiplied by ten. As he had expressed to Heather, Ben was almost always thinking of the effect his death would have on his already grieving family. He called Traci before heading out into the mountains that day but got her voicemail and decided to follow up with a quick email.

"Hey love, I'll be working late tonight and might not be able to get to a phone for a while," Ben wrote to Traci on January 8. "I'll talk to you as soon as I can. I love you."

"Shoot," Traci replied. "I just missed you by a few minutes."

After several close calls on January 8, ODA 1316 returned safely to Mazar-e Sharif only to be informed that they would be departing for another combat mission later that night. Rockets had been landing closer and closer to their base over the last few days, and intelligence was indicating they were almost certainly being fired from a nearby village. As always, there would be almost no time to shower, eat, sleep, and check in with family members back home. The never-ending mission would continue.

"It never fucking stops," one of the Green Berets said.

To make matters worse, the already-tired soldiers had awoken well before dawn, eaten breakfast, and started final preparations for their January 9 mission when commanders informed them that their operation had been delayed for two hours due to dense fog, which was common in those tall mountains. This particular assault would take place in a Balkh Province village nestled right around the country's northern tip near Afghanistan's border with Uzbekistan.

Without pausing to ponder the consequences, Ben collapsed back onto his cot upon being notified of the mission delay. He had war paint camouflaging his face and was already wearing most of his gear, which resulted in several searing aches and pains when he woke up. Sleeping with all that stuff was *not* comfortable, but for

Ben, every minute of shut-eye was precious. He would sleep as long as possible and deal with it later.

"Ben, wake up," said his junior medic, Shane, shaking my brother about two hours later. "It's time to go, brother!"

"Ten-four," Ben said with a yawn.

It was still foggy and mostly dark when Ben and Shane boarded separate helicopters to soar through some of the world's tallest cliffs. Even during what was the twelfth year of America's longest war, the beauty Ben took in on that flight must have been magnificent. It's hard to comprehend how such an awe-inspiring place could be almost constantly gripped by fear and bloodshed.

Someday, Ben hoped, the people of Afghanistan would get a chance to forge their own collective path without being terrorized by the Taliban, al Qaeda, and a new terrorist group—ISIS— that was just starting to emerge. While my brother was not naive enough to think the war would end with the unconditional surrender of each and every terrorist, he did believe that the blood, sweat, and tears of his men would ultimately make a difference.

It's impossible to know exactly what Ben was thinking as the bird carrying him, Clay, two fellow American service members, and some Afghan commandos descended into the Balkh Province valley as the last throes of darkness shielded their presence. Knowing my brother, he was praying for the safety of his teammates.

If they could just get through this one day, the soldiers would almost certainly soon get the chance to see their loved ones. For a fleeting moment, Ben might have allowed himself to imagine running through Seattle's airport toward Traci, Luke, and the kids as they jumped with excitement and waved American flags to celebrate his return.

By the time the helicopter reached the objective, the ramp leading off the back of the bird had jammed. That meant that everyone aboard had to jump out and plunge about ten feet downward into a dry riverbed.

As soon as my brother's boots hit the cold valley's ground, Ben flipped the proverbial switch that had helped him excel under pressure from the very beginning. In an instant, Sergeant First Class Ben Wise was no longer a husband, father, son, or sibling. He was an American warrior.

Pop! Pop! Pop!

The first shots rang through the valley just minutes after Ben, Clay, and their teammates ran west to east after jumping out of the bird. Shane, who couldn't be with Ben and Clay since medics were always split up, was with their twin element about a mile to their west.

Delta Force had arrived in the area before the Green Berets. As one of the military's two top-echelon task forces, every bit as crucial and secretive as SEAL Team 6, Delta Force had invited ODA 1316 to join them on this particular mission. The Delta Force warriors were split between clearing the nearby village of Tandurak and performing overwatch atop the valley's twin cliffs. Those providing overwatch were unable to descend into the narrow valley without first boarding a helicopter.

As the firefight began, Ben and Clay were the U.S. special operators closest to the action. My brother could see snow on the hills and in several shaded areas as the firefight erupted. The only other light was coming from intermittent enemy AK-47 and machine-gun fire, which was directed toward a team of infantry scouts and Afghan commandos that Clay had sent north toward Tandurak. That's where intelligence had indicated those rockets had originated.

Spy satellites had also revealed the set of caves, which Clay pointed out to Ben as their Chinook helicopter was descending into the valley. Because of the relatively small size of the entrances in photos, along with the darkness as the American and Afghan soldiers landed, it was hard to determine just how many caves they were dealing with. All Clay knew for sure was that securing each and every one of them was his team's top priority.

It was unclear exactly where the initial gunfire came from, but one of the Americans had already taken a bullet that had fortunately struck his water pack. Right away, Clay ordered his team to provide cover fire, which would give the scouts and commandos a chance to pull back. Ben immediately dropped to one knee and began shooting at anything that he could see, which wasn't much near those unsecured cave entrances.

"Covering fire!" Ben and Clay yelled as their teammates ran toward them.

As the unharmed scouts and commandos arrived and the sun continued to rise, Clay and Ben became increasingly fixated on those caves. Other than clearing a few buildings on each side of the cave entrances, there wasn't much else they could do until all threats were smoked out of those still-very-dark crevices.

That's when Clay first sent the Afghan commandos, who were carrying heavy machine guns and RPGs, toward the caves. Again, this was supposed to be their fight, with the Delta Force warriors and Green Berets operating as advisers in a supporting role. Clay was reluctant to risk the lives of any Americans until their Afghan counterparts had at least been given the opportunity to seize the valley from whatever terrorist group was controlling it.

Just as Clay and Ben confirmed that they could see at least three cave openings in the massive cliff, they saw another flash of light and accompanying *pop* from one entrance. A split second later, they saw an Afghan commando who had been moments away from firing an RPG into the cave fall squarely on his back. Not only had the partner soldier been wounded, but in the key moments that followed, the lives of every single American and Afghan on the patrol were at risk.

Since his finger was on the trigger, the force of the bullet hitting the Afghan commando caused him to press it as he flew backward while being shot. All of a sudden, ODA 1316 wasn't only under attack from an enemy hiding in the shadows but an explosive device that had been shot up into the morning fog.

"RPG!" Ben yelled.

"Take cover!" Clay followed.

Even the enemy fighters must have retreated into their caves, because the next thirty seconds were almost completely silent. To this day, nobody knows where that RPG landed, because no blast ever followed. Perhaps it was a dud.

Intense fighting resumed as soon as it became clear that an explosion wouldn't kill everyone in the valley. When the Afghan was hit, however, Ben's job—at least for the next few minutes—became not that of a war fighter but a U.S. Army medic tasked with caring for the wounded. My brother's duty was to not only reach that wounded Afghan commando but save his life.

Bullets zipped past my brother as he ran toward the enemy-infested cave entrances and reached the bleeding partner soldier. As Ben dragged him behind a boulder to render aid, he quickly discovered the Afghan had been shot somewhere around his cheek. He was still alive.

"I am here for you," Ben said in Dari to the shaking, scared Afghan soldier. "Just try to relax. Let me help you," my brother continued. "All I need you to do right now is pray."

As the wounded commando asked Allah for mercy, Ben used

his many years of training to somehow stop most of the bleeding and save the Afghan's life. Had the bullet struck his face even half an inch higher, the commando would have been dead before Ben reached him. Thanks to my brother's bravery and also a bit of luck, the soldier survived.

After Ben finished helping the Afghan back to Clay's firing position, where the soldier was subsequently flown out of the valley on a medevac chopper, Ben closed up his medical bag and rejoined the battle. Rifle in hand, it was time to take down this well-armed group of terrorists—once and for all.

The only problem was that the twenty or so remaining Afghan commandos were increasingly spooked after witnessing their battle buddy being shot in the face. One by one, they started to fall back before eventually shutting down.

"What the fuck do we do now?" Clay said to Ben, lamenting that they had a platoon full of largely Afghan fighters instead of U.S. special operators. "It's gonna be hard to take those caves if these guys are quitting on us."

Just then, bullets struck the river valley's frozen mud about a foot from where Ben and Clay were conversing. Once again, they were forced to scramble and take cover while still trying to figure out the next move.

After a few minutes of discussion, the team's CCT had a rather brilliant idea. Rather than lead the patrol into the cave's darkness, which would result in almost certain death, he would ask for a set of Hellfire missiles to be fired into the caves by a group of Apache helicopters reserved for this very mission. The CCT's request was approved just a few minutes after calling it in.

"*Birds inbound!*" Clay shouted into the valley and over the radio. "*Take cover!*"

Ben, whose language training had already paid huge dividends, repeated Clay's command to the Afghan soldiers quietly enough so whoever was hiding in the caves hopefully couldn't hear him.

Moments later, the American helicopters laid waste to what Ben and Clay still thought were three caves. The explosions thundered off the walls of the surrounding cliffs and also a mud wall that was right behind the spot where everyone was taking cover.

Much more concerning than the earsplitting sounds, however, was the shrapnel now flying toward their heads. My brother ducked as jagged pieces of metal flew at lightning speed and repeatedly pierced the mud behind them.

"*Stay down!*" Ben yelled in Dari to the Afghans.

Fires were now visible in the cave entrances, where Ben and Clay could now see and hear a rapid succession of explosions. It was almost certainly enemy ammunition that had been set ablaze by the missiles. There was a less-than-zero chance—or so they believed—that anyone inside any of the three caves could have survived those blasts, let alone the intense heat.

"All right, now let's go clear this fucking village!" Clay shouted after the chaos died down.

Moments later, Ben joined the rest of the team in going door-to-door and rounding up every military-age male, who would be subsequently sent to a nearby mosque for questioning. Clearing a village was pretty much standard procedure by this point in the deployment. To Ben, everything seemed normal except for one thing.

"Hey, Clay, where are all their wives and kids?" Ben asked. "I've seen a few, but shouldn't there be way more of them?"

"Ten-four, good point," Clay said. "Keep your eyes open."

Once the males had been sent down to the mosque, Ben's team turned its attention back to the caves, where the missile-induced fires had almost fully died down. As the commander on the ground, Clay knew every nook and cranny of that dreadful valley had be 100 percent accounted for before he could pull his men out. The only such areas remaining were the set of caves and a nearby building.

They would start—Clay had decided with Ben's input—with the building. Most of the Afghans had calmed down a bit since their fellow commando was shot and saved by Ben, so they once again took the lead.

The plan was for Clay to initially throw a flash-bang grenade, which are essentially distraction devices often used by SWAT teams to create commotion during a police raid. As designed, the grenade would set off nine bright flashes accompanied by deafening bangs to startle and confuse whoever was inside the building.

For whatever reason, the grenade only flashed and banged once. The commandos were nevertheless just as frightened by the sights and sounds as the bad guys were supposed to be. Just like a few minutes earlier, they immediately froze in their tracks.

"What the fuck are you guys doing?" Clay yelled to the Afghans. "Move in!"

Even with Ben repeating his command in Dari, the commandos once again quit on the mission.

Luckily, nobody was inside the building, which meant the only task left was clearing the three caves that had already been bombarded by American missiles. It was an operation that Ben, Clay, the CCT, a Chemical Reconnaissance Detachment (CRD) soldier, and the infantry scouts could hopefully complete on their own before getting back on the birds and leaving the valley, which was still murky and bitterly cold between those huge cliffs despite the sun having risen.

That's when Ben discovered the two additional caves and proceeded—with only a limited amount of help from two or three commandos—to rescue those women and children.

"We've got to get these people out of here," Ben said over the radio to Clay.

As the petrified civilians filed out and were directed toward the mosque, Ben once again radioed Clay, who was on lower ground with another set of suddenly useless commandos.

"There are two more caves up here that haven't been Hellfired," said Ben, referring to the fact that the missiles hadn't reached the new caves he'd just discovered. "I say again, these two entrances have not been Hellfired. Over."

When Ben valiantly volunteered to clear the second cave with two frightened Afghan commandos walking behind him, Clay got extremely nervous. Ben's plan was to throw his frag grenade into the cave and then run around the corner to take cover while any potential gunfire ensued.

Clay and the CCT were only about ten or so yards away by that point, but still on lower ground, which meant they had more protection should someone start shooting out of the entrance. Before Clay could yell out any words of caution to Ben, my brother threw the grenade. That's when Clay and the CCT heard the shots.

Amid frenetic flashes of light, Clay saw my brother fall backward onto the rocks, where he was now at the mercy of an unknown number of enemy fighters who—throughout the morning chaos—had been quietly waiting to strike from the darkness.

Despite Ben's efforts to save a commando earlier in the day, the Afghan commandos behind him took off running at the first sign of danger. While Clay and the CCT desperately wanted to help Ben, they had no choice but to take cover and wait out the agonizing moments that ensued. Had they tried to push forward, they would have almost certainly been killed.

As my brother lay on his back screaming in pain, Clay pleaded with one of the toughest and smartest Green Berets he had ever known.

"Crawl, Ben!" he shouted through tears. "You've got to crawl, brother!"

The gunfire from the cave had only increased over the last few seconds. While Clay and the CCT couldn't tell from their vantage point, several of the bullets were striking Ben as he lay on the cold ground. Until the enemy stopped shooting, there was nothing anyone could do.

Suddenly, all Clay could hear was Ben shouting for help, which meant the enemy was probably reloading. In an instant, both Clay and the CCT jumped up to throw frag and smoke grenades at the cave entrance. As the gunfire quickly resumed, the CCT managed to grab my brother by his body armor and pull him to safety.

Clay then ordered the infantry scouts to maintain steady gunfire on the cave entrance, which would enable the CCT to call in more air strikes. Most important, it would also be Clay's job to call in another medevac helicopter and—until the medic arrived—do his best to administer lifesaving care to my brother.

Like the other Green Berets, Clay had only received standard-issue medical training from Ben and his fellow medics. Ben's junior, Shane, was still on the other side of the valley, where he and his team were working to clear hills and houses. Shane had stopped in his tracks as soon as he heard Clay call out my brother's roster number over the radio and request a medevac, which meant Ben had been wounded. Other than writing down everything Clay was saying over the radio, there was nothing Shane could do to help his senior medic at that early stage. He was simply too far away.

Clay felt as if he were in the middle of a nightmare as he looked down toward my bleeding brother. *This can't be happening to Ben*, he thought. It appeared the shots that had initially knocked Ben down had struck his body armor, which was actually a good initial sign.

It took further investigation for the Green Beret to realize that most of the bullets had struck Ben while he was lying on his back.

When Clay tore my brother's pants off to evaluate the wounds, he discovered a mangled, bloody mess. Amid the pain, Ben asked if his manhood was intact.

"You're good, bro!" Clay said. "You're gonna be fine!"

The rest of Ben's lower extremities were not fine, however. As Clay kept looking, it seemed like bullet holes were everywhere. Clay did exactly what he was trained to do in that situation, though: tie tourniquets and patch up whatever wounds he could see.

When the American infantry soldiers ran out of ammunition, they took the useless Afghan commandos' machine guns so they could continue firing into the cave. Clay then took off running down to the creek bed to pick up a stretcher while the CCT stayed behind and held my brother's hand.

Ben was incoherent by that point due to a heavy dose of battlefield painkillers. I can only pray that he didn't feel too much pain beforehand. I also hope his mind was filled with warm thoughts of Traci, Luke, and the other people he cared about most.

After requesting more fire from the scouts on the ground and the Delta Force warriors on the cliffs, Clay and the CCT teamed up to carry my brother's stretcher through the chaos and to the creek, where the medevac bird was waiting.

"You'll be okay, Ben," Clay said after loading him on the chopper. "I love you, brother!"

As the helicopter carrying my brother rose above the cliffs, a five-hundred-pound bomb decimated the entrance to the cave while Clay, the CCT, CRD, and other soldiers took cover. While the helicopter pilots marveled at the plume of smoke and fire billowing up from the valley, massive boulders, rocks, and tree branches simultaneously rained down on the American and Afghan soldiers from the cliffs.

Soon after the dangerous debris stopped falling, the Delta Force soldiers flew down on a Black Hawk helicopter to lay further waste to the caves, which caused almost the entire side of the mountain to collapse. When the Delta Force guys were done, Clay—with his uniform covered in my brother's blood—moved toward the cave to fire a Carl Gustaf recoilless rifle.

The anti-tank weapon caused two or three ensuing explosions before another group of Afghan soldiers—not the commandos who had quit a few minutes earlier—threw a thermal grenade. The Afghans then crept inside to pull out several bodies piled up at the entrance.

They found several al Qaeda fighters, including one whose body looked like Jell-O but whose chest was amazingly still moving up and down. Before Clay could give an order to administer medical care, an Afghan put five bullets squarely in the bleeding terrorist's torso.

It was nighttime when Clay, the CCT, CRD, Shane, and other team members finally flew out of the still-smoke-filled valley. Because of what everyone suspected about the severity of Ben's injuries, it had been the worst moment of the entire deployment, even more devastating than the day Kevin was shot.

Despite an overwhelming sense of sadness and guilt, most of my brother's teammates initially thought Ben would live. After all, he hadn't been struck above the waist, which meant my brother's likelihood of survival was probably decent despite what would surely be a long, difficult recovery. Perhaps he and Kevin would wind up sharing a hospital room.

When the Green Berets got back to Mazar-e Sharif, everyone started asking Clay what happened as the worried soldiers jumped on their phones to try to get an update on my brother's condition. It was Shane who first found out that Ben would soon be transported to Bagram Airfield for his first set of surgeries. He would then be flown to Landstuhl Regional Medical Center in Germany for what would likely be several more.

Everyone paused when a siren came over the base's radio. It was an urgent call for donations of Ben's blood type. Despite exhaustion, every single Green Beret on the team immediately lined up to get needles stuck in their arms. While none of them knew it at the time, hundreds of American and NATO soldiers of all nationalities were doing the same thing at Bagram.

Shane also learned that he had been designated as my brother's medical escort. He would not fly with Ben from Mazar-e Sharif to Bagram, Shane was told, because of an emergency surgery Ben needed to have during the flight. He would instead meet Ben at Bagram before flying with him to Germany.

As Shane waited to leave Mazar-e Sharif, he decided to go through my brother's gear. He discovered not only Ben's body armor and radio, both of which were riddled with bullets, but his medical bag. The outside was almost entirely soaked with blood.

When Shane opened Ben's bag, he didn't just discover that his blood had soaked through the kit's exterior. He also realized that my brother's tools were still covered in the blood of the Afghan commando whom Ben had treated earlier in the same battle.

During the last day U.S. Army Sergeant First Class Benjamin Brian Wise ever spent at war, he risked not only his life but many subsequent years of happiness with Traci and Luke to fight and bleed with his Afghan partners. He also saved many of their lives, from the commando to those innocent women and children in the first cave he found. For an American soldier, the willingness to put everything on the line for those around you is the true meaning of service.

I love you, Ben.

12

NOT AGAIN

It was around 1:00 a.m. in our five-hundred-square-foot apartment in Kaneohe Bay, Hawaii. I was fast asleep when I felt a nudge on my shoulder.

"Honey, your phone is ringing," Amber said.

I fumbled to the kitchen, found my cell phone, and stepped out onto our patio overlooking the beautiful bay.

"Beau, sweetheart," the voice on the other end of the line said. "I know you were asleep, but you need to wake up. I've got something really important to tell you."

The statement lingered for a brief moment before finally registering. The voice was that of my mother, who was calling from back home in Arkansas.

Minutes earlier, my mom and dad had received a phone call of their own from a strange number. After hearing what the person had to say, my mom had collapsed onto her knees and looked up toward the heavens.

"You will not destroy me," she told God. "You will not destroy my family."

Back on the phone, I was waiting for my mother to deliver what I knew would be some sort of bad news. I could tell by the way her normally composed, distinguished voice was quivering ever so slightly.

"Your brother has been shot in the leg," she said. "That's all we know, but the good news is that he should be okay, honey. Your father and I think Ben will be coming home very soon."

Despite the hesitation, the overall tone in my mom's voice was surprisingly unconcerned, especially considering that she had already lost her oldest son to war. We calmly finished our conversation before I went back to bed.

"Ben got hurt, but everything's okay," I confidently told Amber, jumping back between the sheets. "He's coming home early."

Amber didn't say so at the time, probably because she was still half-asleep, but she was already thinking of something I had said the previous day. On our way to a cookout at the home of one of my fellow marines, I had stopped in my tracks upon being overcome by a strange sensation.

"What's wrong, honey?" Amber said.

"I have this weird feeling," I began.

"What are you talking about?" my wife asked nervously.

"I feel like something's going to happen," I said. "And it's going to affect everyone."

While it was scary to hear that Ben had been wounded just over two years after Jeremy was killed, especially so soon after my premonition, the result of a leg wound would most likely be a minor surgery or two followed by an early flight home to reunite with Traci and the kids. It was a close call, but things could have been a lot worse.

While contemplating the information I had just received, I managed to doze back off.

A few hours later, I awoke restless and worried from my broken sleep. *What if it's worse than Mom thought? What if whoever called*

my parents is downplaying or even hiding the full extent of Ben's in-
juries?

Because of protocol, I figured that Traci had almost certainly
been informed of Ben being wounded before I'd found out. After
picking up the phone to call her and getting a busy signal, I decided
to hold off for a few more hours. I couldn't imagine how hectic things
were in that house and certainly didn't want to add to the confusion.
Instead, I sent Ben's wife a short, simple text message.

"Thinking of you and the kids," I wrote. "Remember that
Amber and I are always here for you, Traci. Love, Beau."

I went to work later that morning and informed my boss,
Master Gunnery Sergeant Bryan, about what had happened to my
brother. He then asked his superiors to keep him updated in real
time on Ben's status.

Over the next few hours, my commanding officer assured
me—with what seemed like absolute certainty—that Ben would
ultimately be okay. To this day, I believe he was telling the truth.
The biggest problem when a U.S. service member is wounded—
especially in the first hours after a battlefield incident—is the spread
of erroneous information. It's often unavoidable during the fog of
war. Plus, some of Ben's teammates were frequently out in the field.

That's when my work phone rang. On the other end of the
line was a woman speaking in a strong, yet subtle tone. She introduced herself as a retired lieutenant colonel who now worked for
the Green Beret Foundation.

After exchanging pleasantries, she informed me that Ben's
wounds were more severe than previously described. My chest and
entire body began to tighten just like in Afghanistan when I had
first received the bad news about Jeremy.

Not again.

The lieutenant colonel then said that for Ben to receive advanced medical procedures of the utmost necessity, he would be transported to Landstuhl Regional Medical Center in Germany. I could be flown there to meet him—on the foundation's dollar—if I chose.

I knew the next step was getting in touch with Traci, but even after the harrowing experience of trying to console Dana following Jeremy's death, I had no idea what to say. The sense of devastation I was feeling was nothing compared to the emotional roller coaster she had been riding since 6:10 a.m. Pacific time, when she was awoken with the horrific news that her husband had been shot.

In fact, Traci initially thought it was Ben who was calling at that ungodly hour because of the weird number on the caller ID. She actually answered the phone upset that Ben would wake her up so early before being jolted to attention by an unfamiliar voice.

"Mrs. Wise?" the caller said.

Traci's stomach sank the very moment she realized Ben wasn't on the other end of the line. Right away, she knew something was wrong.

"What happened to Ben?" she said. "What happened to Ben?"

"Mrs. Wise, I'm sorry, but Sergeant First Class Wise has been shot," the U.S. Army officer said.

As an authentically selfless military wife and member of my family, however, Traci wasn't thinking of herself. She was overcome with worry for my parents, Heather, and me. Most of all, she was thinking of her children—especially young Luke.

As she lay in her still-darkened bedroom, Traci softly repeated two words through her unrelenting tears.

"Not again," she whispered.

I don't know exactly where Traci was when I called to discuss Ben's worsening condition and what I could do to help her cope. I was immediately impressed by Traci's composure and strength as we began to talk. My sister-in-law had been overwhelmed by phone calls since that morning, yet she was somehow managing to stay calm amid the chaos.

"Thanks for calling, Beau," she said. "Where are you?"

"I'm still in Hawaii," I said.

"When can you get here?" she inquired.

"I'm working that out right now with my command, but I don't want you to worry," I said. "One way or another, I'll get to you."

About an hour later, I received an official set of orders from the U.S. Marine Corps to report to Fort Lewis. It was a greatly appreciated gesture, along with the U.S. Army Special Operations Command volunteering to pay for Amber's and my travel costs to Washington State. The Green Beret Foundation and the Special Operations Warrior Foundation, to their infinite credit, would then cover Traci's and my long journey overseas.

"Hey, it's Beau again," I said to Traci. "I don't have any more news on Ben since our last call."

"Where are you?" she said, mirroring our last conversation.

"I'm on my way," I responded.

For the first time all day, I sensed a small sliver of relief in Traci's voice.

"Thank God," she said.

"Amber's coming with me," I continued. "She'll watch the kids while you and I fly to Germany."

"I can't wait to see you," she said. "And I can't wait to meet Amber."

Even under the most trying of circumstances, Traci was looking forward to finally being introduced to my wife. She hadn't been able to attend our impromptu wedding in Hawaii while Ben was deployed.

As Amber and I hurriedly threw some clothes in a couple of

overnight bags, I looked out at Hawaii's bright blue sky and flourishing green mountains. I couldn't help but wonder what had really happened to Ben in Afghanistan's snowcapped cliffs.

That's when my phone rang—again. This time, it was my dad, who first and foremost wanted the latest medical update. When I told him there was nothing new, he explained that he and my mom had gotten stuck on their way from Arkansas to Germany due to passport problems. It would take another twenty-four to forty-eight hours to get everything ironed out.

"I love you, Dad," I said. "Ben is a fighter, and he'll get through this."

"See you soon, son," my father said.

I was silent for a few minutes after we hung up while once again staring out at the lush mountains. After initially allowing doubt to creep in, I grew comforted by the ill-fated idea that no modern military family could possibly be forced to endure this same horror twice.

Back in Arkansas, my sister was experiencing a similar set of emotions after our parents left for their trek to Germany. Just as Ben had asked her to do numerous times for his teammates, Heather got down on her knees and started to pray.

"Lord, you already took Jeremy," she said. "You can't have Ben."

While Amber and I were flying over the Pacific Ocean from Hawaii to Washington State, Traci's cell phone rang. It was someone from the Green Beret team's command to gently inform her of a development that had been unthinkable just a few hours earlier. Both of her husband's legs had just been amputated below the knees.

Like my mom and me, Traci had initially been told that Ben had been shot in the leg. Without speaking directly to a doctor or medic, there was simply no way for my brother's wife or any of us to know how serious Ben's wounds actually were.

Traci became understandably angry upon receiving the news while standing on the second level of her and Ben's three-story home in Puyallup, Washington. She naturally wanted more specifics, but the soldier on the other end of the line didn't have the answers she so desperately needed.

When we arrived at Traci and Ben's house, our chief concern was for the kids. Little Luke was just two years old and far too young to understand what was happening. Twelve-year-old Ryan had heard Traci's first phone conversation after Ben was wounded and was well aware of the situation's seriousness. Ten-year-old Kailen knew something was off when she didn't have to go to school that day, prompting Traci to softly explain to her daughter that Ben had just been shot during a battle in Afghanistan.

By that point, Traci had asked to stop receiving phone calls and designated me as her official source of information. Physically and emotionally, there had simply been too many calls, voicemails, and texts to keep up with, even after the arrival of Ben's wounded friend Kevin and another Green Beret teammate, Sergeant First Class Trevor Hunter. On top of it all, Traci still had to take care of the kids.

After sharing their first of many hugs, Amber did her best to reassure Traci that her children would be in good hands while she was in Germany. Before they had a significant amount of time to get to know each other, however, my cell phone rang yet again.

"Beau, we need to get you and Traci over there right away," the lieutenant colonel said.

I immediately went to another room so the kids couldn't hear the conversation.

"Ma'am, I just have one question," I said. "Have there been any more amputations since the Army talked to Traci?"

"I can confirm there are multiple gunshot wounds to the lower extremities, and both legs have been amputated above the knees," she said. "It's time to get you both on a plane."

I was speechless. I tried to steel myself before going back into the living room, knowing that Traci would pick up on any and all emotions I expressed after the disturbing phone call.

"What happened?" she said.

"We need to go to the airport," I calmly responded.

While Traci was packing, I told her and Amber about the additional amputations. Like my wife and me, Traci was in a state of complete shock and utter disbelief. Amputations above the knee often render the use of prosthetics even more difficult and carry all kinds of additional implications about an amputee being able to live a "normal" life. To that point, relaying the dreadful news to Ben's wife was the worst thing I had ever had to tell a member of my family.

Before we left Puyallup, Traci decided to tell Ryan, who handled the unimaginable update with the maturity of a thirty-year-old. Even amid the panic and grief, Traci was so proud of her son.

After saying goodbye to Ryan, Kailen, Amber, Kevin, and Trevor, Traci and I headed to Seattle. The first part of our journey would be to the nation's capital, where we would catch a flight to Amsterdam. I also needed to update my passport during our layover before we could board the second plane.

The Fisher House Foundation, which had first helped my family two years earlier with lodging for the arrival of Jeremy's casket in Dover, Delaware, generously arranged rooms for Traci and me that evening near Washington Dulles International Airport in Northern Virginia. On the first flight, I could tell that my sister-in-law was extraordinarily sleep deprived, so as soon as we got to the hotel, I gently told her to get some rest.

"We'll be on another plane tomorrow morning," I said after giving her a hug.

Traci and I hadn't been in our respective rooms for more than a few minutes when my dreaded cell phone rang for what seemed the hundredth time. Once again, it was the lieutenant colonel. Her tone was even more serious than the last call.

"Beau, it's more severe than they thought," she said so quietly that she was almost whispering. "One of your brother's legs has been amputated at the mid-thigh and the other at the hip."

What did she just say?

After stumbling around the room for a moment, I collapsed on the bed.

"I know this is terrible news, Beau, but there is no indication that this is going to be fatal," she said. "It's just going to be a very difficult adjustment for Ben and your family."

I didn't know what to say, so I stayed silent.

"Please accept my most sincere apology in advance, but I am required to ask you this question," the lieutenant colonel continued. "Do you know if Ben is an organ donor?"

I was getting angry. Not only was every update worse than the last, but the lady who had repeatedly assured me that everything would be fine was suddenly talking like Ben was going to die. In that moment, I wasn't an enlisted U.S. marine—just a mad, extremely confused brother.

"How should I know?" I said. *Why the fuck would she even ask me that?*

"Beau, again, I'm sorry, but if could you please ask Traci . . . ," she stammered.

"No, I won't ask my brother's wife if he's a fucking organ donor!" I said while gradually losing control of my volume and tone. "I think she's going through enough right now."

I stopped mid-sentence upon realizing that not only was I way out of line but Traci was in the room next to mine. The walls weren't thick enough to shield her from the horrendous news that I was irresponsibly shouting. Seconds later, I could hear Traci sobbing uncontrollably.

"I apologize for my language, ma'am," I said. "But before we discuss anything else, I need to go next door."

"I understand, Beau," she said. "We're going to get you on a different flight to Amsterdam that's leaving tonight, so if you and Traci can please get packed, I'll have someone there to pick you up in about thirty minutes."

We hadn't had time to unpack in the first place, so that wasn't an issue. My first and only priority was going next door to face Traci before we headed back to the airport. When she answered the door, her hair was still wet from a quick shower, and her face was equally soaked with fresh tears. I could tell right away that she had heard every word I had shouted during the phone call.

"I want to know what's happening, Beau," Traci demanded. "And I want to know right now."

"I will tell you everything at the airport," I said, holding Traci's shoulders and looking directly into her tear-filled eyes. "But first, I need you to get your things, because they just changed our next flight to tonight."

"Why?" she said. "What happened?"

After falling onto the bed, Traci began the process of shutting down emotionally. While I could never put myself in the shoes of a grief-stricken military spouse, I had experienced similar feelings shortly after being notified of Jeremy's passing.

To make matters worse, we had to race through the international terminal at Dulles to make our new flight. After being handed my updated passport and being whisked through security, we ran to the gate as I kept a close eye on Traci to make sure she didn't fall. Even while running through the airport, the expression on her face was getting blanker and blanker.

Traci didn't say a word until I checked on her several hours into our flight to Amsterdam.

"Can you sleep?" I said.

"No," Traci said. "Can you?"

After I responded with a "Nope," we began to talk. Before long, Traci and I were having a once-unthinkable conversation about Ben spending the rest of his life in a wheelchair. Every time she started to lose hope, however, I tried to shift our tearful discussion to a positive place.

"If anyone can deal with losing his legs, it's Ben," I said. "You know better than anyone how tough he is. After you bring Ben home, the guys and I will come over and start building ramps," I continued. "If that doesn't work, we'll find a way to get you a new house. The Gary Sinise Foundation and a bunch of awesome charities build 'smart homes' for wounded vets. Ben can do this. And so can we."

Upon arriving in the Netherlands, I realized we only had five minutes to catch our next plane to Frankfurt, Germany. Missing this flight could truly have life-or-death consequences, so once again, I told Traci that we had to run.

During our mad dash through a busy airport in a foreign country neither of us had ever been to, I looked to my left and immediately realized Traci was no longer next to me. After a few moments of frantically looking around, I saw something that was seemingly straight out of a horror movie.

Amid all the commotion, Traci was standing frozen in the middle of the bustling terminal while staring blankly down at the floor. Once and for all, the mind of Ben's wife had almost completely shut down.

Without saying a word, I took Traci's bag and threw it on my back. I briefly considered putting her on my back, too, before deciding on taking her hands and basically dragging her the rest of the way. Traci was so zoned out that she had temporarily forgotten how to walk.

I can't imagine what the many hundreds of onlookers must have thought as I dragged Traci to the gate, which was seconds away from being shut before the agent hurriedly checked our tickets. Thankfully, the compassionate airline employee allowed us to board the Frankfurt-bound flight.

"Do you know what compartment syndrome is?"

Life would never be the same for Ben, Traci, or our family after a doctor uttered those seven words a few minutes after we arrived at Landstuhl Regional Medical Center in Germany.

In addition to Traci and the army surgeon, I was standing with Shane, the junior medic who had gone through Ben's bloody medical bag about seventy-two hours earlier. While I didn't realize it at the time, that was also the approximate amount of time since he had gotten any sleep. From Afghanistan all the way to Germany, Shane had been quietly keeping vigil next to his Green Beret teammate. By being there for Ben from his last encounter with the enemy all the way through the fight for his life, Shane helped teach me the true meaning of battlefield brotherhood.

Even after a detailed medical conversation with Shane and then the dedicated doctors and nurses who were desperately trying to save my brother's life, it never truly felt like we were going to lose Ben. That all changed the moment Traci, Shane, and I walked into the hospital room.

The moment I first laid eyes on my brother is permanently seared in my memory. *This has to be the wrong room,* I thought.

The man in the hospital bed had no legs and was bloated beyond imagination. As we later came to understand, the doctors had no choice but to keep pumping blood, fluids, and epinephrine into Ben's body in the hopes that circulation would soon improve after the removal of his legs. The severe case of compartment syndrome Ben had developed was—please forgive me for this crude explanation—sucking the life out of him.

Traci was initially afraid to approach the man in the bed, who looked absolutely nothing like the Ben she so deeply adored. She was trying hard to make a connection yet couldn't shake the notion that this person wasn't her husband. It was the strangest, most surreal feeling Traci had ever experienced.

While taking her first steps toward the bed, Traci didn't know if she was going throw up, faint, cry, or scream. She summoned up all her considerable courage to move closer and eventually take the hand of the man the doctors said was her husband.

As if she were frozen in time, Traci placed the hand she had given to Ben on their wedding day on top of his. The moment their fingers touched, the sacred bond they shared instantly returned.

Despite the best efforts of some of the world's finest physicians and nurses, none of the countless surgical procedures or medications seemed to be working. Ben's kidneys were failing as he rapidly reached the point of systemic shock.

The smells inside that hospital room were overpowering, as were the sounds of my brother's slowing heart. If there is a hell, this was surely it. Even in Afghanistan, I had never felt so terrified and powerless.

Being in that room was an out-of-body experience for all of us.

It's hard to explain, but it felt like we were watching all of this on television instead of actually being present.

Most of all, I was continually looking for my brother somewhere in that hospital bed. After a few painful minutes, I gave up upon realizing that I simply couldn't find him.

Seeing the person we were told was Ben was the worst moment of my life, yet my pain couldn't even be compared to Traci's. Shane and I took turns holding her up as she shook her head and continually cried.

After regaining her composure, Traci began to recognize her husband by his light brown hair.

"It really is you," she whispered. "I'm here, honey."

Traci eventually began stroking Ben's hair like she had during so many tender moments—from their courtship at Fort Lewis all the way to that baseball game during his last trip home.

"I love you with all my heart, body, and soul," she whispered in her husband's ear.

Traci was coming to terms with the reality that Luke's father would most likely live the rest of his life as a double amputee.

"This man who loved his guitar, who loved tearing apart his amps, throwing his son, touching his wife, would now depend on me for every movement he makes," Traci later told *The Washington Post*.

The reality of Ben and Traci's future was even worse than she'd thought. Before we were sent back to the nearby Fisher House to rest, I told Shane that I had noticed the doses of epinephrine being delivered more and more frequently.

"What does that mean?" I asked my brother's fellow Green Beret.

After taking me aside so Traci couldn't hear us, Shane told me the truth.

Heather, Ben, and Jeremy Wise celebrate a "Harvest Festival" (aka Halloween) in El Dorado, Arkansas.

Clockwise from left: Heather, Ben, Beau, and Jeremy pose for a family photo.

Mary, Jeremy, and Jean Wise at West Point.

Jeremy, Jean, Ben, Beau, Mary, and Heather at their house in Hope, Arkansas, while Ben was on leave from Iraq in 2003.

Jeremy, then a U.S. Navy SEAL, and Heather in Prescott, Arkansas.

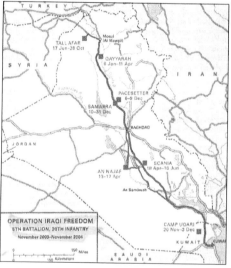

Map of key U.S. Army Fifth Battalion, Twentieth Infantry operations in Iraq in 2003–04.

(U.S. Army Center of Military History)

Ben holds up a copy of *USA Today* while training for his upcoming Iraq deployment on April 10, 2003, at the Yakima Training Center in Washington State.

(Chris "Ven" Galka)

Jeremy, Dana, and Ben in Virginia Beach.

Ben, Ethan, and Jeremy in Virginia Beach.

Jeremy while on a U.S. Navy SEAL Team 4 deployment to Iraq.

Jeremy, Ben, and Beau at Ben's Special Forces graduation at Fort Bragg, North Carolina, in 2008.

Ben and Beau pose for the infamous Yarborough knife photo after his graduation ceremony.

Ben and Jeremy pose together before Ben and Traci's wedding on March 29, 2009, in Washington State.

(Heather Mann Photography)

Jeremy delivers the toast at Ben and Traci's wedding.

(Heather Mann Photography)

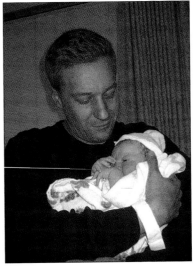

Traci and Ben look into each other's eyes on their wedding day.

(Heather Mann Photography)

Ben holds Luke shortly after his birth on December 15, 2009, in Washington State.

A map of Afghanistan.

(United Nations)

Jeremy while working as a Xe contractor in Afghanistan in 2009.

A map of the CIA compound inside Forward Operating Base Chapman in Khost, Afghanistan.

(Tim Brown/GlobalSecurity.org and GeoEye)

Ben and Beau pay their respects to Jeremy on January 7, 2010, at Naval Amphibious Base Little Creek Chapel in Virginia Beach.

(U.S. Naval Special Warfare Group 2)

Ethan holds the folded American flag at Jeremy's funeral in the spring of 2010 at Albert G. Horton Jr. Memorial Veterans Cemetery in Suffolk, Virginia.

(Katrina Clay)

CIA Director Leon Panetta, left, participates in a ceremony adding twelve new stars, including one representing Jeremy, to the CIA Memorial Wall on June 7, 2010, at CIA headquarters in Langley, Virginia.

(Central Intelligence Agency)

Ben and his fellow U.S. Army Green Berets eat a meal prepared by Afghan commandos.

Ben while deployed to Afghanistan with U.S. Army ODA 1316.

(Kevin Flike)

Ben demonstrates how to provide medical care under fire in Afghanistan in 2010.

(U.S. Navy/Petty Officer 1st Class Mark O'Donald)

Beau giving a route briefing to fellow Marines while training for their Afghanistan deployment at Twentynine Palms, California, in March 2011.

(Isaiah Castro)

Amber and Beau at Pyramid Rock on Marine Corps Base Hawaii in Kaneohe Bay, Hawaii, on April 6, 2011.

Beau mans the turret while on patrol through the Garmsir District of Afghanistan's Helmand Province in the summer of 2011.

(Isaiah Castro)

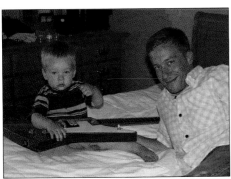

Luke, Ben, and one of Ben's many guitars in between his Afghanistan deployments in Washington State.

Kevin Flike, an Afghan commando, and Ben while deployed to Afghanistan.
(Kevin Flike)

Ben and Luke at a Seattle Mariners–Boston Red Sox Major League Baseball game on August 12, 2011, in Seattle, Washington.

FEB 6

Dr. and Mrs. Jean F. Wise

███████████████

Dear Dr. and Mrs. Wise,

I realize words provide little comfort or solace, but I want to offer you and your family my deepest sympathy and personal condolences during this most difficult time. Our men and women in uniform voluntarily make extraordinary sacrifices in their service to our Nation, and your son made the ultimate sacrifice. I know his loss leaves an enormous void in your lives.

At this critical time in our history, Sergeant First Class Benjamin Wise answered the call to duty and served a cause bigger than himself in Afghanistan. A grateful Nation will never forget his willingness to uphold the values that make America unique in human history.

With my deepest sympathy,

Sincerely,

[handwritten signature]

[handwritten note:] I am so very late in the emotion of losing mother son of yours to combat. As the father of 3 sons, I cannot imagine the pain you must be facing. And yet, I know that like Ben, he did not he wanted — to fight of all of this. He is a true American hero and patriot. God bless him and you.

Letter to Jean and Mary Wise from Defense Secretary Leon Panetta.

February 6, 2012

Mrs. Traci D. Wise

Puyallup, Washington 98374

Dear Traci:

I am deeply saddened by the loss of your husband, Sergeant First Class Benjamin B. Wise, USA. No words can ever ease your sorrow, but please take comfort in knowing that he has honored us all beyond measure.

We will forever remember with humble gratitude his selfless sacrifice in defense of our great Nation, and we will never be able to repay our debt to you. All of us mourn your loss. All of us pay tribute to his faithful devotion to duty.

Michelle joins me in extending our heartfelt sympathy. We pray that the cherished memories of your husband console you as you grieve, and that his brave service to this country brings you pride in this time of sadness. May God bless you and your family.

Sincerely,

Letter to Traci Wise from President Barack Obama.

GEORGE W. BUSH

February 2, 2012

Mrs. Traci D. Wise
Puyallup, Washington

Dear Traci:

I am deeply saddened by the loss of your husband, Sergeant First
Class Benjamin B. Wise, USA.

Ben's noble service in Operation Enduring Freedom has helped to
preserve the security of our homeland and defend the liberties
America holds dear. Our Nation will not forget Ben's selfless
sacrifice and dedication in our efforts to make the world more
peaceful and more free. We will forever honor his memory.

Laura and I send our heartfelt sympathy to you, Luke, Ryan, and
Kailen. We hope you will be comforted by your faith and the love
and support of your family and friends. May God bless you.

Sincerely,

George W. Bush

Letter to Traci from former President George W. Bush.

Luke looks at a portrait of his dad after Ben's passing.

Luke at the A Company, Third Battalion, First Special Forces Group building, dedicated to his father, at Joint Base Lewis-McChord in Washington State on December 7, 2015.

Luke at a bench dedication ceremony for Ben and Jeremy in November 2013 in El Dorado, Arkansas.

Beau visiting his brothers on June 23, 2019.

(Tom Sileo)

Beau's family on the day their daughter's adoption was finalized in Bowie County, Texas, on November 18, 2019.

Beau Wise views his oldest brother Jeremy's star on the CIA Memorial Wall for the first time on May 27, 2021, inside the George Bush Center for Intelligence in Langley, Virginia. *(Central Intelligence Agency)*

Jeremy and Ben are laid to rest side by side at the Albert G. Horton Jr. Memorial Veterans Cemetery in Suffolk, Virginia.

(Tom Sileo)

"It's not good, Beau," he said. "The most important thing you can do right now is let the doctors do their thing and pray."

I could tell by Shane's mannerisms that Ben had entered the sunset of his life, even though I was nowhere near the point of acceptance. When Jeremy died, the news had hit me like a tidal wave. After Ben was wounded, the steady stream of bad news made it feel like I was drowning.

"How is my son, Beau?" my mom said over the phone moments before she and my dad boarded a direct flight from D.C. to Frankfurt.

I tried to be vague before asking to speak to my dad. I wasn't about to let my mother—who had already lost one son to war—spend the next nine hours helplessly pondering the very real possibility of losing a second.

"Please be subtle when you react," I said after she handed the phone to my father. "Dad, Ben has compartment syndrome. Both of his legs have already been fully amputated."

My dad was silent for about five seconds before trying to take the news in stride for his wife's benefit. As a physician himself, however, he instantly knew how serious the situation had become.

"Thanks for the update, Beau. We'll see you in a few hours," Dr. Jean Wise said while trying not to visibly tremble. "I love you."

"Love you too, Dad," I said before hanging up and bursting into tears.

Traci and I had been crying in our respective Fisher House rooms in Germany when I got a gentle knock on the door of my room. It was Shane.

"It's time," he said.

Not again.

Traci hadn't truly slept in about seventy hours, but one last time, I picked her up off the bed and held her tightly as we made the short walk back to the hospital. She was shaking not only from the frigid January air but from the realization that she was probably about to share the final precious moments on earth with her soul mate.

Ben's bloated appearance had somehow worsened since our last visit. The smells were even more intense and the sounds of the medical machines seemed louder until Traci and I eventually saw, smelled, and heard nothing. We both became singularly focused on Ben after the doctors told us this was indeed the end.

As Traci knelt down to once again whisper in Ben's ear while being held by Shane, I temporarily snapped out of my fog to make a last-ditch, desperate plea to the surgeon.

"Please, Doctor, my mom and dad are on a plane," I said. "They are only two hours away from landing in Frankfurt."

"I understand, Corporal," he said. "I can't possibly imagine what you're feeling right now."

"Is there anything at all you can do to keep my brother alive until they get here?" I said. "They already lost one son to this war."

What could the surgeon say? What was happening in this room was almost unprecedented since 9/11. To his credit, however, the doctor explained the likely consequences of another surgical procedure.

"It might give your brother another hour or two," he said. "But anything I do would also cause a significant amount of additional damage and a lot more pain."

That's when Traci intervened.

"That's not Ben," she said, pointing to the hospital bed. "Ben is gone."

Traci was not only right but made a decision no wife should ever have to make with a momentary sense of clarity and everlasting purpose.

In a few excruciating minutes, Traci would be a widow, and my mom and dad would only have one son left.

"We've reached the final phase," the surgeon said to Traci, Shane, and me. "Now is the time to say whatever you would like to say."

After Ben received his last rites, I knelt down next to my second brother. The epinephrine injections were now being administered every sixty seconds, which meant that he was—for all intents and purposes—on 100 percent life support.

"You were always there for me, bro," I said to Ben. "Had you made it out of this room, I want you to know that I would have always been there for you. You and Jerms were the best brothers I ever could have asked for. I hope that someday I can be half the husband, father, son, and brother that you guys were. Goodbye, Benny. I love you. I'll see you again."

Traci moved in next. As her life's worst nightmare unfolded before her tearful eyes, a singular thought began overwhelming her racing, sleep-deprived mind: *I can't ask him to stay.*

"It's okay," she whispered repeatedly into her dying husband's ear. "It's okay. There's nothing on earth here that I can give you that's as great as what's waiting for you," she said before giving Ben one last kiss. "I love you."

Traci, Shane, and I then stepped away from the bed as the surgeon pushed a button to stop the epinephrine injections. Three and a half minutes later, Ben's chest stopped moving.

While it wasn't the first thing that entered my mind as my brother passed, I was subsequently comforted in knowing that Benny and Jerms were back together in a better place.

Traci fell down a few seconds after her husband died. Her knees landed very hard on the hospital room's polished floor, causing Shane and me to immediately help her up and make sure she was okay.

About thirty seconds later, the thought of little Luke suddenly flashed through my mind. Like Ethan, he would be forced to grow up without his father. *Not again.*

This time, it was me who hit the floor. After Shane picked me up, Ben's grieving wife leaped into my arms to console her fallen husband's little brother.

"It's okay," Traci whispered, just as she had to Ben moments earlier. "It's okay."

Upon regaining what was left of my strength, I limped out into the hospital hallway to call Heather, who was waiting for the next update back in Arkansas after just getting off the phone with Jeremy's widow.

"Hey, I just talked to Dana," Heather answered. "We might have found the perfect wheelchair for Ben—"

"Heather, Heather, I need you to stop," I interrupted. "Please listen to what I'm about to say."

My sister immediately paused.

"Ben's gone," I said.

After about a minute of silence that was only pierced by the intermittent sounds of my sister weeping, Heather became enraged. How could God rip someone so precious away from the world, especially after already taking Jeremy? *Not again.*

"Mom and Dad are getting ready to land in Frankfurt," I said. "What on earth am I supposed to say to them?"

"I don't know, Beau," Heather said through tears. "I just don't know."

About an hour after Ben's passing, all I could hear was the roaring engine of a large white Mercedes van being driven by my brother's teammate. Just a few days earlier, Shane was treating wounded American soldiers and Afghan commandos in a valley beneath two cliffs. Now he was tearing down Germany's world-famous auto-bahn.

While Shane's duty was technically to Traci, both she and the deployed Green Beret appreciated the enormity of this *Fast and Furious*–like drive to the airport. In a few minutes, I would be offi-cially informing my parents that they had lost a second son to com-bat. Mary and Jean Wise had just become the only mom and dad since 9/11 to lose two children as a result of the War in Afghan-istan.

What do I say? All I knew for sure was that I didn't want to give them the terrible news on a freezing tarmac in Germany or inside the busy airport.

As if we were deployed together in combat, I "ordered" Shane to get my parents in the van as quickly as possible. For the next few minutes, Shane and I would treat my mom and dad like high-value targets being whisked away for questioning.

We were obviously a lot gentler but somehow managed to get my parents door-to-door within three minutes of them stepping off the plane. Even for a Special Forces soldier and a U.S. marine, it was impressive work in this day and age of post-9/11 airport security.

As soon as the van's door slid shut and the cold outside air began mixing with the heat cranked up in the vehicle's interior, my mom spoke up.

"Beau, how is my son?" she said.

My stomach sank, much like Traci's when she'd gotten the

first phone call more than five days earlier. While my duty as a son and an active-duty American service member was clear, nobody could ever prepare for such a tragic moment.

"Listen, Mom and Dad," I began. "I am so sorry, but Ben died of his wounds an hour ago."

My mom was motionless. My dad, who was then suffering from the early symptoms of Parkinson's disease, was shaking but expressionless. Given what I told him a few hours earlier about compartment syndrome, however, he seemed to know the news was coming. My father had nevertheless been holding out hope of getting one last chance to see his son before Ben slipped away.

"He tried so hard to hang on," I continued. "We wanted to keep him alive for you, but I am terribly sorry. It's over."

My dad began tearing up as my mom tried to mask her anger. She had raised her fist at God only a few days earlier and insisted that he would not destroy the Wise family. While he didn't, this sure came close.

Never during her life's worst nightmares did Mary Wise envision being told that her second little boy was gone inside some rental van that would soon be speeding back down the autobahn. *Not again.*

When we arrived at Landstuhl, the surgeons explained to my parents what had happened. Growing frustrated with the layman's terms he was hearing, my dad interrupted.

"I'm a doctor," he said. "Please talk to me like a doctor."

A few minutes later, my dad fully understood why his son had died. He was coming to grips with what had happened when his wife once again spoke up.

"Can I see my son?" she said.

I immediately put my arms around my mother and asked her to listen carefully to what I was about to say.

"Mom, I need you to trust me on this," I said. "I don't think it's wise for you to go in there. Let Dad go. He can explain the details to you later if you want, but I don't want what's inside that room to be the lasting image of your son."

Without saying anything in response, my mom nodded and walked out of the hospital with my brother's teammate Trevor, who had formally escorted my parents to Germany. A few minutes later, my mom was hugging and consoling her daughter-in-law, which would give Shane a chance to finally get some sleep after the most emotionally trying set of duties a deployed soldier could be asked to perform.

First, Shane and I brought my dad to spend a few difficult but tender minutes with Ben.

"Let's go see my son," he said just before walking inside the room.

My father was weak from not only Parkinson's but the long journey overseas coupled with the passing of his second son. My normally stoic dad was crying when he walked into the hospital room, but undeterred by Ben's still extremely bloated face and torso.

"Oh, buddy," he said. "Oh, Ben—you're still my handsome boy."

After a few minutes full of the rawest mixture of emotion and shock, my dad picked up his cane and wobbled over to the Fisher House to be with his wife and daughter-in-law. Before Shane led my dad away, I had one final request.

"I want us to be Ben's guardian angels," I said to Shane. "I want you and me to take my brother home."

The military eventually approved my request. I didn't have my proper Marine Corps uniform with me, which was required while escorting a casualty to Dover Air Force Base. Shane and Trevor quickly solved that problem by convincing Landstuhl's tailor to sew me a new uniform. I don't think my family could have made it through those harrowing six days in Europe without the help of my fallen brother's teammates, who repeatedly went above and beyond.

What Shane and I couldn't have known in the first few days after Ben's passing was that our jobs as guardian angels would soon be much bigger than escorting a fallen soldier who happened to be my brother.

U.S. Army Sergeant First Class Benjamin Brian Wise succumbed to the wounds he suffered on January 9 in Afghanistan's Balkh Province at Landstuhl Regional Medical Center in Germany on January 15, 2012. Four days later, six of my fellow Hawaii-based U.S. Marines were killed in a CH-53 helicopter crash in Helmand Province, where I had just finished my second combat deployment.

Ben wouldn't want the end of this chapter to be about him. He would want us to honor the six brave marines whose flag-draped caskets would soon fly next to his on a giant 747 jet bound for the country each service member had died to defend.

Captain Daniel Bartle, 27, Ferndale, Washington
Captain Nathan McHone, 29, Crystal Lake, Illinois
Master Sergeant Travis Riddick, 40, Centerville, Iowa
Corporal Jesse Stites, 23, North Beach, Maryland
Corporal Kevin Reinhard, 25, Colonia, New Jersey
Corporal Joseph Logan, 22, Willis, Texas

I didn't just have the honor of helping escort one fallen brother from Germany to Dover, Delaware. I had the distinct privilege of flying home with seven.

13

SOLE SURVIVOR

Which one is Ben?

After finally leaving Germany for another day and a half of travel to Dover Air Force Base, I was the guardian angel not only for Ben but those six fallen marines. The only problem was that I wasn't sure which unmarked flag-draped coffin was carrying my brother. Not knowing exactly where he was made me frustrated and anxious.

When you're a guardian angel, you must always stay close to the caskets you're responsible for watching over. That meant Shane and I stayed on the plane when the 747 stopped to refuel while picking up a group of returning U.S. service members in Romania. Every waking hour would be spent staring at the Stars and Stripes covering the remains of all seven fallen American heroes.

At some point after leaving Romania, a few guys—I'm not sure who they were—came downstairs to "smoke and joke," as we called it in the Marine Corps. While they probably didn't initially realize that the jet was carrying precious cargo, I almost lost it when one of them nonchalantly walked by us without seeming to pay any mind to the seven fallen heroes he had just passed.

Without hesitation, I stood up and started raising my voice while pointing toward the small group of returning U.S. troops.

"Look here, you motherfuckers," I began.

Much like the teammate in Afghanistan who'd ordered me to stand down shortly after Jeremy's death, Shane immediately intervened.

"Go," he said, pointing to the stairs. "Go up top."

After one last glare at the troops who had drawn my ire, I followed Shane's order. He presumably gave the service members a stern talking-to, while adding that one of those coffins belonged to my second brother to be killed in Afghanistan. I can't imagine how bad those guys must have felt as Shane made his way upstairs to check on me.

Shane managed to calm me down shortly after taking his seat. He could tell I was frustrated, angry, and still hungover after what wound up being a weeklong bender in Germany. I thought I could drink away at least some of the pain, which of course didn't work, although boozing to the point of passing out was just about the only way I could get some shut-eye.

"I'm the last one," I said to Shane, who had already gone above the call of duty to console Ben's wife, my parents, and me since leaving Afghanistan. "How will I be the oldest son? How will I be Heather's only brother and Traci's and Dana's only brother-in-law?"

Between this rant and my outburst downstairs, Shane could tell I had reached a breaking point.

"Seriously, Beau," he said. "You need to get some sleep."

Once again, I followed Shane's order. Over the next few hours, I somehow managed to get my first non-alcohol-induced sleep in about two weeks.

When I woke up, we were about an hour from landing on the East Coast, where I knew my parents were waiting at the same Fisher House in Dover, Delaware, where we had all stayed after Jeremy was killed. While my mom and dad were treated like royalty by the Fisher House staff, and by employees of the USO and other compassionate charities, being back at Dover two years later felt like a recurring nightmare. No parents—military or otherwise—should have to go through the living hell that my mother and father experienced.

Upon collecting my thoughts, I went back downstairs to check on Ben and the six marines. When I realized nobody else was around, I lowered my head to say a prayer for the families of the fallen, including my own. The pain everyone was about to experience when we landed in Delaware was a feeling I knew all too well.

Shane was awake when I went back upstairs. After clearing the cobwebs, he began to explain the delicate, detailed procedures for dignified transfer ceremonies, on which he had been briefed while I was busy drinking myself into oblivion in Europe. I had already witnessed one such ceremony, but as a member of the military tasked with ensuring that protocol was followed, things were much different.

There was some daylight when we landed at Dover Air Force Base, even though I initially had no clue whether it was dawn or dusk. A few minutes after getting off the plane, Shane and I were taken to an office where an army chaplain was waiting to greet us. After shaking our hands and offering his condolences, the chaplain looked in my direction to relay some orders that originated from well above our pay grades.

"Corporal, you have done your duty as a guardian angel," he said. "Now your only job is to worry about your family."

While I appreciated the military's gesture, I had hoped to participate in the actual dignified transfer ceremony even though I was a bit nervous about whether I could keep my still-raw emotions in check. Still, orders were orders, and I knew my parents would be comforted and relieved to have their only living son standing beside them as Ben's flag-draped casket was carried down the jet's ramp into the frigid nighttime air.

My brother's wife had been escorted back to Washington State by Trevor. Toward the end of their flight, Traci put her hand on the arm of Ben's teammate and asked him a poignant, very difficult question.

"Why do you guys do it?" she said. "Why do you volunteer to do this job when this is sometimes the end result?"

Trevor was initially lost for words before stammering out an answer.

"I know it sounds like a cliché, especially right now," the Green Beret said. "But everything about wanting to serve for God and country and for the guys on your right and left really is true."

Traci thanked Trevor and nodded to signal that even amid her relentless grief, she understood the ethos of an American warrior.

Just as Jeremy was my primary counselor during the "good times," Ben often took on the same role in the "bad times," especially in our big brother's absence. Learning of this conversation after the fact, I recalled the advice that Ben had given me when I'd asked what it was like to deploy as a married man. As many veterans can attest, there is an enormous difference between going overseas as a bachelor and deploying as a husband, wife, father, or mother. I wish I could have been there to help Trevor comfort Traci in Ben's own words.

"You fear what may happen to you when you're gone. You fear

what may happen to your brother when you're home," Ben once told me. "It's not in the nature of a warrior to sit still. I'll do everything in my power to come home to my family. God forbid I have to make that choice, but if I must, I pray that I'll always find the strength to put my brother before myself."

Shortly after arriving in Puyallup, Traci decided that instead of turning around and flying all the way back to the East Coast, she would stay home with the kids for the time being after a physically and emotionally grueling overseas journey. Throughout the sad events in Dover, however, Traci, Luke, Ryan, and Kailen were never out of our minds. Ben was a soldier, son, and brother, but first and foremost, he was a husband and father. That's how all of us knew he wanted to be remembered.

I was having a cup of coffee that evening when a U.S. Army colonel suddenly entered the building I was sitting inside. After standing at attention and being told, "At ease, gents," the colonel asked Shane and me to sit down.

"I just want you to know that the commandant [of the Marine Corps] is en route," he said. "He would like to pay his respects to your brother and also meet you guys."

While most ordinary Americans probably didn't know his name at the time, the commandant was and is a godlike figure inside the Marine Corps. I had never met General James F. Amos—or any commandant, for that matter—so you can probably imagine my shock and trepidation upon being told that I was about to get the opportunity to salute him.

"Is he coming here for us, sir?" I asked the colonel.

"I think he was initially coming for the families of the six marines," the colonel said. "But then he heard about what's happened to you and your parents. When you meet him, remember that you're now here as a family member, not a service member," he continued. "Stay seated when the commandant approaches you."

Yeah, right, I thought. Regardless of the situation, failing to stand in the presence of the commandant was abhorrent to all my training and seasoning as a United States Marine. When I saw General Amos, there was no chance I would do anything but stand and salute.

A few days earlier at the Pentagon, the last name Wise once again crossed the desk of Leon Panetta, who had transitioned from CIA director to secretary of defense shortly after the retirement of longtime defense secretary Robert Gates. Panetta, who had been unanimously confirmed despite the deepening partisan divide in Washington, vividly recounted the moment he learned of my brother's passing in *Worthy Fights.*

> One day in early 2012, I was sitting at my desk and con-
> templating the file before me. It told the story of Benja-
> min Wise, a sergeant first class who had been on patrol in
> Balkh Province, Afghanistan, when his unit came under
> enemy fire. He was hit and rushed to Germany for med-
> ical treatment, only to die of his wounds. Ben left behind
> a wife, two sons, and a daughter. He was the son of Jean
> and Mary Wise, who raised him, along with two brothers
> and a sister, in a small town outside Little Rock, Arkansas.
> They were a religious family, and a patriotic one.
>   As I read the material before me, I was suddenly
> struck by a sense that I knew this family. I called in Jeremy
> [Bash, the Department of Defense's chief of staff]. We
> leafed through the file and confirmed my worst fear: Ben

Wise was the younger brother of Jeremy Wise, one of the security officers we had lost in the Khost bombing two years earlier, on one of the most awful days in the history of the CIA.

Not only had the thirty-fifth commandant of the Marine Corps almost certainly received the news directly from Secretary Panetta, but at some point, General Amos subsequently realized that a third Wise brother was serving under his command.

Back at Dover, I was fidgety and extremely unsettled. In the moments following the news of the commandant's impending arrival, I admit to not thinking very much about my parents or the gravity of the overall situation. I was an active-duty marine who suddenly realized that he hadn't shaved in several days and looked like a pile of dog shit moments before facing my boss.

"I need my kit bag," I said to Shane, who said he didn't know where it was. "I need a razor—please help me find a razor."

While I had appreciated the efforts of the tailor in Germany, my uniform had been hastily sewed and was—as a result—full of mistakes. None was more glaring than my uniform saying *U.S. Marine* instead of *U.S. Marines*, which the commandant would almost certainly notice.

If you have never served in the military, my panic about these seemingly meaningless details—especially given the extenuating circumstances—might seem a bit ridiculous. Yet inside the armed forces and particularly the Marine Corps, the small stuff means everything.

As always, Shane managed to calm me down.

"Don't sweat it, Beau," he said, patting me on the back. "This is the one time in your military career that you don't have to worry about any of this crap. The commandant won't care."

A few hours later, during which I managed to finally find a disposable razor and get a quick shave, my suddenly smooth face was being hit by blasts of cold wind on the freezing Dover Air Force Base tarmac. I had stood in almost this exact spot two years earlier. Perhaps for that reason, the words of one of the fallen CIA officers' wives began echoing through my mind.

"Kill them all," she had said. "Go over there and kill all those motherfuckers."

I felt an enormous sense of failure for not doing more damage to the enemy during my two subsequent combat deployments. Not only had I failed the grieving spouse of Jeremy's fallen teammate, now the terrorists had killed my second brother, too.

As we waited for the commandant's arrival, all I could think about was how eager I was to return to Afghanistan and rejoin the fight. In my cloudy, grief-stricken mind, I recklessly made plans to shoot anything that moved over there and not care about the consequences.

Just then, a black limousine emerged from the darkness and rolled onto the mostly dark tarmac. I saw not only General Amos and his wife, Bonnie, but the stars and bars of many high-ranking Marine Corps leaders.

One of the dignitaries was then colonel James Bierman, who had commanded my battalion before becoming military secretary to the commandant of the Marine Corps. Colonel Bierman, who eventually rose to major general, was and is one of our nation's most respected marines. He was also just about the only familiar face on that tarmac other than my parents.

Without thinking, I reached out and gave the colonel a huge hug. It wasn't proper protocol, but Colonel Bierman nevertheless hugged me back before sharing his condolences.

The sergeant major of the Marine Corps—another godlike figure in my world—appeared before my family next.

"Stay strong," he said as I saluted and stood at attention.

Finally, the commandant and Mrs. Amos reached us as I started sweating bullets despite the frigid conditions. I was lucky I found that razor, because the first thing my boss did was put his white-gloved hand on my face.

"What a handsome boy," he said. "Thank you for your service, Corporal."

The next set of memories will stay with me until the day I die.

After General and Mrs. Amos hugged my mother and shook my father's hand, the commandant—wearing his majestic, heavily decorated dress uniform—got down on one knee. He then looked up at my mom, who was numb not only from the cold but from being back on that dreaded blacktop so soon after her oldest son's remains had returned to American soil.

"I am very, very sorry," General Amos said to my mom.

Seemingly in slow motion, the commandant then pointed in my direction.

"Mrs. Wise, you have my word: Beau's not going *anywhere* for a long, long time," my boss said.

Just like that, everything I had trained and worked so hard for during the previous five years vanished into the darkness. A million thoughts ran through my mind in those next few moments as I violated protocol by snapping my head in the direction of the commandant. *Did I really just hear him say that?*

Seconds later, my eyes met Shane's, who was standing off to the side. "It's okay," he mouthed through the cold air. Then, just after all of us sat down, I felt my dad's cold hand on my shaking knee. He didn't speak, but in my head, I could hear him saying something to the effect of "I understand that you're upset, Beau, but the commandant is right."

As my angry eyes shifted to the other Marine Corps leaders

in attendance, I noticed that many were in tears. They had been deeply moved by not only what they had witnessed on that frigid runway but by the nearly unprecedented post-9/11 tragedy that had befallen my parents and our entire family.

Still, it was impossible not to think about what had just happened to my ill-fated future as an aspiring Marine Corps gunner. For whatever reason, the sinking feeling became official when I saw the commandant basically pick up my dad from his chair while Mrs. Amos took my mom by the hand and led her toward the plane from which Ben's flag-draped casket would soon emerge. My boss had just made a solemn promise to my mourning mother, and there was no way he would ever go back on it.

Oh my God, I thought. *It's really over.*

My thoughts abruptly shifted as we reached the 747 and realized that the families of all six fallen marines had just witnessed the dignified transfers of their loved ones. Like two years earlier, my parents and I saw and heard the cries of devastated dads, moms, spouses, siblings, and—worst of all—children.

When my eyes met theirs, even though they had no idea I had just flown from Germany with their departed heroes, my heart was filled with nothing but sadness and sympathy.

In that moment, I also thought back to being aggravated by initially not knowing which coffin Ben was inside. As soon as I saw the faces of those grieving Gold Star family members, however, all my frustration vanished.

It doesn't matter which one is Ben, I thought. *It never did.*

After the Bartle, McHone, Riddick, Stites, Reinhard, and Logan families boarded a bus to take them back inside and out of the cheerless cold, it was time for Ben to return to the soil of the country he had fought for since that altercation with Jeremy after he'd first enlisted. Their fight back in Arkansas, which I had witnessed, felt like a lifetime ago. In reality, it was two.

General Amos stood and saluted about ten paces behind my parents and me as Ben's American flag–covered coffin was slowly marched off the plane by six uniformed U.S. Air Force airmen. Their collective breath was visible through the frosty nighttime air, which only added to the surreal nature of the tragedy we were watching unfold before our eyes. *Not again.*

When the dignified transfer ceremony concluded, General and Mrs. Amos graciously gave us a ride back to the Fisher House inside the commandant's limousine. It took all my willpower as a highly trained U.S. marine to prevent myself from pleading with my boss to reconsider his apparent decision to render me ineligible for combat duty. Perhaps it hadn't even been his call in the first place, I thought.

Back in the nation's capital, the only man my boss answered to other than the president of the United States—Secretary Panetta— sat down at his desk shortly after his worst fears about my family had been realized.

This was the second letter I was writing to this same mother and father. In two years and fifteen days, Jean and Mary Wise had given their country two of their four children.

I sat alone for a few minutes imagining the depth and pain of that sacrifice. I remembered my anxiety when my son went off to war, and thought of the many Americans who care so deeply for their country that they risk everything—their families, their happiness—for its security. I thought of my own father, shoving off from Italy in search of a country that would give him an opportunity he never thought possible anywhere but here. I thought of my own attempt to return that gift by embarking on a career of public service. And I realized with a sharp pain in my heart that Jeremy and Ben had both been in harm's way because of orders I had given, issued in the interests of protecting their country, our country. The letter before me expressed the appreciation of a grateful nation, but even that seemed small compared with the magnitude of this family's contribution.

The secretary of defense's letter was both authentic and comforting.

Dear Dr. and Mrs. Wise,

I realize words provide little comfort or solace, but I want to offer you and your family my deepest sympathy and personal condolences during this most difficult time. Our men and women in uniform voluntarily make extraordinary sacrifices in their service to our Nation, and your son made the ultimate sacrifice. I know his loss leaves an enormous void in your lives.

At this critical time in our history, Sergeant First Class Benjamin Wise answered the call to duty and served a cause bigger than himself in Afghanistan. A grateful Nation will never forget his willingness to uphold the values that make America unique in human history.

With my deepest sympathy,
Sincerely,
Leon E. Panetta

Secretary Panetta's heartfelt note to my mom and dad didn't end there. He described the painstaking process of finishing his letter in *Worthy Fights*.

After a few moments, I added a handwritten note:

"I am so very lost in my emotion of losing another son of yours to combat. As the father of three sons, I cannot imagine the pain you must be feeling. And yet, I know that like Jeremy, Ben was doing what he wanted—to fight for all of us. He is a true American hero and patriot. God bless him and you."

Ben and Jeremy Wise left behind parents and wives and children, and they will be forever missed. There is solace, I hope, in the categorical fact that their fights were worthy, and that service to this nation is service well rendered.

I finished my note, put down my pen, and called home.

While Secretary Panetta was writing his letter to my parents, several of our country's foremost leaders in the post-9/11 war on terrorism were doing the same.

Dear Mr. and Mrs. Wise,

I recently learned about Ben's loss as a result of combat operations in Afghanistan. Please accept my sympathies, as well as the sympathies of the entire Central Intelligence Agency. I understand Ben was an outstanding medic and Soldier and an exemplary leader, performing the hardest work that this Nation asks of any of its citizens.

Rest assured, the CIA continues to hold dearly to the memory of Jeremy's service and his sacrifice, on behalf of the Agency and our country. I know this letter offers little comfort to you at this time. Nothing I can say will help ease the pain you or your family are experiencing due to the ultimate sacrifices made by your two sons in our Nation's defense. I want to ensure you understand that you, Ben, Jeremy and your family will always remain in our prayers.

I know you will always remain proud of the sacrifice Ben made in support of our country. He did what few today would do—he answered his Nation's call, and we will always honor his memory.

With my deepest sympathy,
David H. Petraeus

David Petraeus was not only the director of the CIA but a retired U.S. Army general who had helped turn the tide against the insurgency in Iraq before eventually taking command of all American and NATO forces in Afghanistan. I had a specific memory of Ben telling me how much he respected the military leadership of General Petraeus before one of our Afghanistan deployments, which made his letter even more meaningful.

"We mourn Ben's loss with you and your family," General Petraeus wrote by hand beside his signature. He also sent a similar letter to Traci.

In addition to Secretary of the Army John M. McHugh and Army Chief of Staff Ray Odierno, a retired general who once commanded all U.S. forces in Iraq, Traci received a letter from the two most recent presidents of the United States.

Dear Traci:

I am deeply saddened by the loss of your husband, Sergeant First Class Benjamin B. Wise, USA.

Ben's noble service in Operation Enduring Freedom has

*helped to preserve the security of our homeland and defend the
liberties America holds dear. Our Nation will not forget Ben's
selfless sacrifice and dedication in our efforts to make the world
more peaceful and more free. We will forever honor his memory.
Laura and I send our heartfelt sympathy to you, Luke,
Ryan, and Kailen. We hope you will be comforted by your
faith and the love and support of your family and friends.
May God bless you.*

Sincerely,
George W. Bush

Despite having been out of office for three years when Ben was
killed, the nation's forty-third president took the time to graciously
console my sister-in-law and thus our entire family. I am grateful to
President and Mrs. Bush for their extraordinary kindness.

President Bush's successor, President Barack Obama, first con-
soled my parents at Langley by speaking the name of Jeremy and
his fallen CIA colleagues. The commander in chief would do so
again in his February 6, 2012, letter to Traci.

Dear Traci:

*I am deeply saddened by the loss of your husband, Sergeant
First Class Benjamin B. Wise, USA. No words can ever ease
your sorrow, but please take comfort in knowing that he has
honored us all beyond measure.*

*We will forever remember with humble gratitude his
selfless sacrifice in defense of our great Nation, and we will
never be able to repay our debt to you. All of us mourn your
loss. All of us pay tribute to his faithful devotion to duty.*

Michelle joins me in extending our heartfelt sympathy.

We pray that the cherished memories of your husband console you as you grieve, and that his brave service to this country brings you pride in this time of sadness. May God bless you and your family.

Sincerely,

Barack Obama

Thank you for the compassion you showed my family after the deaths of my brothers, President and Mrs. Obama.

One of the last official condolence letters my parents received was from the commandant, who had presumably taken a few days to collect his thoughts after meeting and standing beside us during that bitterly cold, heartbreaking night at Dover Air Force Base.

Dear Dr. and Mrs. Wise,

It is with heavy hearts that my wife, Bonnie, and I send our condolences as you mourn the loss of your son, Ben. Your family has paid an immeasurable price for the freedom of our Nation. We realize that there are no words that will ease the pain of losing two sons, but we would be deeply remiss not to offer our heartfelt sympathy and our boundless gratitude for your family's service and sacrifice.

Ben leaves behind a legacy of determination and selfless courage. He is one of our Nation's heroes, and we hope that fond memories of the honorable life he lived will bring some measure of comfort.

With Beau serving in the ranks of our Corps, we embrace your entire family as a part of our Marine Corps family and we grieve with you. Please know that you are in our thoughts and prayers during this difficult time. If there is anything we can do, please do not hesitate to ask.

With deepest sympathy,
James F. Amos
General, US Marine Corps
Commandant of the Marine Corps

Like Secretary Panetta and General Petraeus, the commandant included a handwritten note below his typed letter. The eleven extra words included by General Amos left no doubt that my life and career in my beloved United States Marine Corps would never be the same.

"You have my word that we will take care of Beau!" he wrote.

With all due respect to the commandant, I didn't need anyone to "take care of" me. I needed—or at least thought I needed—to keep the memory of my two fallen brothers alive by following in their footsteps on the battlefield.

Aside from the obvious, my family's story was nothing like *Saving Private Ryan*. Jeremy, Ben, and I volunteered to serve with full knowledge of the potential consequences. I still shudder when people compare me to the fictional character played by Matt Damon or the idea that someone needed to come and rescue me after Ben was killed.

Still, there was no denying the fact that in the blink of an eye, I was removed from combat under the same Department of Defense policy that serves as *Saving Private Ryan*'s heart and soul. While I was suddenly a "sole survivor" in the eyes of the Pentagon, it felt more like my soul had been permanently ripped away.

Both of my brothers were American heroes who had given everything—their bodies, their minds, their futures, and many subsequent years with their wives and kids—to defend freedom and our flag. As a sole survivor who would never again be allowed to fight for those sacred ideals, I firmly believed that I had been cheated out of my only chance to cement Jeremy's and Ben's selfless legacies.

At the time, I remember thinking it wasn't fair. To be even more candid, I felt in my heart that it was wrong.

U.S. Marine Corporal Matthew "Beau" Wise being barred from combat definitely wasn't what I wanted. While Jeremy and Ben would have probably been glad that I was forced to stop deploying, especially considering the emotional well-being of my wife, parents, and Heather, I also think that if either of them had been put in my shoes, they would have felt just as angry and frustrated to be sitting on the sidelines while their respective units went back to war.

In complete spiritual and emotional anguish, I boarded yet another flight; this one bound for Virginia Beach. Once there, I would bury my second brother in just over two years.

14

DE OPPRESSO LIBER

Three years after Ben was killed, I was sitting alone in the dark living room of our apartment just outside Camp Robinson in Arkansas, where I was listening to the ominous opening bass chords of Filter's "Hey Man Nice Shot." The 1995 alternative rock hit had been one of Ben's and my favorites since childhood and later helped him get fired up for dangerous missions as a Green Beret medic and sniper.

The song's opening lyrics—"I wish I would have met you, now it's a little late"—reminded me of young Luke, who had been all but robbed of his chance to know the dauntless, devoted dad who loved him so much.

After spending two years in Washington State, where Amber and I did our best to help Traci raise Luke, Ryan, and Kailen as a single mom, I subsequently requested another transfer to be near my dad, whose body was then being ravaged by Parkinson's in addition to the unrelenting grief that haunted us all.

Much like when we were out in Washington, Amber was doing most of the heavy lifting to help my family. I spent most of my nonworking hours drinking heavily, which was starting to negatively affect everything from my military career to my marriage. Not only was I routinely showing up hungover to early-morning training exercises, my wife would often find me passed out on the couch after long nights of alcohol abuse.

This particular evening marked a low point since my second brother's passing. After polishing off a liter of Jack Daniel's, which had become an almost nightly ritual, I drunkenly decided to pull out my beige M1911 pistol and place it on the table in front of me.

Jeremy died in late 2009. Ben died in early 2012. By the start of 2015, it had become clear that our dad didn't have much time left on earth, either. At that point, the thought of yet another Wise family funeral was simply too much to bear. *Not again.*

Now sipping a beer, I pulled out a DVD of Ben's memorial services that had been recorded by the U.S. Army. As soon as it started to play, the awful memories hit me like a freight train as my foggy mind became increasingly impaired by both booze and misery.

As one of Ben's Green Beret teammates spoke, I looked down at the yellowish handle of my pistol, which was sitting next to the empty bottle of liquor. If I picked up the gun, put it to my head, and pulled the trigger, all my pain would go away. I would never again have to think about my brothers' deaths and funerals or those harrowing final images of Ben from that hospital room.

I also wouldn't have to watch my father suffer and ultimately be buried while my mother and sister wept. In my intoxicated mind, that pistol suddenly looked like the only way out.

Before picking up the gun, I decided to watch more of the video. The DVD's sights and sounds took me right back to Virginia Beach, where for the second time in just over two years, I had laid an older brother to rest.

* * *

Ben's last will and testament contained four highly specific requests.

1. He wanted to be buried in a suit, not his U.S. Army uniform.
2. He wanted to be buried with his Bible.
3. He wanted to be buried next to Jeremy.
4. He wanted a Van Halen song played at his funeral.

Ben's flag-draped casket arrived in Virginia a few days after my career as a Marine Corps gunner effectively ended in Dover. In keeping with Ben's wishes to be buried in civilian clothing to emphasize his role as a husband and father rather than that of a war fighter, I opted to also wear a suit on that gray, chilly January 2012 day.

Sergeant First Class Trevor Hunter, who was in his full U.S. Army Green Beret uniform, stood at attention next to me as Ben's coffin was delicately taken off the private plane and put in a hearse, which would then be driven to a nearby funeral home. The Patriot Guard Riders—a magnificent group of loyal Americans who step forward to assist families of the fallen during military funerals—protected the vehicle carrying my brother by encircling it with motorcycles.

With most of his team still en route from Afghanistan, it was decided that Ben would have multiple memorial services, starting in Virginia Beach before his burial next to Jeremy in nearby Suffolk. ODA 1316 and other Green Beret leaders would then gather the following month out at Fort Lewis to bid a final farewell to their selfless teammate, who had touched so many lives since enlisting a decade earlier.

Like every event following Ben's passing, the memorial services were surreal and would blend together in my memory. Never before or since those few weeks have I felt like such an outsider instead of an active participant. Rather than stand up and speak at the ceremonies, I would seek out an empty corner and stand there looking down until it was time to shake hands and thank everyone for coming. After all, what was there to say? Both of my brothers were dead.

To their eternal credit, Ben's teammates and another incredibly brave member of my family felt differently. There was no way they would allow my second brother to be buried without first seizing their shared opportunities to tell the world what they thought of him.

After opening remarks from a U.S. Army chaplain at one of the services, during which a family member took a crying little Luke out of the chapel so Traci could stay seated just inches from her husband's Stars and Stripes–covered casket, a tribute video was played. It included the Van Halen song "Top of the World," which made both Traci and me smile for the first time in what seemed like many months. While one of Ben's four wishes had technically been fulfilled, my brother would have been pissed off that it was a song recorded with Sammy Hagar on vocals. He liked Sammy but was a much bigger fan of the band's original lineup, including lead singer David Lee Roth. Traci and I chuckled as the "Van Hagar" song echoed through the chapel.

After the video tribute was over, a uniformed Green Beret began limping from the pew and toward the podium. It was one of Ben's closest battle buddies, Staff Sergeant Kevin Flike, who had postponed a scheduled surgery at the Mayo Clinic in Minnesota to fly across the country and honor his fallen friend.

Kevin was in enormous pain, both physically and emotionally, as he struggled to reach the spot where he would deliver the remarks he had so carefully written. The feelings racing through his mind since receiving the news that Ben had been shot had been far worse than being shot himself. The soldier's wounded stomach was queasy, and his fractured hip was throbbing. As a testament to the kind of warriors who made up Ben's ODA, however, almost no one noticed that Kevin was hurting so badly that he almost collapsed on his way up to the podium.

Flanked by two cross-shaped wreaths and military flags, Ben's beloved brother-in-arms began to speak.

"My name is Kevin Flike," the wounded hero said. "I had the privilege of being on the same team as Ben. The first day that I walked into our team room, Ben was the first person to speak to me. He looked up from the computer and asked, 'Can I help you?' At the time, Ben was probably asking this question just wondering, 'Who is this new guy standing in the doorway?' However these four words—'Can I help you?'—came to define my relationship with Ben Wise."

Despite secretly struggling to stay on his feet, Kevin eulogized Ben with passion and poise.

> 1 John 3:18 says, "Let us not love with words or tongue, but with actions and in truth." Ben did not have to say that he was a Christian; his selfless service and love for others showed that he could walk with Christ.
>
> When Ben was done with his work, he would ask everyone else on the team if they needed help, even though this might mean missing a few extra hours of sleep or free time. If someone was working, Ben was right there helping them.
>
> When Ben arrived in Afghanistan for our first deployment, he was undergoing the tragedy of losing his brother Jeremy. Despite being exhausted from the arduous

journey from the States and the loss of his brother, the first thing Ben did when he arrived to our firebase was spend hours with me working on my shooting. Ben had a lot more experience than me, but rather than chastise me for being the new guy, he shared his knowledge with me and made himself available whenever I had any questions.

Through both deployments, Ben also made himself emotionally available to everyone on the team. Ben was a man you could go to when you were having problems. He was genuinely interested in what you had to say. If he asked you how you were doing, he really wanted to know how you were doing. A relationship with Ben carried a deeper meaning—and there was nothing superficial about it.

Kevin tried to keep his composure as he looked down from the podium and toward my parents, Heather, Traci, and me.

Ben loved his family. He often talked about his mother, father, sister, brothers, wife, and children. During deployments, Ben spent a lot of his free time looking at pictures of his family. Whenever he received a new picture or video of his family, he was sure to show it to everyone. As soon as Ben was finished using a computer, his last act was usually to set the computer's background to a picture of his family. His voice would become animated. Ben was truly a great family man.

As a medic, Ben was responsible for the physical well-being of the team. However, he took it upon himself to make sure that our mental well-being was also being taken care of. Ben always knew when to interject humor into a situation . . . Ben frequently gave out free hugs if he

thought your spirits needed to be lifted. Even when someone was fuming with anger, a free hug from Ben seemed
to calm everyone down.

Kevin went on to tell a humorous story about Ben taping photos of Ewoks around the base after the Green Berets started growing beards while deployed to Afghanistan. He thought several of
his teammates were starting to resemble the *Star Wars* characters,
which quickly became a running joke inside ODA 1316.

Ben's humor was not limited to large-scale pranks such as
this one. He was also king of the one-liners. He had incredible timing and knew exactly when to make his deliv-
ery. Ben's actions helped us get through long deployments
and picked us up when we were down. Ben's humor made
the good times great and the hard times better.

Hebrews 11:1 says, "Faith is being sure of what we
hope for and certain of what we do not see." Ben's faith
was unshakable. Despite hardship and tragedy, Ben carried on an amazing relationship with Christ.

Before missions, Ben would seek out other teammates and myself in order to pray. Ben was devoted to
reading the Word and often discussed it with others and
myself. Ben would often talk to me about what book he
was reading, and the verses that stuck out to him. Sometimes the discussions were long and sometimes they were
short; however, they were always full of meaning—each
one allowed insight to Ben's relationship with Christ.

The wounded soldier then talked about their Bible study
group, which Ben carried on in the weeks and months after his

friend was shot. Next, Kevin discussed the impact that Jeremy had on my second-oldest brother. He said Ben was comforted by Jeremy's renewed faith in God shortly before his death, much like my father had noted during the funeral service two years earlier.

Kevin cleared his throat before closing his powerful speech. He was relieved that he could stay standing without asking for help but overwhelmed with sadness and grief as he once again looked toward my family.

A few years ago, when I walked into our team room, Ben asked if he could help me. Well, he certainly has. Ben's life will serve as an inspiration for not only myself but for so many others. Ben has set forth an example of a devoted family man, selfless citizen, and follower of Christ. For the rest of my life, I will strive to follow the example that Ben Wise has set forth.

Ben was my teammate, my friend, and my brother. I love you, Ben. I miss you, and I will always strive to be the man you are. Thank you, and God bless.

With that, Kevin limped back to his seat.

In an ultimate tribute to their brotherly bond and enduring friendship, Traci decided to bury Ben with Kevin's Bible after being informed by the army that Ben's belongings would not arrive home from Afghanistan in time for the funeral. For eternity, Ben would rest with the thick NIV Bible that he and Kevin once used to share the word of God in the mountains of Afghanistan with their fellow deployed soldiers.

At some point after sitting down to finally rest his shattered hip and stomach, Kevin heard the words Ben once spoke to him.

"You have to read the Bible like it's a love letter from God to you," Ben said. "Pore over every word and search for the meaning of every sentence—every nuance."

For the rest of his life, Kevin would pore over not only the Bible but the treasured moments he shared with his fallen friend.

Trevor took the podium next. The seasoned warrior, who was bigger than Kevin or probably anyone else in the chapel, was overwhelmed with emotion and barely able to speak at times. He also glanced nervously in our direction toward the end of his remarks.

"We will always remember Ben as a great medic, as a lively, loyal teammate, and most of all as a friend," Trevor said before walking away in tears.

The chaplain gave Trevor a pat on the back as he exited the podium area. I wish I could have done the same. To this day, I consider Trevor not only a friend but a hero and a brother.

Despite being overwhelmed with emotion, Trevor didn't go back to his seat. He walked straight toward my sister, took her hand, and helped guide her toward the podium.

Heather, who had started her eulogy to Jeremy by saying that "if I didn't talk, I know I'd regret it my whole life," was now facing a second unthinkable tragedy just over two years later. Just like in 2010, my sister summoned all her strength to share a few consequential words before her brother was buried.

"I had the honor of speaking at Jeremy's funeral, and that was so much easier, because with Jeremy, you mostly wouldn't have to guess what he was thinking because he would just tell you," Heather said with Ben's casket just a few inches in front of her. "Ben was quieter. He was talkative, but just softer."

Understandably, Heather was even more emotional than two

years earlier. Like the rest of us, she simply couldn't believe all of this was happening. *Not again.*

After a lengthy pause, Heather resumed her eulogy. As she wept, so did Trevor, who had taken a seat to her immediate right, along with almost everyone else in the chapel. No sister should ever have to bury one brother, let alone two.

"He never left my side," Heather said of Ben. "Even when he was deployed, he just had this way of being with you."

As she had personally witnessed in the last few months, Heather spoke of her brother's constant concern for the welfare of others rather than his own.

"If you were close to Ben, he was thinking about you, even if you didn't know that he was," she said.

Heather then shared the story about Ben calling twice from Afghanistan to ask her to pray for Kevin, who had no idea his teammate's sister even knew who he was, let alone that he had been shot. Even while dealing with his ongoing combat deployment, Ben had taken the time to call home to ask her to pray for someone she had never met.

"And that was Ben," Heather said.

In closing, my sister eloquently eulogized Ben in a delicate, deeply personal way that only she was capable of doing.

"My brother Ben had a pure heart," Heather said as her strong voice began to crack. "In childhood, if he made a mistake, it was with his head; it wasn't with his heart. He was one of the best people I have ever known in my entire life."

I love you, Biggie. And so did Jeremy and Ben.

I was worn out by the time I found myself in the back of that limousine uttering almost exactly the same words as Ben had two years earlier: "I can't believe I'm the oldest brother now."

In what seemed like the blink of an eye, I was heading down the same road toward the same cemetery to bury the same brother who had sat next to me during the same ride less than two years earlier. I felt sick to my stomach.

When my family arrived at the Albert G. Horton Jr. Memorial Veterans Cemetery in Suffolk, Virginia, I knew right away that something was wrong. The limousine was taking us to a cemetery plot that was nowhere near where Jeremy had been laid to rest in 2010. Traci, my mom, and Heather immediately burst into tears upon realizing that Ben's final wish had apparently not been granted.

"Jeremy's over there," I told the cemetery director, pointing toward the section where my oldest brother was buried at the time.

As is sometimes the case when dealing with several layers of government and military bureaucracy, the extenuating circumstances of Ben's death and his final wishes had not been relayed to cemetery officials with the necessary sense of urgency.

After a few minutes of pleading her case with a cemetery official, my grieving mother had enough.

"I'm going to get on the phone and take care of this right now," she said.

Everyone, including me, was silent. Who could my mother possibly be calling?

Unbeknownst to any of us, Arkansas governor Mike Beebe had told my mom that if she ever needed anything, all she had to do was dial a private number he had provided shortly after learning of our family's twin tragedies. Sure enough, the governor's office sprang to action the very moment they heard about the cemetery confusion.

Within minutes, Governor Beebe was on the phone with Virginia governor Bob McDonnell, and the two state leaders quickly solved the problem. A few days later, they had decided, Jeremy and

Ben would be reunited. My family and I will forever be grateful to Governors McDonnell and Beebe for stepping in to ensure that my brothers would always be together.

A decision was subsequently made to move Jeremy to section four, row twenty-five, of the cemetery, where Ben would then be laid to rest beside his grave. While the additional delay was frustrating and painful for everyone, especially with Ben's and Jeremy's children to worry about, the wait was worth it.

The graveside service was dignified, but also short and sweet. After the agony of Jeremy's funeral less than two years earlier and waiting longer to bury Ben in the same cemetery, none of us saw the need to drag things out.

I looked over at Dana and nine-year-old Ethan as the pastor read from 1 Corinthians 13, which was already etched on my oldest brother's headstone.

"When I was a child, I talked like a child, I thought like a child, I reasoned like a child," verse 11 goes. "When I became a man, I put the ways of childhood behind me."

The moment that reading echoed through the cold, quiet cemetery, my mind flashed back to something Jeremy often said to Ben and me: "It's time to grow up." Whether it was me struggling to find my path in life or Ben deciding when to enlist, both of us could always count on Jeremy chiming in with some semblance of those five words.

Boom. Boom. Boom.

For the second time in twenty-one months, a twenty-one-gun salute was performed by the U.S. Navy in honor of Jeremy Jason Wise. The earsplitting sounds made all of us shudder even more than the winter day's cold air.

Next, it was time to read some of Ben's favorite Bible verses from Philippians 3:12–21, which is etched on his tombstone.

"But our citizenship is in heaven," verses 20 and 21 read. "And we eagerly await a Savior from there, the Lord Jesus Christ, who, by the power that enables him to bring everything under his control, will transform our lowly bodies so that they will be like his glorious body."

Having been one of the few people to see Ben's body just before and after he died, the verses he chose gave me enormous comfort. As Traci had said in Germany, the man in the bed wasn't Ben. In heaven, he would not only have his legs back but his big brother. For at least that one moment, I found some semblance of peace.

Boom. Boom. Boom.

With the day's second twenty-one-gun salute, Benjamin Brian Wise was laid to rest at the age of thirty-four next to his big brother.

When I looked toward Traci, Luke, Ryan, and Kailen, I saw their sadness, but I also knew they would be okay. Not only would Amber and I soon move out to Washington State but what Traci had been through between the news of Ben's wounds and his passing had made an already tough military wife even stronger. The rest of her life would be hard, but in the end, Traci would prevail.

As for my parents and sister, I knew their unshakable faith would help guide them through the darkness. The only question was about the severity of the Parkinson's disease that had already begun its assault on my emotionally devastated dad.

When it was time to leave the cemetery, I took one last look at the stately space now occupied by my older brothers. Like the bedroom they had first shared as boys growing up in Arkansas, they were finally back by each other's sides. In that moment, I longed for Jeremy to look at me and say, "You can hang out with us tonight," like he had so many years earlier. Perhaps I will drag a mattress out to the cemetery someday for a sleepover like when we were kids.

As the limo slowly rolled out of the Albert G. Horton Jr. Memorial Veterans Cemetery, I once again read the words of President Abraham Lincoln: "Honor to the soldier and sailor everywhere, who bravely bears his country's cause."

Jeremy and Ben Wise were not flawless men, but as warriors, they were the epitome of bravery and honor. I only wish I got to spend more time with them both.

The final official U.S. military ceremony following Ben's death was held at Fort Lewis on February 8, 2012. Even though Amber and I were already in the process of moving from Hawaii to Washington State, I was honored to accept the Green Beret team's invitation to my brother's West Coast memorial service.

The setting was the most dramatic of any military gathering I had ever been a part of. Between two large, framed photos of Ben in uniform were the U.S. and Green Beret colors, along with the Battlefield Cross, which consists of a helmet, rifle, boots, and the fallen hero's dog tag.

I was nervous and intimidated as the ceremony was set to begin, especially when I was almost immediately approached by a three-star general. He was wearing his beautifully decorated U.S. Army dress uniform.

After shaking my hand, the general put a pin on my Marine Corps uniform. It said, "De Oppresso Liber," which is Latin for "to liberate the oppressed." That is the sacred adage of the U.S. Army Special Forces community, which meant more to Ben than anything other than his wife and children.

"You're one of us now, brother," the general said to me.

"Thank you, General," I nervously stammered. "Thanks for honoring my brother, sir."

A few moments later, I took a seat next to Traci, and the memorial service began.

"We thank you for the life and service of Sergeant First Class Benjamin Wise," an army chaplain prayed. "Thank you for endowing him with the gift of courage, faithfulness, and compassion."

Lewis North Chapel was filled with some of the nation's most experienced, elite soldiers, including the rest of ODA 1316, which had by then fully returned from Afghanistan. One by one, commanding officers and Ben's trusted teammates spoke about the impact my brother had on their lives and careers.

"Ben's actions on the ninth of January are indicative of how Ben lived as a warrior, husband, son, brother, and father," one of Ben's commanders said. "Caring for others and leading from the front while always adhering to the Special Forces motto: the quiet professional."

"Ben, you will not be forgotten," the officer said in closing. "De Oppresso Liber."

One of Ben's fellow Green Berets drove home the fact that when it came to his pedigree as both a medic and sniper, Ben was truly the best of the best.

"I'll always remember our trip to Thailand together," the soldier said. "Not only did Ben prove his superior medical knowledge while acting as a primary mentor and instructor to the Thai special forces . . . he held the top shooting score for the detachment while instructing the Thai soldiers in combat marksmanship and close-quarters combat."

The Green Beret went on to say, "I was still getting to know Ben at the time. And that day, I learned how truly exceptional he was as he motivated me through the grueling event and the intense Thai heat."

The sorrowful soldier then began to talk about serving with my brother in battle.

"During our first trip to Afghanistan together, Ben and I led a platoon of Afghan commandos during a six-hour firefight," he said. "Ben and I maneuvered our platoon on the Taliban insurgents, getting within hand grenade distance of the enemy. That day was some of the most close and intense fighting I had experienced personally since 2003 during the Iraqi invasion. Despite the heavy volume of fire, Ben demonstrated extreme bravery," the soldier said before pausing to hold back tears. "The whole time keeping his composure, [Ben directed] our commandos in the most extreme circumstance. I watched as they emulated everything that Ben did."

This large, blond-haired Special Forces warrior reminded me a lot of Jeremy, which was cemented by what he said in closing.

"Ben was our brother and a good friend," the soldier said, pausing, this time no longer able to contain his emotions. "We'll always love you, Ben. We'll always miss you."

The next Green Beret to speak echoed his teammate's high praise.

"Ben was a natural leader and a trusted teammate," the soldier said. "He was always ready to volunteer for any detail, and the team sergeant could always trust Ben to bring honor to the team by living the team motto: 'Find a way, make a way.' The loss of Ben and Ben's leadership is a tremendous blow to our team, ODA 1316. Ben was a very important person to all the men of 1316. He was a key personality in all our lives and in the lives of our team's alumni."

Another army chaplain spoke last.

"He is now a citizen of heaven with a glorious, transformed

body, looking down on earth. I'm looking forward to that day when I see him face-to-face as citizens of heaven, enjoying our eternal retirement together," the chaplain said of Ben. "We're grieving today because his physical presence is not with us on this earth. But at the same time, we must focus on what Ben would want us to do as he looks down upon us from heaven. That is to do right in the sight of God as we serve the calling of our great nation: as quiet professionals and as we take care of the responsibilities of our families and the world God has given us. In fact, this was what Ben was all about."

As I looked down at my new "De Oppresso Liber" pin, Colonel Brian Vines, deputy commander of the First Special Forces Group, joined his fellow speakers in perfectly summing up Ben's life and military career.

"Sergeant First Class Wise was and will always be remembered as an American soldier, a Special Forces medic, a teammate to the men of ODA 1316, a combat-proven warrior, a Silver Star recipient, and a husband, a son, a brother, and a friend," Colonel Vines said. "He, like his brother Jeremy, answered his nation's call to arms and sacrificed all . . . to liberate the oppressed."

After the memorial service, one last twenty-one-gun salute shattered the silence of the arctic air outside the Lewis North Chapel.
Boom. Boom. Boom.

The same sound was seconds from filling my Arkansas living room as I made my final decision about whether to end my own life. Instead of a twenty-one-gun salute, my time on earth was about to end with a single bang heard only by my still-sleeping wife.

As I had initially stared down at my gun, which was still on the living room table, I felt numbness brought on by years of grief, as well as far too much alcohol. It wasn't until I watched the memorial video and thought more about my brothers' final acts that the deadness inside my head slowly began to subside.

Jeremy's final moments had been spent trying to disarm an al Qaeda terrorist who had a suicide bomb strapped to his chest. Ben's series of courageous closing deeds—saving not only the Afghan commando but those innocent civilians before volunteering to approach the second cave—precisely defined the phrase he lived and died for: "De Oppresso Liber."

That's when I picked up my M1911 pistol.

If I pulled the trigger, my last act would be blowing my brains out while leaving my devastated wife to clean up the mess. I would also rob my parents of their third and last living son. *Not again.*

Just then, I heard a pair of voices.

"It's time to grow up," Jeremy and Ben said in unison.

Before allowing myself a split second to change my mind, I dropped the magazine into my left hand and rapidly ejected the chamber round into the same hand. Next, I placed the magazine and my pistol on the coffee table and briefly paused to stare at the hollow-point bullet I had ejected from my faithful sidearm.

As I walked to the kitchen to dump the rest of my beer into the sink, *not again* were the only two words I could muster until quietly opening the bedroom door and approaching my wife by the bedside. After she woke up and realized what was happening, I put the empty firearm into her hands.

"Hide this," I told Amber. "Don't give it back to me until you think it's safe for me to have a gun again."

Without saying a word, Amber took the pistol and got it as far away from me as possible.

I spent the rest of the night in the guest bedroom, where I lay down on the bed and started to cry. Even though it had been three years since Ben's death, that night—during which a vivid memory of my brothers' voices helped stop me from making the horrible mistake of killing myself—was the first time I was able to truly mourn their deaths.

Jeremy and Ben Wise saved a lot of lives during their eight combined combat deployments and more than fourteen years spent defending our nation. The last life they saved was mine.

AFTERWORD

A WORD ON THE WISES

I was promoted to the rank of sergeant shortly after Ben died. I left the active-duty ranks in 2016 and the marines as a whole three years later, but I will always be thankful for my opportunity to serve in the beloved Corps. Semper fidelis.

I also went on to become a father. In 2017, Amber and I adopted our son and then—while this book was being written—adopted our daughter. Even though our kids never got to meet my brothers, they will most certainly grow up learning about the heroism of Uncle Jeremy and Uncle Ben.

U.S. Army Sergeant First Class Ben Wise was posthumously awarded the Silver Star for gallantry in action by Army Secretary McHugh on February 1, 2012.

U.S. Navy Special Warfare Operator First Class (SEAL) Jeremy Wise was posthumously awarded the CIA equivalent to the Silver Star—the Intelligence Star—for extraordinary heroism in 2010.

In addition to his star on the CIA Memorial Wall at Langley and Jeremy's name being etched in the CIA's Book of Honor, the Intelligence Star is an extremely rare award. According to *Source-*

Watch, "only a few hundred persons have received this award during the entire history of the CIA."

Ben's additional army decorations include two Bronze Star Medals, the Purple Heart, the NATO Medal, three Army Commendation Medals, three Army Good Conduct Medals, the National Defense Service Medal, three Iraq Campaign Medals with Bronze Service Stars, two Afghan Campaign Medals with Bronze Service Stars, the Global War on Terror Service Medal, multiple Meritorious Service Medals, two Overseas Service Ribbons, two Noncommissioned Officer Professional Development Ribbons, the Army Service Ribbon, the Special Forces Tab, the Combat Infantryman Badge, the Expert Infantryman Badge, the Combat and Special Skill Badge, the Presidential Unit Citation, and the Parachutist Badge.

Jeremy's additional navy awards include two Navy and Marine Commendation Medals with Vs for valor, the Pistol Marksmanship Medal, the Rifle Marksmanship Medal, two Sea Service Deployment Ribbons, the Global War on Terrorism Service Medal, the Iraq Campaign Medal, the Afghanistan Campaign Medal, the National Defense Service Medal, the Navy Good Conduct Medal, the Combat Action Ribbon, three Navy and Marine Corps Achievement Medals, and the Joint Service Achievement Medal.

Ben was honored with a place in the Arkansas Military Veterans' Hall of Fame. As Jeremy was not a current service member when he was killed in action, he is unfortunately ineligible for the same honor.

Both of my brothers were honored by Arkansas Speaker of the House Matthew Shepherd and Governor Asa Hutchinson, who respectively passed and signed a resolution officially recognizing the sacrifices of Jeremy and Ben.

Ben was later honored by the First Special Forces Group,

which dedicated A Company's Third Battalion headquarters in his honor: SFC Benjamin B. Wise Hall.

Jeremy and Ben's alma mater, Hendrix College, revived their football program in 2013 and dedicated it to three distinguished alums to give their lives in service of our great nation: Jeremy, Ben, and Lieutenant Robert Young, who was killed in World War I. Hendrix's football facility is now known as Young-Wise Memorial Stadium.

Shortly after Ben was killed, a U.S. military outpost in Afghanistan's Balkh Province was renamed Camp Wise. A plaque in front of the installation said CAMP WISE: BROTHERS-IN-ARMS, before listing Ben and Jeremy's names and the dates and circumstances of their ultimate sacrifices.

In 2010, then CIA director Leon Panetta flew all the way to Khost, Afghanistan, to dedicate a plaque honoring fallen CIA heroes Harold Brown Jr., Elizabeth Hanson, Darren LaBonte, Jennifer Lynne Matthews, Dane Clark Paresi, Scott Michael Roberson, and Jeremy.

The plaque quotes Isaiah 6:8: "And I heard the voice of the Lord, saying, 'Whom shall I send, and who will go for us?' Then I said, 'Here I am; send me.'"

As we were writing this book, Jeremy Bash, who served as chief of staff at both the CIA and Department of Defense, told my coauthor, Tom Sileo, that in nearly every speech given by him and Secretary Panetta since leaving office, they not only make a point to quote Isaiah 6:8 but to also specifically mention Jeremy and Ben. Thank you, Secretary Panetta and Mr. Bash, for continuing to honor my brothers.

Our sister Heather still lives in Arkansas, where she is the head trainer at a local fitness club. Jeremy's widow, Dana, is remarried and still lives in Virginia with her husband and children, including Ethan.

Traci now lives in Arizona with her children. In 2013, Traci posted a photo of Luke sitting in front of a framed photo of his father that subsequently went viral on Facebook, Twitter, Instagram, and other social media platforms.

"Found my son sitting having a moment with his daddy the other day," Traci wrote. "We lost him January 15 in Afghanistan . . . we cannot forget about the incredible loss these children must undertake."

Not a day goes by that I don't think of Luke, Ethan, and all the wonderful kids Ben and Jeremy helped raise. When they're old enough to read this book, I hope it will make them proud of the dads and uncles who loved them beyond measure.

My mom, Mary Wise, still lives in Arkansas. Incredibly, she has maintained her unshakable faith despite experiencing heartbreak like no wife or mother should ever have to endure. As she said to God after Ben was shot, "You will not destroy me. You will not destroy my family." He hasn't.

My father, Dr. Jean Wise, passed away at the age of seventy-one on September 12, 2016, due to complications from Parkinson's disease. He was laid to rest in Magnolia, Arkansas.

While he left behind a beloved wife, daughter, son, and grandchildren, my dad has finally been reunited with his two boys in a much better place. Indeed, Dad, you raised godly sons. I hope I can one day live up to the shining examples set by you, Jeremy, and Ben.

Many will see the title of this book and think the third Wise man is me, but it's not. It's my dad.

ACKNOWLEDGMENTS

BEAU WISE

To my loving and supportive mother, Mary, and sister, Heather: thank you both for consistently encouraging me in my walk with Christ. I don't know how it is that neither of your relationships with God seemed to ever be shaken, but in truth, you're both stronger than I've ever been. I'm proud to be your son and brother. We've certainly learned the hard way that there's never any promise of fair seas. In retrospect, I'm just grateful that I had you two to fall back on through the roughest times. I pray we all become more and more grateful for the smallest of blessings and that I become a better son and brother to you more and more every day. I love you both dearly.

Ever since I received the news of my oldest brother's death in the chaplain's little plywood office in Helmand Province, Afghanistan, countless relatives and friends have rallied to support my family. To this day, it has never ceased. Throughout all the turmoil, we've been so blessed with love and support while struggling with the loss of not just two but three heroic men.

To those who never let my parents grieve alone—the Ralsh, Stuckey, Davidson, Sewell, and Kuntz families—I am eternally grateful for all you've done for my parents, Heather, Dana, Traci, and the children.

To my dearest cousins, who are more like brothers and sisters: thank you for always reaching out, even in the darkest of times. Leah Evashuck, Nathan Fletcher, Jonathon Farley, Brandon and Justin Sewell, and your beautiful families: I thank God every day for having such an amazing support network in our lives. It was your phone calls and text messages, including one in particular from Nate—"Don't go through this alone, brother. Call me!"—that helped pull me out of my darkest hole. I am grateful beyond measure.

Sherrie, Barbara, and Johnny: Leaving my parents behind and moving to Washington under the circumstances in 2012 was one of the hardest decisions I've ever had to make. I'm not sure I would have made that decision if you hadn't been there. Knowing the Morgan family would be drawn to the support of your sister gave me the assurance Amber and I needed in our decision to help Traci raise the newest addition to the Wise family.

In January 2012, I was formally placed on sole survivor status against my wishes. My initial response was devastation. I was scared of losing my Marine Corps family. Looking back, I have no idea how I could have possibly coped with either loss without my marine brethren beside me, but now know the relationships made in the Corps run deeper than our service status at any given time.

General Amos, sir, I now fully appreciate that the decision you made was not driven by politics, public relations, or military strategy. It was a human decision. It's taken me some time, but I now believe that every decision you made was for the benefit of my parents and family as a whole. Thank you for putting their welfare ahead of my own selfish ambitions, and thank you for protecting me from myself. I may not have realized it at the time, but I am eternally grateful.

General Bierman, you were larger than life when I arrived in the fleet. First Battalion, Third Marines sang your praises from the first day I arrived on board MCBH, and it didn't take long for me to figure out why. On that cold, dark day in Dover, seeing you shortly after escorting my brother Ben and our marine brethren home from Afghanistan and Germany made me feel like I had when I'd returned to my patrol base after burying Jeremy. I've tried to carry the Third Marine culture with me throughout my career. My greatest ambition has been to be a mentor and teacher first and a disciplinarian second. I learned that from you, sir.

If there was one acquaintance that was long overdue on my part, it's Bob Jordan. Even though Jeremy and Ben are gone, they're still connecting me to amazing people. You and your beautiful family have devoted your entire lives to the service of our great nation and the memory of great patriots like Jeremy and Ben. I had heard the name "Father Bob" so many times, and now I've finally had the distinct privilege of meeting your family and sharing so many wonderful stories about a man so dear to us both. You've truly been one of the most invaluable resources to this book.

From my three different active-duty stations, I heard the same name associated with travel from my parents. There was always some event to honor my brothers that I would hear about. From Gold Star banquets to CIA memorials and dedications, Secretary Leon Panetta was a name commonly heard in my calls home. Sir, I'm not sure how this is possible, but it seems like you've been by my parents' side through the worst of times as much as or more than I have, in some cases. I'm eternally grateful to you, sir, for all your efforts in the preservation of the memories of both my brothers and the tender care and friendship you showed my parents along the way. Thanks so much to you and Mr. Jeremy Bash for supporting my family, and thank you both so much for aiding us with this project.

I hope and pray that this book can help fellow Gold Star family members. I think that was the number-one goal for Tom and myself from the start. One strong piece of advice that Jeremy used to give me when he wanted me to grow up was, "There's no such thing as a paradigm shift. Change takes work. There is only the daily grind." After we lost Jeremy and I returned to my little patrol base in Afghanistan, I went to a friend and fellow marine who had lost a brother in Iraq a few years earlier, and I asked him for advice on coping with the loss. His response was, "One day at a time." Every day lived is an honor to the memory of those we mourn. Cherish them and carry them with us . . . one day at a time.

After we lost Jeremy and Ben, we were approached by various journalists from *The Washington Post:* Joby Warrick, Ian Shapira, Whitney Shefte, and Ricky Carioti. If not for you, I may have never found the courage to speak out in the first place. All of you have done so much to preserve Jeremy's and Ben's memories. Ian and Joby, your assistance in this project has been invaluable to not only Tom and me but to my family as well. Thank you for always seizing the opportunity to honor my brothers and their families.

It was in the middle of Ian's *Post* tribute to Jeremy and Ben that he informed me of another family with very similar circumstances. I pray every day for the Hubbard family, as well as the Westbrooks and Velezes, who have also endured such horrific wartime tragedies. My son and daughter will both be raised with the knowledge of the costly price of freedom. I hope our paths cross in the near future. I pray to God: please heal our families and grant all of us peace. One day, may all of us be made whole and joyously reunited.

To my agent, E. J. McCarthy, and my editor, Marc Resnick, along with everyone at St. Martin's Press: something tells me I've been spoiled by this process. I suppose I thought there would be more friction along the way. Instead, all of you have been nothing but supportive and a dream to work with. Marc, you were the only editor who led with the question, "Do you have any kids?" In the middle of that conference call, I texted Tom and said, "I think he's our guy!" Tom wholeheartedly agreed, and there's been no doubt ever since. Thank you for enthusiastically helping us tell this story of two great patriots.

To all the members of the U.S. Navy, U.S. Army, U. S. Marine Corps, and special operations communities: when your brother called for help, you rallied. I hope this book does honor to all our fraternities and our entire military family. There have been so many photos, texts, emails, letters, and documents that you sent—even some from overseas. To all those reading this, there were SEALs and Green Berets trying to contribute to the preservation of the memories of their brothers while actively deployed to war zones. This book wouldn't be what it now is without you.

Kevin Flike, Trevor Hunter, Shane, Clay, John, Joel, Joe McCarty, Chris "Ven" Galka, Robbie Walden, Matt Hudgeons, Paul Sebastian, Judson, Danny, Troy, Phil, and Zadoc: there wouldn't be a book without you guys! On behalf of Jeremy, Ben, Heather, my parents, and myself, we will never forget that you were there for my brothers when they were here and the way you've continued to honor them both long after they passed. Thank you, brothers.

There are so many people who rallied to contribute to this effort even after the manuscript was written. Thank you to Casey Tillman, Eric Balser, Israel Marales, Patrick Hayes, Isaiah Castro, and Frank Woodmancy, for all your help.

To my USMC brethren, this book coincidentally marks the end of my Marine Corps career. It breaks my heart to leave, but it's with great pride I can say that I truly believe my piece of the Corps is in better condition than when I found it. I fucking love machine guns, baby! There is no better MOS than 0331. To all my comrades at 1/3, MCSF Bn Bangor, India Co. 3/23, and all others scattered abroad: before you make a decision, look left and right before you look up and down. Hoorah and semper fidelis!

In the summer of 2018, I was contacted by Traci about a journalist who wanted to write "something" about Jeremy and Ben. Skeptical as usual, I agreed to talk.

Tom, I wasn't halfway through reading *8 Seconds of Courage* before I was completely taken in by both the elegance of your pen and your patriotic zeal for those who serve our country. I'm so honored to have met your family, who welcomed me into their homes without ever having met me. Thank you for being patient with me in the chapters that weren't so easy. This has been one of the most taxing and rewarding processes of my life.

Looking back at what good friends we've become, there's no way I could've gone through this without you. I hope someday that I can repay you for all that you've done for my brothers and my family! I know I've said many times that I wish you could have met them. After reviewing the full manuscript, I can't help but think what my father would say and how proud he would have been to have you tell this story. So on behalf of the entire Wise family to yours, God bless you. Not all patriots wear uniforms.

To my best friend, soul mate, and wife, Amber, I'm more in love with you now than the day we first got married. The day we eloped to Honolulu was one of the most amazing days, next to adopting our beautiful son and daughter. I can't believe that God sent me someone strong enough to walk with me through all that we've been through. Who could've imagined that a path so horrific would have led to where we are now? You've always pushed me back to the Father. Our children could never wish for or find a better mother. I want you to know, there is no way that I would have made it this far without you. Thank you for staying by my side and leading in the times when I was too weak. I look forward to every day that I get to spend with you and the kids for the rest of our lives.

In 2013, Amber and I learned that biological children from our marriage was definitively never going to happen. This came as a huge blow to us, yet our devotion to each other never wavered, and God answered our prayers and rewarded us with two beautiful children. The process was far from simple and would have never been possible if I hadn't been lucky enough to marry into one of the most amazing families. Cyndi and Dennis: there would be no kids in our life without you and no home filled with the joyous laughter we get to experience on a daily basis. It is truly impossible for me to imagine life without my children or their amazing grandparents.

The most painful thing anyone in this family has experienced hasn't been the thought of a sibling losing brothers or parents losing sons. The thought of sons losing their fathers has repeatedly brought every one of us to our knees.

Luke and Ethan, I hate that you have to go through this life without Ben and Jeremy. I'm sorry for not being able to be there for you as often as I've wanted to. You're the bravest boys that I've ever known.

For a year and a half, Tom and I have worked as diligently as we could to honor your fathers. I hope one day that this book will help bring you closer to each of them.

I find some comfort at least knowing that Ben and Jeremy left you in the hands of the strongest and most loving mothers, Traci and Dana. You deserve to know the character and caliber of men they were. Hopefully, this will help you as you navigate the storms ahead.

Don't be afraid to grieve, Luke and Ethan. We're all here whenever you need us. Carry the name you were given with pride, but most importantly—in keeping with the wishes of both your fathers—it's okay to call on the memories of our loved ones lost, so long as we call on our Blessed Savior, first and foremost. Stay the course! I love you both like my own children. Hebrews 12:1–2.

TOM SILEO

On July 13, 2018, I sent a Facebook message to Gold Star wife Sonya Williams, widow of U.S. Army Staff Sergeant Jesse L. Williams. The brave soldier had served with Ben during their 2003/04 combat deployment and subsequently made the ultimate sacrifice on April 8, 2007, in Baqubah, Iraq, where he was killed by an enemy sniper at the age of twenty-five. I wrote a syndicated column called "The Jesse Room" about the soldier, Sonya, and their daughter, Amaya, in 2012.

Nobody helped get the ball rolling on this project more than Sonya, who first put me in touch with her friend and fellow Gold Star wife Traci Wise. Sonya: I will always be grateful for your help, courage, and willingness to share the memory of your husband with me and the rest of the world. None of us will ever forget Staff Sergeant Jesse L. Williams.

I remember my first phone call with Traci like it was yesterday. Even while separated by thousands of miles, I heard the unmistakable strength in her voice. Traci: thank you not only for putting me in touch with Beau but for serving as the backbone of this book from the very beginning. Hopefully, the pages of *Three Wise Men* do justice to not only Ben's brilliance as a husband, father, and "quiet professional" but the unimaginable pain you endured and the courage you summoned in response. Luke, Ryan, and Kailen are lucky to have you as their mom.

Beau: becoming your coauthor and friend has been the honor of a lifetime. I will always remember our first research trip to Virginia Beach and D.C., where we saw the Washington Nationals beat the Atlanta Braves on June 21, 2019. Little did we know that just over four months later, we would not only be making substantial progress on this book but FaceTiming each other on the night the Nats won their first-ever World Series championship.

You, Amber, your children, and your entire family embody everything that is great about America. From the bottom of my heart, thank you for your service to our country and for allowing me to play a small part in helping you share Jeremy, Ben, and your dad with the world.

To Beau's mom, Mary, and his sister, Heather: it has been both an honor and a pleasure getting to know both of you during the course of writing this book with Beau. I hope and pray we adequately emphasized your huge roles in this American story of sacrifice. God bless you both.

To all the selfless soldiers, sailors, SEALs, and Green Berets who took time to speak with us while researching this book: thank you so much for your service to our country and your willingness to take time out of your busy lives to share memories of Jeremy, Ben, and your various deployments. It was a privilege to learn so much about the meaning of brotherhood, friendship, and sacrifice from all of you.

To my literary agent, E. J. McCarthy: thank you for believing in me and my fervent desire to continue writing books that honor America's true heroes. From *Brothers Forever* all the way to *Three Wise Men*, your treasured support, guidance, and friendship have been indispensable in establishing my career as an author. Thank you.

To Marc Resnick and the entire St. Martin's Press team: I am extremely grateful that you—above all others—stepped forward to publish and spread the word about *Three Wise Men*. I hope to work with all of you on many future projects.

To my mom, Diane, her husband, Bruce, my dad, Bob, my sister, Lauren, and her husband, Mark: thank you for your constant support and especially for welcoming Beau during our first research trip.

On another personal note, a major family event occurred while Beau and I were writing this book. Not only did my wife and I learn that she was pregnant with a baby girl, but tests subsequently confirmed that our daughter, Natalie, has Down syndrome.

To my wife, Lisa: the strength you have shown throughout this painful but enlightening ordeal reminds me of Traci Wise. You never gave up, and inspired everyone around you—including me—to find the bright side of an indescribably difficult situation.

Natalie: you, along with your big sister, Reagan, mean everything to your mom and me. We love you!

One of the first non–family members I told about the earth-shattering news my family received in August 2019 was Beau Wise. Every step of the way, he encouraged me as my wife and I experienced shock, grief, confusion, anger, sadness, and—eventually—clarity and resolve.

Thank you for your compassion and friendship, Beau. I can't wait until my daughters are old enough to read *Three Wise Men* and understand what the word *hero* truly means.

Beau Wise

SERGEANT BEAU WISE served on active duty in the Marine Corps from 2008 to 2016 with First Battalion / Third Marines; Marine Corps Security Forces; and India Company Third Battalion / Twenty-third Marines. He is the only known American service member to receive the Department of Defense's "Sole Survivor" designation as a result of the nineteen-plus-year war in Afghanistan. *Three Wise Men* is his first book.

Tom Sileo

TOM SILEO is an author, contributing senior editor of *The Stream*, and recipient of the Marine Corps Heritage Foundation's 2016 General Oliver P. Smith Award for distinguished reporting. Tom has written several books, including *Brothers Forever* and *Be Bold*.